GCSE Edexcel
French

Like the *Tour de France*, revising for GCSE French can feel like a hard slog.
Luckily, this brilliant CGP book is packed with all the study notes and practice
questions you'll need for the Edexcel Grade 9-1 exams in 2018 and beyond!

We've also included **free audio files** to go with the listening questions.
You'll find them on the CD-ROM — or you can download them from this page:

www.cgpbooks.co.uk/GCSEFrenchAudio

How to access your free Online Edition

You can read this entire book on your PC, Mac or tablet, with handy links to all the
online audio files. Just go to **cgpbooks.co.uk/extras** and enter this code:

0341 5A25 8882 7398

By the way, this code only works for one person. If somebody else has used
this book before you, they might have already claimed the Online Edition.

Complete
Revision & Practice
Everything you need to pass the exams!

Contents

Contents

Published by CGP

Editors:
Lucy Forsyth
Hannah Roscoe
Matt Topping

Contributors:
Marie-Laure Delvallée
Sophie Desgland
Jackie Shaw
Sarah Sweeney

With thanks to Christine Bodin, Sharon Knight, Jennifer Underwood and Karen Wells for the proofreading.
With thanks to Jan Greenway for the copyright research.

Acknowledgements:

Audio produced by Naomi Laredo of Small Print.

*Recorded, edited and mastered by Graham Williams of The Speech Recording Studio,
with the assistance of Andy Le Vien at RMS Studios.*

Voice Artists:

Danièle Bourdais

François Darriet

Jason Grangier

Perle Solvés

CD-ROM edited and mastered by Neil Hastings.

Edexcel material is reproduced by permission of Edexcel.

With thanks to iStock.com for permission to use the images on pages 50, 58, 71, 92, 95, 160 & 165

Abridged and adapted extract from 'Madame Bovary', on page 24, by Gustave Flaubert.

Abridged and adapted extract from 'Les Misérables', on page 54, by Victor Hugo.

Abridged and adapted extract from 'Un Mariage', on page 169, by Ernest Laut.

Abridged and adapted extract from 'Les trois mousquetaires', on page 176, by Alexandre Dumas.

Abridged and adapted extract from 'Le tour du monde en quatre-vingts jours', on page 63, by Jules Verne.

*Every effort has been made to locate copyright holders and obtain permission to reproduce sources. For those sources where it has
been difficult to trace the originator of the work, we would be grateful for information. If any copyright holder would like us to
make an amendment to the acknowledgements, please notify us and we will gladly update the book at the next reprint. Thank you.*

Numbers

Understanding how numbers work in French is really important — they're not as simple as they are in English.

Un, deux, trois — One, two, three

0	zéro				
1	un				
2	deux	11	onze	20	vingt
3	trois	12	douze	30	trente
4	quatre	13	treize	40	quarante
5	cinq	14	quatorze	50	cinquante
6	six	15	quinze	60	soixante
7	sept	16	seize	70	soixante-dix
8	huit	17	dix-sept	80	quatre-vingts
9	neuf	18	dix-huit	90	quatre-vingt-dix
10	dix	19	dix-neuf		

① 11 to 16 all end in 'ze'. But 17, 18 and 19 are 'ten-seven' etc.

② Except 'vingt', most of the 'tens' end in 'nte'. Also, '70' is 'sixty-ten', '80' is 'four-20s', and '90' is 'four-20-ten'.

Grammar — 'un' / 'une'

For feminine nouns, use '<u>une</u>' and '<u>et une</u>' instead of '<u>un</u>' and '<u>et un</u>':
Il y a <u>vingt et une</u> filles et <u>vingt et un</u> garçons.
There are <u>21</u> girls and <u>21</u> boys.

③ In-between numbers are formed like English ones, but add 'et un' for numbers ending in '1'.

21 vingt et un
22 vingt-deux

④ For the 70s and 90s, add 11-19 to 'soixante' and 'quatre-vingt' (like 'quatre-vingts' (*80*) but without the 's'). '81' and '91' bend the rule explained in point 3 — they miss out the 'et', e.g. quatre-vingt-un (*81*).

71 soixante et onze 91 quatre-vingt-onze 100 cent 10.000 dix mille
72 soixante-douze 98 quatre-vingt-dix-huit 1000 mille 1.000.000 un million

⑤ For hundreds and thousands, put cent, deux cent, mille (etc.) before the number.

623 six cent vingt-trois 1947 mille neuf cent quarante-sept

In French, long numbers are broken up by full stops instead of commas. Also, French decimals use commas instead of decimal points.

Add '-ième' to the number to say second, third etc.

Here are a few more handy words to <u>spice up</u> your French. Watch out for 'first' — it doesn't follow the rule.

Use 'premier' for masculine nouns and 'première' for feminine ones.

1st	premier / première	5th	cinquième	10th	dixième
2nd	deuxième	6th	sixième	99th	quatre-vingt-dix-neuvième
3rd	troisième	7th	septième		
4th	quatrième	8th	huitième		
		9th	neuvième		

A 'u' is added to 'cinq'.

une douzaine	*a dozen*
une dizaine	*about ten*
une vingtaine	*about twenty*
un nombre de	*a number of*
des dizaines	*lots / dozens*

Numbers ending in 'e' lose the e.
The 'f' in 'neuf' changes to a 'v'.

Read, write, repeat — you simply have to know these numbers...

Read Mathieu's social media profile, and answer the questions **in French**. Write the numbers in full.

Salut ! Je m'appelle Mathieu, et j'ai dix-sept ans. Je suis le quatrième enfant de la famille — j'ai trois sœurs aînées. Nous habitons dans la première maison de la rue Phillipe — c'est la troisième rue après le parc. Il y a une vingtaine de maisons dans la rue.

e.g. Quel âge a Mathieu ? **Il a dix-sept ans.**
1. Il a combien de frères et de sœurs ? [1]
2. Quelle est sa maison ? [1]
3. Où se trouve la rue où Mathieu habite ? [1]
4. Combien de maisons y-a-t-il dans la rue ? [1]

Times and Dates

Times and dates are essential for your exam — make sure you know how to use both in French.

Quelle heure est-il? — What time is it?

1) There are different ways to tell the time in French. Make sure you <u>learn</u> all of them. To say 'it's...o'clock' use '<u>il est...heure(s)</u>'.

Il est une heure.	*It's 1 o'clock.*
Il est vingt heures.	*It's 8 pm.*

> To say 'in the evening' without referring to a specific hour of the day, just say 'le soir'. E.g. 'Le soir, j'ai dormi.' (*In the evening, I slept.*) The same rule applies for 'in the morning' and 'in the afternoon'.

2) Use this vocab to say '<u>quarter past</u>', '<u>half past</u>' and '<u>quarter to</u>'.

et quart	*quarter past*
et demie	*half past*
moins le quart	*quarter to*
du matin	*in the morning*
de l'après-midi	*in the afternoon*
du soir	*in the evening*

Il est deux heures et quart.	*It's quarter past two.*
Il est deux heures et demie.	*It's half past two.*
Il est trois heures moins le quart.	*It's quarter to three.*
Il est cinq heures du soir.	*It's five in the evening.*

Être à l'heure — To be on time

1) To say '<u>...minutes past</u>', you say the hour, then the number of minutes. You don't need any <u>extra</u> words.

Il est trois heures douze.	*It's 03:12.*
Il est vingt heures trente-trois.	*It's 20:33.*

The French use the 24-hour clock a lot — so make sure you can use it.

2) Use '<u>moins...</u>' *(less)* to say '<u>...to</u>'.

Il est onze heures moins dix.	*It's ten to eleven.*

Grammar — 'à' with times

You use '<u>à</u>' with times to say '<u>at</u>'.
à dix heures   *at ten o'clock*

Les jours de la semaine — The days of the week

In French, the days of the week are always <u>lower case</u>. They're also all <u>masculine</u>.

lundi	*Monday*
mardi	*Tuesday*
mercredi	*Wednesday*
jeudi	*Thursday*
vendredi	*Friday*
samedi	*Saturday*
dimanche	*Sunday*

Grammar — le lundi (Mondays)

To say something happens regularly on a certain day, use the <u>masculine definite article</u> ('le') with the day — <u>not a plural</u>.
Le lundi, je fais du sport.
On Mondays, I do sport.

aujourd'hui	*today*
demain	*tomorrow*
hier	*yesterday*
après-demain	*the day after tomorrow*
avant-hier	*the day before yesterday*
la semaine	*the week*
le week-end	*the weekend*

Je pars mardi.	*I'm leaving on Tuesday.*
Le week-end, j'aime faire la grasse matinée.	*At the weekend, I like to have a lie-in.*
Elle voit son père le dimanche.	*She sees her father on Sundays.*

the next day — le lendemain

During the week — Pendant la semaine

every day — tous les jours

Times and Dates

Here are some more vocab and phrases you can use to talk about times and dates.

Les mois de l'année — The months of the year

Months and seasons are <u>masculine</u> and <u>don't</u> begin with <u>capital letters</u>.

janvier	January	juillet	July	(en) hiver	(in) winter
février	February	août	August	(au) printemps	(in) spring
mars	March	septembre	September	(en) été	(in) summer
avril	April	octobre	October	(en) automne	(in) autumn
mai	May	novembre	November		
juin	June	décembre	December		

Watch out — 'in spring' is 'au printemps'.
All of the other seasons use 'en'.

Quelle est la date? — What's the date?

In French, you say '<u>the nine April</u>' or '<u>the seventeen November</u>'. The exception to this rule is the <u>first day</u> of a month, where you use '<u>le premier</u>' (*the first*), like you would in English.

Aujourd'hui c'est le quinze mai. *Today is the 15th of May.*

the first of August — le premier août

Mon frère est né le vingt-cinq février mille neuf cent quatre-vingt-dix-huit. *My brother was born on the 25th of February 1998.*

in the 90s — dans les années quatre-vingt-dix
in the year 2000 — en l'an deux mille

Ce matin / ce soir — This morning / this evening

These time phrases are really useful for <u>making arrangements</u>... and for your <u>exams</u>.

ce matin	*this morning*	la semaine prochaine	*next week*
cet après-midi	*this afternoon*	la semaine dernière	*last week*
ce soir	*this evening / tonight*	toujours	*always*
demain matin	*tomorrow morning*	quelquefois	*sometimes*
cette semaine	*this week*	(assez) souvent	*(quite) often*
ce week-end	*this weekend*	(assez) rarement	*(quite) rarely*

Qu'est-ce que tu fais ce soir? *What are you doing this evening?*

Le soir, je vais souvent au cinéma. *In the evening, I often go to the cinema.*

La semaine prochaine, je vais danser. *Next week, I'm going to dance.*

this weekend — ce week-end
rarely — rarement
This afternoon — Cet après-midi

Don't forget to be on time for your exams...

LISTENING 01

Listen to this French school-radio broadcast. Answer the questions **in English**.

You'll find the audio tracks on your CD-ROM, or at www.cgpbooks.co.uk/ GCSEFrenchAudio.

e.g. For how long will the headmaster talk? **five minutes**

1 a. When do most students get up? *[1]*
b. When do lessons start? *[1]*
c. On which days do dance classes take place? *[1]*
d. When was the school established? *[1]*

Questions

Knowing how to ask questions is key in any language. And it's not just the words that matter...

Les mots interrogatifs — Question words

quand?	*when?*
pourquoi?	*why?*
où?	*where?*
comment?	*how?*
combien?	*how much / many?*
qui?	*who?*
quoi?	*what?*
que?	*what?*
quel?	*which?*

These are known as interrogatives.

Grammar — quel, quelle, quels, quelles

'Quel' means 'which' or 'what'. It's an interrogative adjective, so it agrees with the noun it refers to. It has masculine, feminine, singular and plural forms:

quel (masc. singular)	quels (masc. plural)
quelle (fem. singular)	quelles (fem. plural)

Quelles filles aiment chanter?
Which girls like singing?

'Filles' (*girls*) is feminine and plural, so 'quelles' is used.

Pourquoi es-tu en retard? *Why are you late?*

Qui vient avec moi? *Who's coming with me?*

Où est la plage? *Where is the beach?*

Ask questions by changing your tone of voice

1) The easiest way to ask a question in French is to say a normal sentence, but make your voice go up at the end. This works well for questions that are answered yes or no.

Tu as faim? *Are you hungry?*

C'est loin? *Is it far?*

Tu travailles le week-end? *Do you work at the weekend?*

In writing, the only difference between this question and the statement 'C'est loin.' (*It's far*.) is the question mark.

2) To answer 'yes' to a question containing a negative, use 'si'.

Est-ce que tu n'as pas faim? — Si, j'ai faim. *Aren't you hungry? — Yes, I'm hungry.*

Use 'est-ce que' or 'qu'est-ce que' for questions

1) You can also turn a statement into a yes or no question by using 'est-ce que'.

Est-ce que tu as des frères ou des sœurs? *Do you have any brothers or sisters?*

Est-ce que tu aimes jouer au tennis? *Do you like playing tennis?*

You can use 'qu'est-ce qui' to ask 'what' when it's the subject of the sentence. See p.115 for more about using 'qui' and 'que' in questions.

2) You usually use 'qu'est-ce que' if your question starts with 'what'.

Qu'est-ce que tu fais dans ton temps libre? *What do you do in your free time?*

Questions

Now you've learnt the basics, you can start developing your questions.

Put the verb first to form a question

You can ask questions in French by <u>swapping</u> the <u>verb</u> (see p.122) and the <u>subject</u> (the person or thing doing the action) around. Don't forget to add the <u>hyphen</u>, though.

Fais-tu du sport?	*Do you do any sport?*
Pouvez-vous m'aider?	*Can you help me?*
Aimes-tu le hip-hop?	*Do you like hip-hop?*

If the verb ends in a <u>vowel</u> and is followed by <u>il</u>, <u>elle</u> or <u>on</u>, you add a '<u>t</u>' to make it <u>easier to say</u>:

A-t-il fini ses devoirs?
Has he finished his homework?

Qu'est-ce que c'est? — What is it?

Here are some useful <u>questions</u> that you might want to ask:

À quelle heure?	*At what time?*	C'est de quelle couleur?	*What colour is it?*
Quelle heure est-il?	*What time is it?*	D'où?	*From where?*
C'est combien?	*How much is it?*	Pour combien de temps?	*For how long?*
C'est quelle date?	*What is the date?*	Que veut dire...?	*What does...mean?*
C'est quel jour?	*What day is it?*	Ça s'écrit comment?	*How is that written?*

Question	**Simple Answer**	**Extended Answer**
D'où viens-tu?	Je viens de Millom.	Je viens de Millom, dans le nord-ouest de l'Angleterre. C'est une petite ville rurale.
Where are you from?	*I'm from Millom.*	*I'm from Millom, in north-west England. It's a small, rural town.*

 SPEAKING

You'll have to ask two questions in the role play...

Here's a role play that Marie did with her teacher.

Teacher : Est-ce que tu fais du sport ?

Marie : Oui, je fais du ski. Normalement je vais à **la piste de ski**[1] le lundi et le mercredi soir.

Teacher : Où est la piste de ski ?

Marie : La piste de ski **se trouve**[2] en centre-ville, près de la piscine.

Teacher : C'est loin de ta maison ?

Marie : Non, au contraire, c'est à quinze minutes à pied. C'est très pratique. Et vous, est-ce que vous aimez faire du ski ?

Teacher : Oui, j'aime bien faire du ski en vacances.

Marie : Qu'est-ce que vous pensez du football ?

Teacher : Le football ne me plaît pas. C'est ennuyeux.

Grade 8-9

[1] ski slope
[2] is (literally 'finds itself')

There's more info about role plays on p.144.

Tick list:
✓ correctly formed question
✓ time phrases
✓ present tense

To improve:
+ use an opinion phrase e.g. 'à mon avis...'

Use the instructions below to prepare your own role play. Address your friend as 'tu' and speak for about two minutes. [10 marks]

Tu parles du sport avec un(e) ami(e) français(e).
- *la natation — l'heure*
- *quand — jour(s)*
- *!*
- *? natation — opinion*
- *? sport préféré*

'!' means you'll need to answer a question you haven't prepared. When you see '?' you need to ask a question.

Being Polite

Politeness makes a big difference — not everyone you talk to will be a friend. Here's a run-down of how to adjust your speech in different situations.

Bonjour...au revoir — Hello...goodbye

<u>Learn</u> these phrases — they're <u>crucial</u>.

bonjour	*hello*	au revoir	*goodbye*
salut	*hi*	à bientôt	*see you soon*
allô	*hello (on phone)*	à tout à l'heure	*see you soon / later*
bienvenue	*welcome*	à demain	*see you tomorrow*
bonsoir	*good evening*	Bon voyage!	*Have a good trip!*
bonne nuit	*good night*	Bonne chance!	*Good luck!*

Comment ça va? — How are you?

Make your conversation <u>sparkle</u> by using these little <u>gems</u>.

Comment ça va?	*How are you?*
Comment allez-vous?	*How are you? (formal)*
Et toi?	*And you? (informal)*
Et vous?	*And you? (formal)*
Ça va bien, merci.	*(I am) fine, thanks.*
Ça ne va pas bien.	*(I am) not well.*
Pas mal.	*Not bad.*
Je ne sais pas.	*I don't know.*
Super!	*Great!*
Je me sens...	*I feel...*
Comme ci, comme ça.	*OK.*

Grammar — using 'tu' and 'vous'

There are two ways of saying '<u>you</u>' in French. '<u>Tu</u>' is <u>singular</u> and <u>informal</u>. You should use it with a <u>friend</u> or <u>family member</u>. '<u>Vous</u>' is for <u>more than one person</u>, or for one person in a <u>formal</u> situation, e.g. a <u>stranger</u> or <u>someone older</u> than you.

Comment ça va?	*How are you? (informal)*
Je me sens fantastique.	*I feel fantastic.*
Pas mal.	*Not bad.*

How are you? (formal) — Comment allez-vous?

awful — affreux / affreuse

well — bien

Puis-je vous présenter...? — May I introduce...?

Puis-je vous présenter Dave?	*May I introduce Dave?*
Voici Dave.	*This is Dave.*
enchanté(e)	*pleased to meet you*

'Enchanté' agrees with the gender of the speaker. It needs an extra 'e' ('enchantée') if the person saying it is female.

The <u>conversation</u> below shows how these phrases are used:

Madame Rollet :	Salut Delphine, comment ça va?	*Hi Delphine, how are you?*
Delphine :	Ça va bien. Comment allez-vous?	*I'm fine. How are you?*
Madame Rollet :	Comme ci, comme ça.	*O.K.*
Delphine :	Puis-je vous présenter Bruno?	*May I introduce Bruno?*
Madame Rollet :	Enchantée.	*Pleased to meet you.*

Delphine uses the polite 'vous' form — Madame Rollet is older than her.

If you're talking to someone you call 'tu', you say 'Puis-je te présenter...?' — it's informal.

Being Polite

This page is about asking politely. These handy words and phrases will help you avoid causing offence.

Je voudrais — I would like

1) 'Je voudrais' and 'j'aimerais' (I would like) are more polite than 'je veux' (I want).

Je voudrais une tasse de thé.	*I would like a cup of tea.*
J'aimerais de l'eau.	*I would like some water.*

We would like — Nous voudrions

He would like — Il aimerait

'Je voudrais' and 'j'aimerais' are in the conditional tense. See p.135 for more.

2) 'Puis-je...' and 'Est-ce que je peux...' both mean 'May I...'.

See p.4-5 for more about questions.

Puis-je avoir un café?	*May I have a coffee?*

Est-ce que je peux m'asseoir?	*May I sit down?*

S'il vous plaît — Please

Don't forget these useful polite words — they could make all the difference...

s'il vous plaît	*please (formal)*	d'accord	*OK / fine*
s'il te plaît	*please (informal)*	pardon	*excuse me (informal)*
merci (beaucoup)	*thank you (very much)*	excusez-moi	*excuse me (polite)*
de rien	*you're welcome*	Je suis désolé(e).	*I'm sorry.*

'Désolé' has to agree with the subject, so you add an 'e' if you're female.

Je vous écoute — I'm listening

Here are some handy phrases to use for formal phone calls or emails.

à l'appareil	*on the line / speaking*	ne quittez pas	*stay on the line*
un instant	*one moment*	à l'attention de	*for the attention of*
je reviens tout de suite	*I'll be right back*	suite à	*further to / following*

Knowing how to use 'tu' and 'vous' correctly is important...

Here's a script for you. Jean is introducing his friend, Michel, to his girlfriend, Aurélie.

Jean : Salut Michel ! Comment ça va ? *(Grade 4-5)*

Michel : Oui, ça va bien merci — c'est le week-end ! Et toi ?

Jean : Pas trop mal. Puis-je te présenter Aurélie, ma **petite-amie**[1] ?

Michel : Enchanté.

Aurélie : Enchantée.

Michel : Comment allez-vous, Aurélie ?

Aurélie : Super, merci, mais **j'ai faim**[2].

Jean : Allons **chercher**[3] un sandwich. À tout à l'heure, Michel.

Michel : À bientôt !

[1] girlfriend
[2] I'm hungry
[3] to get

Tick list:
✓ variety of polite phrases
✓ gender agreement of enchanté(e)

To improve:
+ more detail to develop the ideas
+ different tenses (add a past or future)

Now it's your turn:

Écris un script au sujet de deux personnes qui se présentent pour la première fois.
*Écris environ **40** mots **en français**.* [10 marks]

To get more tenses in your answer, you could make plans to meet in the future, or one person could say where they used to live. Try to include as many of the phrases you learnt on p.6 and 7 as you can.

Opinions

Having an opinion is a great way to pick up lots of marks in the exam, so don't hold back on giving your views. Just make sure that you use a cracking variety of phrases and vocab to really impress the examiner.

Qu'est-ce que tu penses de...? — What do you think of...?

There are lots of ways to ask someone their opinion in French... and to give your own.

Qu'est-ce que tu penses de...?	*What do you think of...?*
Quel est ton avis sur...?	*What's your opinion of...?*
Qu'est-ce que tu penses?	*What do you think?*
Comment trouves-tu...?	*How do you find...?*
Est-ce que tu le / la trouves sympa?	*Do you think he / she is nice?*

Je pense que...	*I think that...*
À mon avis...	*In my opinion...*
Je trouve que...	*I find that...*
Je crois que...	*I believe that...*
Personnellement...	*Personally...*

Qu'est-ce que tu penses de mon frère?
What do you think of my brother? → Je pense qu'il est très sympa.
I think that he's very nice.

Speak your mind — it'll sound impressive

Here's how to say what you like and dislike.

J'adore...	*I love...*
J'aime...	*I like / love...*
J'aime bien...	*I like...*
Ça me plaît.	*I like it.*
Je m'intéresse à...	*I'm interested in...*
Je trouve...chouette	*I find...great*

Je n'aime pas...	*I don't like...*
Ça ne me plaît pas.	*I don't like it.*
Ça ne m'intéresse pas.	*It doesn't interest me.*
Je trouve...affreux / affreuse	*I find...awful*
Je déteste...	*I hate...*
Ça ne me dit rien.	*It means nothing to me.*

Be careful — 'j'aime Pierre' can mean 'I like Pierre' OR 'I love Pierre'. If you only like him, it's safer to say 'je trouve Pierre sympathique' ('*I think Pierre is nice*') or 'j'aime bien Pierre' ('*I like Pierre*'). Otherwise you might be giving out the wrong message...

J'adore jouer au basket.	*I love playing basketball.*	*I like* — J'aime bien
Je m'intéresse à la musique.	*I'm interested in music.*	*I'm not interested in* — Je ne m'intéresse pas à
Je déteste les films d'horreur.	*I hate horror films.*	*I find... awful.* — Je trouve... affreux.

Es-tu d'accord? — Do you agree?

absolument	*absolutely*	bien sûr	*of course*	moi non plus	*me neither*
bien entendu	*of course*	ça dépend	*it depends*	ça m'est égal	*I don't care*

Es-tu d'accord avec moi?	*Do you agree with me?*	*with that* — avec ça
Bien sûr.	*Of course.*	*It depends.* — Ça dépend.

Section One — General Stuff

Opinions

Don't forget to back up your opinions — it's not enough just to say what you think.
Being able to justify and develop those opinions is crucial for earning extra marks.

Parce que — Because

The best way to justify your opinion is to give a reason. 'Parce que' and 'car' both mean __because__.

J'aime ce film parce que les acteurs sont formidables.	*I like this film because the actors are great.*
Je trouve ce film affreux car l'histoire est ennuyeuse.	*I think this film is awful because the story is boring.*

Use describing words to explain your opinions

Here are some __describing words__ that you can use to __explain__ your opinion.

affreux / affreuse	*awful*
amical(e)	*friendly*
amusant(e)	*funny*
barbant(e)	*boring*
beau / belle	*handsome / beautiful*
bon(ne)	*good*
chouette, super	*great*
doué(e)	*gifted / talented*
ennuyeux / ennuyeuse	*boring*
fantastique	*fantastic*
formidable	*great*
génial(e)	*brilliant*
mauvais(e)	*bad*
sympa, sympathique	*nice (person)*

Ce film me plaît parce que les acteurs sont doués.	*I like this film because the actors are talented.*

Remember, adjectives (describing words) need to agree with the noun they refer to — see p.101 for more.

These __phrases__ might come in handy, too:

Ça m'énerve.	*It gets on my nerves.*
Ça me fait rire.	*It makes me laugh.*

Je n'aime pas ce film car ça m'énerve.	*I don't like this film because it gets on my nerves.*

Always make sure you can justify your opinions...

Sophie and Mayeul are talking about a French actor, Maurice le Pain.
Have a look at the text, then answer the questions **in English**.

Sophie : Quel est ton avis sur Maurice le Pain ?

Mayeul : Ça dépend. Je pense qu'il est assez bon dans les films d'action, mais je ne l'aime pas dans les comédies. Il n'est pas très amusant.

Sophie : Je ne suis pas d'accord ! C'est mon acteur préféré parce qu'il est vraiment doué. Ses films sont toujours formidables.

Mayeul : Il te plaît car il est beau. Moi, je préfère les acteurs qui ont du vrai talent.

Sophie : Tu es envieux ! Toutes mes amies adorent Maurice aussi. Nous le trouvons chouette.

e.g. What does Mayeul think about Maurice le Pain in action films?
He thinks he's quite good.

1. Why doesn't Mayeul like Maurice le Pain in comedies? [1]

2. Why is Maurice Sophie's favourite actor? [1]

3. What does Sophie say about Maurice le Pain's films? [1]

4. Why does Mayeul think that Sophie likes Maurice le Pain? [1]

5. What do Sophie's friends think of Maurice? [1]

Putting it All Together

You could get asked your opinion on any of the GCSE topics, so make sure you can bring all the stuff on these pages together. You won't get top marks if you make a statement that you can't back up properly.

Talking about books, films, music...

In the exam, you might get asked if you <u>like</u> or <u>dislike</u> a band, film, book etc. If you don't have an opinion, just make one up. You won't get any marks for <u>shrugging</u>...

ce film	*this film*	ce groupe	*this band*
ce journal	*this newspaper*	cette équipe	*this team*
ce livre	*this book*	cet acteur	*this actor*
ce roman	*this novel*	cette actrice	*this actress*
ce magazine	*this magazine*	ce chanteur	*this singer (male)*
cette émission	*this programme*	cette chanteuse	*this singer (female)*
cette chanson	*this song*	cette vedette	*this star / celebrity*

'Ce' ('this' / 'that') becomes 'cette' in front of feminine nouns. For masculine nouns starting with a vowel, use 'cet'. See p.103 for more info.

Quel est ton avis sur cette équipe?	*What's your opinion of this team?*
J'aime bien cette équipe. À mon avis, les joueurs sont doués.	*I like this team. In my opinion, the players are gifted.*

À mon avis — In my opinion

Question	Simple Answer	Extended Answer
Qu'est-ce que tu penses de la musique classique?	C'est ennuyeux et agaçant.	À mon avis, la musique classique est ennuyeuse.
What do you think of classical music?	*It's boring and annoying.*	*In my opinion, classical music is boring.*

Qu'est-ce que tu penses de ce magazine?	*What do you think of this magazine?*	*this actor* — cet acteur
J'adore cette émission parce que ça me fait rire.	*I love this programme because it makes me laugh.*	*it makes me cry* — ça me fait pleurer
Je trouve ce chanteur affreux car sa musique est ennuyeuse.	*I find this singer awful because his music is boring.*	*he is arrogant* — il est arrogant

TRACK LISTENING 02

Show the examiner that you can express your opinions...

Deux amis parlent de leurs passe-temps.
Complète les phrases en choisissant des mots dans la case.

1(i) a. Blandine aime bien jouer avec .... [1]
      b. Elle n'aime pas toujours faire du .... [1]
      c. Elle préfère .... [1]

  (ii) a. En général, Marc pense que le sport est .... [1]
        b. Marc aime bien .... [1]
        c. À son avis, les comédies sont .... [1]

formidables
ennuyeux
son équipe   lire
agaçantes
regarder des films
sport   natation
relaxant
intéressant   le foot

Listening Questions

Practice exam questions are a brilliant way to prepare for the real things. We've got four pages coming up that give you some realistic tasks to tackle for each of the four GCSE French papers. Good luck!

1 You overhear Paul talking on the phone about his weekend.
Answer the questions **in English**.

TRACK LISTENING 03

Example: How many T-shirts did Paul buy? ......*two*......

a Roughly how many DVDs did he buy? .... *[1 mark]*

b How much did his shopping cost in total? .... *[1 mark]*

c How many friends did Paul see on Saturday evening? .... *[1 mark]*

2 While on a bus in Paris, you overhear two people talking about a singer.
For each question, put a cross in each of the **two** correct boxes.

TRACK LISTENING 04

(i) What does Claire say about Lilette Laurent?

A	My favourite singer is Lilette Laurent.	
B	I think Lilette Laurent writes her own songs.	
C	I think her new song is terrible.	
D	I saw a programme about Lilette Laurent.	

[2 marks]

(ii) What are Georges's opinions?

A	All that celebrities care about is music.	
B	Lilette Laurent's songs are very catchy.	
C	I think Lilette Laurent is fairly pretty.	
D	I like rock music.	

[2 marks]

Speaking Question

For the Speaking Question pages, you'll need to get a friend or a parent to read the teacher's role, so you can pretend it's a real assessment. Before the conversation starts, give yourself a couple minutes to read through the candidate's role, and think about what you're going to say.

Candidate's Role

- Your teacher will play the role of your French friend. They will speak first.

- You must use *tu* to address your friend.

- – ! – means you will have to respond to something you have not prepared.

- – ? – means you will have to ask your friend a question.

> Tu organises une excursion au cinéma avec un(e) ami(e).
>
> - Genre de film que tu préfères — raison
> - Se rencontrer — quand
> - !
> - ? Transport au cinéma
> - ? Après le film — activité

Teacher's Role

- You begin the role play using the introductory text below.

- You should address the candidate as *tu*.

- Do not supply the candidate with key vocabulary.

- You must ask the questions below exactly as they are written.

> Introductory text: *Tu organises une excursion au cinéma avec un(e) ami(e).*
> *Moi, je suis ton ami(e).*
>
> - Quel genre de film préfères-tu ?
> - On se retrouve à quelle heure ?
> - ! Est-ce que tu veux inviter quelqu'un d'autre ?
> - ? Allow the candidate to ask you how you will get to the cinema.
> - ? Allow the candidate to ask you what you will do after the film.

Reading Questions

1 Read this chatroom conversation three teenagers had about their families.

Marie	J'habite avec mes grand-parents. Ma grand-mère a soixante-dix ans et mon grand-père a soixante-treize ans. Ils sont très sympathiques.
Claude	J'ai une assez grande famille. D'abord il y a mon frère aîné, qui a vingt ans. Puis il y a moi, et j'ai dix-sept ans. J'ai aussi une petite sœur, qui a quatorze ans, et un petit frère, qui a douze ans.
Ahmed	Je n'ai ni frères ni sœurs. J'habite avec ma mère, qui a quarante-sept ans. Moi, j'ai quinze ans. Nous avons un vieux chat, qui est plus âgé que moi — il a seize ans. Notre petite famille est harmonieuse.

How old are the following people / animals? Write the numbers in digits.

Example: Marie's grandmother ......70......

a Marie's grandfather ....

d Claude's sister ....

b Claude's older brother ....

e Ahmed's mother ....

c Claude ....

f Ahmed's cat .... *[6 marks]*

2 Lis ce que ces personnes ont écrit dans un forum sur leurs passe-temps.
Réponds aux questions **en français**.

Je fais souvent du sport. Le mardi soir, je fais de la natation. Ça commence à sept heures. Ce week-end, il y a un concours et je vais y participer. — **Aurélie**

Moi, j'aime la musique. Le lundi soir et le samedi matin, je joue de la trompette dans un orchestre. La semaine prochaine il y aura un grand concert. — **Damien**

a Quand est-ce qu'Aurélie fait de la natation ? .... *[2 marks]*

b Qu'est-ce qu'elle fait ce week-end ? .... *[1 mark]*

c Quand est-ce que Damien joue dans l'orchestre ? .... *[2 marks]*

d Quand est le concert ? .... *[1 mark]*

Writing Questions

1   Traduis le passage suivant **en français** :

> On Mondays, I see my friends. Last week, we watched an action film.
> This weekend, I am going to go shopping with my cousins.

....

....

....

....

....

[6 marks]

2   Traduis le passage suivant **en français** :

> My favourite sport is rugby because it is very exciting. I have been playing rugby for seven
> years. At the weekend I like to watch sport on television with my friends, but I'm not interested
> in football. I think that the players are arrogant. In the future, I would like to be a teacher.

....

....

....

....

....

....

[12 marks]

Revision Summary for Section One

These questions are here to help you find out what you know well, and what might need some more work. Once you've had a go at all of them, have another look through the section and revise the bits you found tricky. Tick off the questions you can answer, then put a tick by the page title when you've finished all the questions in that section.

Numbers (p.1) ☑

1) Count out loud from 1–20 in French. ☑
2) How do you say these numbers in French?
   a) 35   b) 71   c) 86   d) 112   e) 2000 ☑
3) How would you say 'ninth' in French? ☑

Times and Dates (p.2-3) ☑

4) Your friend says: 'Je vais aller au parc à huit heures du soir.' Translate her sentence into English. ☑
5) Using the 24-hour clock, say 'it's four forty-five pm' in French. ☑
6) State all of the days of the week in French, from Monday to Sunday. ☑
7) How do you say the following time expressions in French?
   a) yesterday   b) tomorrow   c) the weekend ☑
8) If something happened 'avant-hier', when did it happen? ☑
9) Say all of the months of the year in French, from January to December. ☑
10) Quelle est la date de ton anniversaire? Réponds en français. ☑

Questions (p.4-5) ☑

11) To ask a question just by changing the tone of your voice, what do you need to do? ☑
12) 'Tu joues' means 'you play' or 'you are playing'. What do these questions mean in English?
   a) Pourquoi tu joues?   c) Où est-ce que tu joues?   e) Est-ce que tu joues?
   b) Quand est-ce que tu joues?   d) Joues-tu bien?   f) De quoi joues-tu? ☑

Being Polite (p.6-7) ☑

13) What's the French for...? a) see you soon   b) see you tomorrow   c) good luck ☑
14) You're speaking to your head teacher. Which of the following questions would be most appropriate?
   a) Comment ça va?   b) Comment allez-vous? ☑
15) What's the English for...? a) Je voudrais...   b) Est-ce que je peux...?   c) s'il vous plaît ☑

Opinions (p.8-10) ☑

16) How would you ask someone, in French, what they think of rap music ('la musique rap')?
   Give as many different ways as you can think of. ☑
17) Translate these phrases into English:
   a) je pense que   b) à mon avis   c) je crois que   d) personnellement ☑
18) Translate these opinions about pop music ('la musique pop') into French.
   a) I love pop music.   c) I'm interested in pop music.   e) I find pop music great.
   b) I don't like pop music.   d) I find pop music awful.   f) It means nothing to me. ☑
19) Your friend says: 'Moi, je préfère la musique rock car c'est formidable.' What's he saying? ☑
20) Think of an actor or singer you like, and explain why you like them (in French). ☑
21) Answer this question in French: 'Quel est ton avis sur les films d'action?' ☑

About Yourself

Learning to tell the examiner about yourself is really important. Don't worry if you don't have much to say — just make stuff up so you can show off your knowledge of French vocab and grammar.

Je m'appelle... — My name is...

s'appeler	to be called
avoir... ans	to be... years old
le nom	surname
le prénom	first name
né(e) le...	born on the...
l'anniversaire (m)	birthday

Grammar — saying your age

In French, you don't say how old you <u>are</u> — you say how many years you <u>have</u>. This means you need to use the verb '<u>avoir</u>' (to have).

Quel âge <u>as</u>-tu? ⟹ **J'<u>ai</u> seize ans.**

How old <u>are</u> you? ⟹ *I <u>am</u> sixteen years old.*

> For more on numbers and dates see p.1-3.

Je m'appelle Sara et j'habite à Natland.

J'ai quinze ans, et je suis né(e) le neuf juin 2001.

Mon anniversaire, c'est le deux février.

Je suis britannique mais je suis d'origine asiatique.

I'm called Sara and I live in Natland.

I'm fifteen years old, and I was born on the ninth of June 2001.

My birthday is on the second of February.

I'm British but I'm of Asian origin.

> near to Kendal — près de Kendal
>
> 'Né(e)' needs an extra 'e' on the end if you're female (see p.128).
>
> *English* — anglais(e)
> *Welsh* — gallois(e)
> *Scottish* — écossais(e)
> *Irish* — irlandais(e)

> See p.189-190 for a list of more nationalities.

Ça s'écrit... — That's spelt...

You might be asked to <u>spell out</u> your <u>name</u>, or another piece of information you've given. Generally, the French alphabet is <u>very similar</u> to English, but there are a few <u>tricky letters</u> to watch out for:

A — 'aah'	H — 'ash'	O — 'oh'	V — 'vay'
B — 'beh'	I — 'ee'	P — 'pay'	W — 'doobluh vay'
C — 'seh'	J — 'djee'	Q — 'koo'	X — 'eex'
D — 'deh'	K — 'kah'	R — 'air'	Y — 'eegrek'
E — 'euh'	L — 'ell'	S — 'ess'	Z — 'zed'
F — 'eff'	M — 'em'	T — 'tay'	
G — 'djay'	N — 'en'	U — 'oo'	

> In French, it's 'double V', not 'double U'.

Grammar — accents

For letters with accents, say the <u>letter</u> followed by the <u>accent</u>:

è — '*euh accent <u>grave</u>*'
é — '*euh accent <u>aigu</u>*'
ê — '*euh accent <u>circonflexe</u>*'
ë — '*euh <u>tréma</u>*'
ç — '*seh <u>cédille</u>*'

SPEAKING

French letters can be tricky, so learn how to say them...

Read the question and Sophie's response below.
Parle-moi un peu de toi-même.

Je m'appelle Sophie. Ça s'écrit S-O-P-H-I-E. Je suis née le trois mars deux mille un et j'ai presque seize ans. Je suis anglaise et j'habite actuellement à Manchester, en Angleterre. Pourtant, je suis d'origine asiatique et mes parents sont nés à Hong Kong.

Grade 6-7

Tick list:
✓ tenses: present, perfect
✓ correct formation of dates
✓ conjunctions link phrases together
✓ correct adjective agreement

To improve:
+ more varied conjunctions

Now try to answer the same question.
Aim to talk for about two minutes. [10 marks]

You could say things like your name, age and where you're from.

Your Family

You need to be able to describe your family as well as yourself. This topic is a favourite with the examiners — so learn it well and keep coming back to test yourself on the vocab on this page.

La famille proche — Close relatives

le père	*father*	la nièce	*niece*
la mère	*mother*	le beau-père	*step-father*
le frère	*brother*	la belle-mère	*step-mother*
la sœur	*sister*	le demi-frère	*half-brother*
le fils / la fille unique	*only child*	la demi-sœur	*half-sister*
le grand-père	*grandfather*	le jumeau	*twin brother*
la grand-mère	*grandmother*	la jumelle	*twin sister*
le / la petit(e) ami(e)	*boyfriend / girlfriend*	le / la partenaire	*partner*
le neveu	*nephew*	aîné(e)	*elder*

To say 'I'm an only child' in French, you don't need an article, e.g. 'je suis fils unique'.

When you're talking about something or someone that belongs to you, e.g. 'my sister', you need to use a possessive adjective (see p.103).

Parle-moi de ta famille — Tell me about your family

Question

As-tu une grande famille?
Have you got a big family?

Simple Answer

J'ai une petite famille — nous sommes quatre.

I've got a small family — there are four of us.

Extended Answer

J'ai une petite famille car ma mère est fille unique. J'ai un petit frère et une cousine. J'ai aussi une petite amie qui s'appelle Amy.

I've got a small family because my mum is an only child. I have a little brother and one cousin (female). I've also got a girlfriend called Amy.

Dans ma famille, il y a neuf personnes.

In my family, there are nine people.

J'ai une grande famille car mes parents sont séparés et ils se sont tous les deux remariés.

I have a big family because my parents are separated and they have both remarried.

don't live together — ne vivent pas ensemble

are divorced — sont divorcés

J'ai deux frères qui sont plus âgés que moi.

I've got two brothers who are older than me.

younger — plus jeunes

Le partenaire de ma mère vient d'Italie, donc j'ai de la famille à l'étranger.

My mum's partner comes from Italy, so I have some family abroad.

isn't British — n'est pas britannique

Grammar — comparisons

To <u>compare</u> one person or thing to another, use '<u>plus</u> / <u>moins...que</u>' (*more / less...than*) with an <u>adjective</u> in the middle.

Elle est plus <u>âgée</u> / <u>jeune</u> que moi.
She is <u>older</u> / <u>younger</u> than me.

Don't just list your family members — add in details as well...

A French friend has written a blog post and wants you to translate it **into English**. *[7 marks]*

Dans ma famille, il y a trois personnes — ma mère, mon père et moi. Malheureusement, je n'ai ni frères ni sœurs donc je suis fils unique. Par contre, j'ai beaucoup de cousins et je les vois souvent. Le week-end dernier, par exemple, nous sommes allés au cinéma ensemble et nous nous sommes très bien amusés.

Look out for any changes in tense.

Describing People

Now you know how to name people in French, you can begin to describe them. This page will help you to gain marks by describing people accurately with lots of fancy vocab. Read on for more...

On décrit les autres — Describing others

It's really likely that you'll have to <u>describe</u> your family and friends, so learn these useful <u>adjectives</u>:

<u>les yeux (m):</u>
marron / noisette
<u>les cheveux (m):</u>
roux / bruns / blonds
longs / mi-longs / courts
teints / bouclés / frisés / raides
la barbe
joli(e)
beau / belle
laid(e)
grand(e)
petit(e)
clair(e) / foncé(e)
de taille (f) moyenne

<u>eyes:</u>
brown / hazel
<u>hair:</u>
ginger / brown / blond
long / medium-length / short
dyed / curly / curly / straight
beard
pretty
handsome / beautiful
ugly
tall
short
light / dark
average height

> **Grammar** — agreements
>
> Adjectives <u>agree</u> with the <u>person or thing</u> they're describing — if it's <u>feminine</u>, you need to add an '<u>e</u>' onto the <u>end of the adjective</u>. If it's <u>plural</u>, add an '<u>s</u>'. If it's <u>feminine and plural</u>, add '<u>es</u>'.
>
> **Ma copine est très petite.**
> **My girlfriend is very short.**
>
> **Elle a les cheveux longs.**
> **She has long hair.**

'Marron' (brown) and 'noisette' (hazel) never agree with the noun they're describing.

Ils sont comment? — What are they like?

'Gros' (fat) becomes 'grosse' when it agrees with a feminine noun.

Ma sœur est assez grande et jolie. Elle a les yeux noisette et les cheveux longs et ondulés.

My sister is quite tall and pretty. She has hazel eyes and long, wavy hair.

Ma meilleure copine a les yeux marron et les cheveux bruns. Elle porte des lunettes.

My best friend has brown eyes and brown hair. She wears glasses.

Mon frère aîné a beaucoup de boutons sur le visage et il a une moustache.

My older brother has lots of spots on his face and he has a moustache.

Elles sont toutes les deux de taille moyenne.

They're both average height.

fat — grosse
slim — mince

jewellery — des bijoux (m)

a scar — une cicatrice
a mole — un grain de beauté

very beautiful — très belles

Remember — you need to make all the adjectives agree...

In this extract from a podcast, Fabien is being interviewed about his family.

Find the true statement from the pair below.

e.g. A. Fabien lives with his parents.   **B.** Fabien lives by himself.   **A**

1. *There are two true statements in each list below. Choose the correct statements from each list.*

(i) A. It's never quiet at Fabien's house.
    B. Fabien is the youngest child at home.
    C. His sisters have blue eyes.
    D. Fabien's half-brother is older than him.
    E. His half-brother lives at home.   [2]

(ii) A. Fabien's mother has long hair.
    B. His mother has curly hair.
    C. Fabien's father is tall.
    D. His father has a beard.
    E. Fabien looks like his father.   [2]

Personalities

It's what's on the inside that counts, so it's probably a good idea to learn how to describe your personality. It isn't always easy to sum up your wonderful self in a few words, but use this page as a starting point.

Les personnalités (f) — Personalities

Adjectives need to agree with the nouns they're describing. See p.101 for more.

gentil / gentille	*nice*	bavard(e)	*chatty / talkative*	égoïste	*selfish*
vif / vive	*lively*	aimable	*kind*	jaloux / jalouse	*jealous*
heureux / heureuse	*happy*	compréhensif / compréhensive	*understanding*	bête	*stupid / silly*
				fou / folle	*mad / crazy*

Question
Tu as quel genre de caractère?
What kind of personality do you have?

Simple Answer
Je suis gentil(le) et un peu bavard(e).
I'm nice and a bit chatty.

Extended Answer
Je suis assez vif / vive et bavard(e). Mes amis me disent que je suis vraiment généreux / généreuse, mais je sais que je suis parfois égoïste.
I'm quite lively and talkative. My friends tell me that I'm really generous, but I know that I'm sometimes selfish.

Grammar — imperfect tense
To describe someone in the past, use the imperfect tense (see p.129).
Elle était vive et bavarde.
She was lively and talkative.

Grammar — false friends
Some French words sound like English words, but have a different meaning.

sensible	*sensitive (not sensible)*
le caractère	*personality (not a fictional character)*
grand(e)	*big / tall (not grand)*

Parler des autres — To talk about others

It's useful to be able to say what other people are like too.

Mon frère est égoïste et il ne pense jamais aux autres. Pourtant, je suis très fier / fière de ma famille.

My brother is selfish and he never thinks about others. However, I'm very proud of my family.

Ma meilleure copine, Ann, est vraiment aimable et elle est toujours là pour moi quand j'ai un problème.

My best friend, Ann, is really kind and she is always there for me when I have a problem.

WRITING — Say how people have changed so you can use different tenses...
Pierre has written a blog entry about his best friend.

Mon meilleur ami s'appelle Sunil. Il est sportif, intelligent et toujours heureux. Pourtant, au collège, il est un peu bavard et bête. Cependant il n'est jamais égoïste. Il veut toujours aider les autres et faire de bonnes actions. Le week-end, on va souvent au cinéma et on joue au foot ensemble dans le parc.

Grade 6-7

Tick list:
✓ good use of connectives
✓ wide range of adjectives

To improve:
+ use at least two tenses

Tu décris ton / ta meilleur(e) ami(e) pour ton blog.
*Tu **dois** faire référence aux points suivants :*
- *l'apparence et la personnalité de ton ami(e)*
- *pourquoi il / elle est ton / ta meilleur(e) ami(e)*
- *ce que vous faites ensemble le week-end*
- *ce que vous ferez ensemble dans l'avenir.*

*Écris **80-90** mots environ **en français**.* [20 marks]

Connectives can help you to express an opinion.
cependant / pourtant	*however*
de plus	*moreover*
donc	*so / therefore*

Pets

Pets are often considered as part of the family and they could appear in one of your exams. Even if you don't have a pet, you can still give your opinion and say whether or not you'd like one, and why.

Les animaux domestiques — Pets

la tortue	*tortoise*	l'oiseau (m)	*bird*
le cochon d'Inde	*guinea pig*	le cheval	*horse*
le lapin	*rabbit*	le poil	*animal hair*
le poisson rouge	*goldfish*	sage	*well-behaved*
le poisson tropical	*tropical fish*	méchant(e)	*naughty / nasty*
le chat	*cat*	effronté(e)	*cheeky*
le chien	*dog*	fidèle	*loyal / faithful*
le hamster	*hamster*	paresseux /	
le serpent	*snake*	paresseuse	*lazy*

Grammar — irregular adjectives

Some adjectives have <u>irregular feminine</u> forms (see p.101-102):

blanc (m) / blanche (f)	*white*
vieux (m) / vieille (f)	*old*
fou (m) / folle (f)	*mad*
beau (m) / belle (f)	*beautiful*

Question	**Simple Answer**	**Extended Answer**
As-tu un animal domestique?	Oui, j'ai deux chats.	Oui, j'ai deux chats chez moi. Ils sont blancs, à poils longs et assez vieux. J'avais un chien aussi, mais il est mort il y a cinq ans.
Do you have a pet?	*Yes, I have two cats.*	*Yes, I've got two cats at home. They are white, long-haired and quite old. I used to have a dog too, but he died five years ago.*

Ils sont comment? — What are they like?

You should be able to describe your pet's <u>personality</u>, as well as their appearance.

J'ai un chien qui s'appelle César, et il a trois ans. Il est très vif. Je l'adore car il est mon meilleur ami.	I have a dog called César, and he's three years old. He's very lively. I love him because he's my best friend.

I like to play with him — j'aime jouer avec lui

Malheureusement, je n'ai plus d'animaux, mais quand j'étais plus petit(e) j'avais un lapin. Il était très méchant!	Unfortunately, I don't have any pets anymore, but when I was younger I had a rabbit. He was very nasty!

I can't have any pets anymore — je ne peux plus avoir d'animaux

Moi, je n'aime pas les animaux domestiques. Ils ont une mauvaise odeur, et ils ne sont pas hygiéniques.	I don't like pets. They smell bad, and they're unhygienic.

I'm allergic to them — j'y suis allergique

J'adore les animaux domestiques, surtout les chiens. Ils sont toujours marrants et fidèles.	I love pets, especially dogs. They're always funny and loyal.

affectionate — affectueux

Justify your opinions with 'parce que' and 'car'...

Listen to Romain talking about pets and answer the questions **in English**.

1 a. What does Romain do to help his neighbour? [1]

b. What reason does Romain give for Duc's misbehaviour? [1]

c. Why does Romain like guinea pigs? Give **one** reason. [1]

d. Which pets would Romain like to have when he's older? Give **two** details. [2]

Style and Fashion

Don't just describe your wardrobe in detail here — fashion is at the heart of tons of important debates (the importance of image, how celebrities influence others...), so make sure you've got some opinions ready.

Décris ton style — Describe your style

For more about clothes, see p.32 and p.186.

porter	*to wear*	la bague	*ring*	le costume	*suit*
se maquiller	*to put on make-up*	le maquillage	*make-up*	le parfum	*perfume*
le rouge à lèvres	*lipstick*	la jupe	*skirt*	le tatouage	*tattoo*
les bijoux (m)	*jewellery*	le short	*shorts*	la mode	*fashion*
les boucles (f) d'oreille	*earrings*	le collant	*tights*	teint	*dyed (hair)*

Grammar — 'en...' (made of...)

In French, use '<u>en</u>' to describe what something's made of.

en laine (f)	*made of wool*
en velours (m)	*made of velvet*
en cuir (m)	*made of leather*
en coton (m)	*made of cotton*

Je me fais couper les cheveux tous les mois. C'est cher, mais ça en vaut la peine.

I get my hair cut every month. It's expensive, but it's worth it.

Je voudrais un tatouage au poignet. Je vais le dessiner moi-même — ce sera une expression de ma personnalité.

I'd like a tattoo on my wrist. I'm going to design it myself — it'll be an expression of my personality.

La mode, est-elle importante? — Is fashion important?

The importance of <u>fashion</u> is a popular debate, so it's a good idea to <u>prepare</u> your opinion.

Pour moi, c'est très important d'être à la mode. Je fais toujours attention à ce que je porte, et j'aime être chic.

For me, it's very important to be fashionable. I am always careful with what I wear, and I like to be smart.

I'm passionate about fashion — Je suis passionné(e) par la mode

Moi, je ne m'intéresse pas à la mode. Je choisis toujours des vêtements confortables plutôt que les vêtements à la mode.

I'm not interested in fashion. I always choose comfortable clothes rather than fashionable ones.

practical — pratiques
second hand — d'occasion

Selon moi, ce n'est pas nécessaire de se maquiller pour être beau.

In my opinion, it isn't necessary to put on make-up to be beautiful.

make-up improves self-confidence — le maquillage améliore la confiance en soi

---

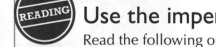 **READING**

Use the imperfect tense to talk about what you used to wear...

Read the following online comments about fashion.

Pauline : Je suis passionnée par les vêtements et les bijoux ! J'aime porter des vêtements en velours parce que c'est à la mode. Par contre, je ne porte jamais de laine car personne de chic n'en porte aujourd'hui.

Jérôme : Moi, j'aime être individuel — je ne choisis pas des vêtements parce qu'ils sont à la mode, mais plutôt car je les aime. Cependant, j'aime me faire couper les cheveux et j'ai trois piercings et un tatouage.

Sylvie : Pour moi, l'apparence physique n'est pas très importante. Je préfère passer du temps en essayant d'être une personne gentille et sympathique plutôt qu'en choisissant des vêtements chics.

Who says each of these things about fashion? Choose either Pauline, Jérôme or Sylvie.

e.g. ....Pauline.... is passionate about fashion.

1. .... doesn't care about clothes. [1]
2. .... enjoys going to the hairdresser's. [1]
3. .... has a personal style. [1]
4. .... is influenced by others. [1]

Relationships

The examiners are also pretty interested in your relationships with other people. Luckily, this page will give you the chance to practise some of those pesky reflexive verbs you know and love. Get reading...

Les amis et les modèles — Friends and role models

se disputer	*to argue*
s'entendre (avec)	*to get on (with)*
connaître	*to know (a person)*
être fâché(e)	*to be angry*
se faire des amis	*to make friends*
casse-pieds	*a pain in the neck*
le sens de l'humour	*sense of humour*
jaloux / jalouse	*jealous*
équilibré(e)	*well-balanced*
soutenir	*to support*

> **Grammar** — reflexive verbs
>
> Reflexive verbs (see p.133) have an <u>extra part</u> — a <u>reflexive pronoun</u>.
>
> **Je <u>m'</u>entends bien avec...**   ***I get on well with...***
>
> **Nous <u>nous</u> disputons souvent.**   ***We often argue.***
>
> In the <u>perfect tense</u> (see p.127-128), the pronoun goes <u>before</u> the present tense part of 'être' (*to be*).
>
> **Il <u>s'</u>est fait facilement des amis.**   ***He made friends easily.***

Mes modèles sont très influents. Ils m'inspirent à travailler dur car je veux être comme eux.

My role models are very influential. They inspire me to work hard because I want to be like them.

Je n'admire pas de célébrités. À mon avis, elles sont souvent gâtées et prétentieuses.

I don't admire celebrities. In my opinion, they are often spoilt and pretentious.

Tu t'entends bien avec...? — Do you get on well with...?

Tu t'entends bien avec ta famille?

Do you get on well with your family?

Je m'entends bien avec mes parents.

I get on well with my parents.

I have a good relationship — J'ai un bon rapport

Quelquefois je me dispute avec ma sœur aînée parce qu'elle est vraiment gâtée.

Sometimes I argue with my older sister because she is really spoilt.

doesn't have a sense of humour — n'a pas le sens de l'humour

SPEAKING — Use 'être' with reflexives in the perfect tense...

Read Ava's response to the picture task, then follow the instructions below.

Décris-moi la photo. La famille, semble-t-elle comme la tienne ?

Sur la photo, il y a une famille de cinq personnes — trois femmes et deux enfants. **Parmi**[1] les enfants, il y a un garçon et une fille. Le garçon **a l'air**[2] plus jeune que la fille. Ils ont l'air heureux et on dirait qu'ils s'entendent bien ensemble.

Grade 8-9

[1]Amongst
[2]looks
[3]even so
[4]cute

Moi, je m'entends très bien avec ma famille aussi. Mon père est plus strict que ma mère, mais il est raisonnable **quand même**[3]. Ma sœur est **mignonne**[4], mais elle m'énerve quelquefois.

Tick list:
✓ good use of comparatives like 'plus que'
✓ accurate use of reflexive verbs

Regarde la photo et prépare des réponses sur les points suivants :

- *la description de la photo*
- *si la famille est comme la tienne*
- *si tu t'entendais bien avec ta famille quand tu étais plus jeune*
- *une activité que tu feras avec ta famille cette semaine*
- *!*

[24 marks]

To improve:
+ include a past tense

You'll always be asked to describe the photo. Use 'Sur la photo, il y a...' to get started. Include as much detail as you can — look at the example for inspiration.

Socialising with Friends and Family

This may be a cruel topic to discuss while you're revising, but you can go back to having a social life soon...

Est-ce que tu es un(e) bon(ne) ami(e)? — Are you a good friend?

passer du temps avec	*to spend time with*	l'amitié (f)	*friendship*
traîner avec	*to hang out with*	indépendant(e)	*independent*
participer à	*to take part in*	joyeux / joyeuse	*happy*
la fête familiale	*family celebration*	le surnom	*nickname*

Question

Selon toi, quelles sont les qualités d'un(e) bon(ne) ami(e)?
In your opinion, what are the qualities of a good friend?

Simple Answer

Un(e) bon(ne) ami(e) te soutient toujours, et il / elle te fait rire.
A good friend always supports you, and they make you laugh.

Extended Answer

Un(e) bon(ne) ami(e) est quelqu'un qui te soutient et qui t'écoute. Il / elle est hônnete et il / elle te donne des conseils. Mais, à mon avis, la qualité la plus importante, c'est qu'il / elle a le même sens de l'humour que toi.

A good friend is someone who supports you and listens to you. They are honest and give you advice. But, in my opinion, the most important quality is that they have the same sense of humour as you.

> **Grammar** — verb + infintive
>
> When one verb <u>follows another</u>, the second verb is always in the <u>infinitive</u> (see p.124).
>
> **Il faut avoir** les mêmes intérêts.
> *<u>You must have</u> the same interests.*
>
> **Mon meilleur copain me <u>fait rire</u>.**
> *My best friend <u>makes</u> me <u>laugh</u>.*

Que fais-tu le week-end? — What do you do at the weekend?

Normalement, je passe le week-end en famille car je ne vois guère mes parents pendant la semaine. J'adore ça — je prends des nouvelles de tout le monde.

Quand j'étais plus jeune, je passais beaucoup de temps en famille le week-end, mais maintenant, l'amitié est plus importante pour moi.

Le dimanche, je rends visite à mon grand-père. Je l'aide en faisant les tâches ménagères, et il cuisine pour moi.

Normally, I spend the weekend with my family because I hardly see my parents in the week. I love it — I catch up with everyone.

When I was younger, I used to spend a lot of time with my family at the weekend, but now, friendship is more important for me.

On Sundays, I visit my grandad. I help him by doing the housework, and he cooks for me.

WRITING

When you use 'il faut', put the verb that follows in the infinitive...

Philippe a écrit un blog sur les activités qu'il fait avec sa famille.

Je suis très sociable, et pendant mon temps libre je sors beaucoup avec mes copains. Je vais chez eux le soir pendant la semaine. Le week-end, j'essaie de passer un peu de temps en famille, mais c'est difficile car j'ai deux petits frères et mes parents sont souvent **occupés**[1].

Quand j'étais plus petit, je passais plus de temps en famille — le samedi soir nous regardions un film ensemble. Maintenant, je préfère sortir avec mes copains.

Grade 6-7

[1]busy

Tick list:
✓ tenses: present, imperfect
✓ time expressions ('pendant', 'le week-end')

To improve:
+ include conditional, future and perfect tenses
+ more advanced conjunctions

Écris un blog sur les qualités d'un(e) bon(ne) ami(e). Tu **dois** faire référence aux points suivants :

- *les qualités d'un(e) bon(ne) ami(e)*
- *si tu es un(e) bon(ne) ami(e)*
- *ce que tu fais avec tes ami(e)s*
- *tes projets pour l'été avec tes ami(e)s.*

Écris **80-90** mots environ en **français**.   [20 marks]

Don't forget to justify your opinions using 'parce que' and 'car'.

Partnership

Seeing as Paris is the city of love, we couldn't let this topic slip by. Plus, you might have to talk about your views on love and marriage in the exam, so you need to know this stuff inside out and back to front.

Le mariage — Marriage

l'amour (m)	*love*	les fiançailles (f)	*engagement*	la femme	*wife*
célibataire	*single*	les noces (f)	*wedding*	épouser	*to marry*
la confiance	*trust*	le mari	*husband*	se marier	*to get married*

Le mariage montre au monde qu'on s'aime. Cependant, à mon avis, le mariage commence à devenir démodé.

Marriage shows the world that you love each other. However, in my opinion, marriage is starting to become old-fashioned.

these days / today — de nos jours

Les noces sont trop chères. Avec l'argent, je préférerais acheter une maison.

Weddings are too expensive. With the money, I would prefer to buy a house.

I think that — Je pense que

Je crois que le mariage est important, il donne de la structure à la vie de famille.

I believe that marriage is important, it gives structure to family life.

In my opinion — Selon moi

Question

Tu voudrais te marier un jour?

Do you want to get married one day?

Simple Answer

Oui, à l'avenir je voudrais me marier et avoir des enfants.

Yes, in the future I'd like to get married and have children.

Grammar — talking about the future

There are lots of different ways to talk about your <u>future plans</u>. You can use:

- The <u>future tense</u> (see p.126): **je serai**   *I will be*
- Or the <u>conditional tense</u> (see p.135): **je voudrais**   *I would like*
- Or use '<u>j'espère</u>' (*I hope*) <u>+ infinitive</u>: **J'espère me marier un jour.**
  I hope to get married one day.

Extended Answers

Oui, pour moi le mariage est très important, et à l'avenir j'espère rencontrer l'homme / la femme de mes rêves et rester avec lui / elle pour toujours. Franchement, je ne comprends pas ceux qui ne veulent pas se marier.

Yes, marriage is very important for me, and in the future I hope to meet the man / woman of my dreams and stay with him / her forever. Frankly, I don't understand those people who don't want to get married.

Moi, je ne veux pas du tout me marier. Par contre, pour moi, ce qui est plus important c'est l'amour et la confiance. On peut être avec quelqu'un et avoir des enfants sans l'épouser.

I really don't want to get married. On the other hand, for me, what's more important is love and trust. You can be with someone and have children without marrying them.

 READING

This is the perfect opportunity for you to use the future tense...

Read this extract from 'Madame Bovary' by Gustave Flaubert and choose the correct phrases.

Emma a, au contraire, désiré se marier à minuit, **aux flambeaux**[1]; mais le père Rouault n'a rien compris à cette idée. Il y avait donc des noces, où quarante-trois personnes sont venues, où l'on est resté seize heures à table, qui a recommencé le lendemain et quelque peu les jours suivants.

[1]in torchlight

1. Emma wanted to get married...
   A. the next day.
   B. in sixteen hours.
   C. at midnight.   [1]

2. Emma's wedding...
   A. was short and simple.
   B. suited her father's wishes.
   C. was exactly the way she wanted it.   [1]

Listening Questions

Time to put what you've learnt to the test. Have a go at answering these practice questions —
if you struggle with something, read through the section again and then have another stab at it.

1   Samir et Maya parlent de la mode. Complète les phrases en choisissant un
     mot ou des mots dans la case. Il y a des mots que tu n'utiliseras pas.

~~importante~~	blouson	la bijouterie
coiffer	ennuyeux	couper les cheveux
les magazines	gilet	passionnants

Example: Samir dit que la mode est vraiment ....importante........ .

a   Il cherche les styles à la mode dans ....   *[1 mark]*

b   Il aimerait un nouveau ....   *[1 mark]*

c   Maya ne pense pas que les vêtements à la mode soient ....   *[1 mark]*

d   Maya aime se faire ....   *[1 mark]*

2   Pascale is talking about her friends and family.
     Put a cross in the correct box to complete the sentences.

a   She sees her grandparents...

A	at family parties.	
B	during the school holidays.	
C	every day.	

[1 mark]

b   Pascale's aunt...

A	lives far away.	
B	just got married.	
C	has two children.	

[1 mark]

c   Pascale and Kelise both enjoy...

A	playing the piano.	
B	classical music.	
C	singing in a choir.	

[1 mark]

Speaking Question

Candidate's Role

- Your teacher will play the role of your French friend. They will speak first.

- You must use *tu* to address your friend.

- – ! – means you will have to respond to something you have not prepared.

- – ? – means you will have to ask your friend a question.

> Tu parles de ta famille avec un(e) ami(e) français(e).
>
> - Ta famille — description
>
> - Famille — importance
>
> - !
>
> - ? Frères et sœurs
>
> - ? Enfants dans le futur

Teacher's Role

- You begin the role play using the introductory text below.

- You should address the candidate as *tu*.

- Do not supply the candidate with key vocabulary.

- You must ask the questions below exactly as they are written.

> Introductory text: *Tu parles de ta famille avec un(e) ami(e) français(e).*
> *Moi, je suis ton ami(e).*
>
> - Comment est ta famille ?
>
> - Ta famille est-elle importante pour toi ? Pourquoi ?
>
> - ! Parle-moi d'une activité que tu as faite récemment avec ta famille.
>
> - ? Allow the candidate to ask you if you have any siblings.
>
> - ? Allow the candidate to ask you if you want to have children in the future.

Reading Questions

1   Lis l'email de Tania qui parle d'elle-même. Réponds aux questions **en français**.

> Je m'appelle Tania, j'ai seize ans et je suis française. J'habite dans une
> petite ville près de La Rochelle avec ma famille. Je suis assez grande, mais je
> ne suis pas aussi grande que mon frère. Il aime toujours me rappeler qu'il est
> déjà plus grand que notre père même s'il n'a que quatorze ans. Mes cheveux
> sont blonds et courts, et j'ai les yeux verts. Je suis sportive et j'aime nager
> et jouer au football. Je joue au football tous les samedis depuis trois ans.

a   Comment est Tania ? Donne **un** détail.

....   *[1 mark]*

b   Son frère est très fier. Pourquoi ?

....   *[1 mark]*

c   Qu'est-ce qu'elle dit sur le football ? Donne **un** détail.

....   *[1 mark]*

2   Lis ces commentaires des jeunes sur leurs animaux domestiques.

Claude	J'ai un lapin. C'est un lapin mignon, mais un peu ennuyeux, il passe tout le temps à manger ou à dormir.
Lena	Mon chien s'appelle Hugo. Il est très fidèle et n'est jamais têtu. Pourtant, il est super aventureux donc il a besoin de promenades très longues.
Faiz	J'adore mes poissons rouges. Ils ne font pas grand chose, c'est vrai, mais je suis très paresseux et c'est facile de m'en occuper.
Naima	J'ai un lézard, et de temps en temps il est de mauvaise humeur — il m'a mordu hier. Cependant, c'est un animal que je pourrais regarder pendant des heures.

Qui est la personne correcte? Choisis entre : Lena, Faiz et Naima.

Example: L'animal domestique de ....Claude......... n'est pas très passionnant.

a   .... est fasciné(e) par son animal domestique.   *[1 mark]*

b   .... doit prendre de l'exercice à cause de son animal domestique.   *[1 mark]*

c   .... n'aimerait pas avoir un animal domestique qui a besoin de

beaucoup d'activité.   *[1 mark]*

Writing Questions

1   Ton / ta correspondant(e) t'a posé des questions sur le mariage.
    Écris un email au sujet d'un mariage récent dans ta famille.

    Tu **dois** faire référence aux points suivants :

    • les personnes qui se sont mariées

    • tes sentiments pendant la cérémonie

    • ton opinion au sujet du mariage en général

    • les qualités de ton / ta partenaire idéal(e).

    Écris 80-90 mots environ **en français**.   *[20 marks]*

2   Traduis le passage suivant **en français** :

    > I met my two best friends at a youth club. Edith is very funny and chatty, like me.
    > Delphine is shy but kind and generous. They are very different but they are very nice and
    > we spend lots of time together. We get on well. Sometimes it is difficult to make friends.

    ....

    ....

    ....

    ....

    ....

    ....

                                                                  [12 marks]

Revision Summary for Section Two

These questions bring together everything you've learnt in this section, so they're good at highlighting any bits you still need to brush up on. Don't worry if some questions are a little hard — have a go at them and then flick back through the section to revisit anything you're not sure about.

About Yourself (p.16) ☑

1) How would you say your name, age and birthday to a French person you've just met? ☑
2) Now tell them where you live, and what nationality you are. ☑
3) Spell your first name and surname out loud using the French alphabet. ☑

Your Family (p.17) ☑

4) As-tu une grande famille? Réponds en français. Utilise des phrases complètes. ☑
5) If Jonty is 'ton petit ami', what is he? ☑
6) Your penfriend tells you: 'Mes parents ne vivent pas ensemble, donc j'habite avec ma mère. Mon frère n'habite pas à la maison car il est plus âgé que moi.' What's she saying? ☑

Describing People and Personalities (p.18-19) ☑

7) Your best friend has light, curly hair and hazel eyes. She's quite tall and wears lots of jewellery. She is lively, but sometimes she is too sensitive. How would you describe her in French? ☑
8) How would you say the following words in French? a) short b) ugly c) average height ☑
9) 'Est-ce que tu ressembles à tes parents?' Translate the question into English and answer it in French. ☑
10) Write three sentences in French describing your personality. ☑

Pets (p.20) ☑

11) Julien tells you: 'J'ai un grand chien qui s'appelle Maurice. D'habitude, il est sage, mais parfois il est un peu effronté. Nous jouons ensemble dans le jardin.' What do you know about his pet? ☑
12) In French, say whether or not you would like to have a pet in the future, and explain why. ☑

Style and Fashion (p.21) ☑

13) Translate the following into English: a) une bague   b) des bijoux   c) un tatouage   d) teint ☑
14) La mode est-elle importante pour toi? Pourquoi / Pourquoi pas? Réponds en français. ☑

Relationships and Socialising (p.22-23) ☑

15) You don't get on with your brother. Out of the sentences below, which one would best describe your relationship?
   a) J'ai un bon rapport avec lui.   c) Il se fait facilement des amis.
   b) Nous nous disputons souvent.   d) Il est fou. ☑
16) Est-ce que tu t'entends bien avec tes parents? Réponds en deux phrases en français. ☑
17) In French, say whether you prefer spending time with your friends or your family, and why. ☑

Partnership (p.24) ☑

18) Describe your ideal partner. Think about their personality as well as their appearance. ☑
19) In French, jot down two reasons for marriage and two reasons against it. ☑
20) 'J'espère me marier un jour, mais je vais attendre jusqu'à l'âge de trente ans. Je veux être sûr de trouver la femme de mes rêves.' What does Jean think about marriage? ☑

Everyday Life

Tidying, cleaning, cooking... I'm sure you do all those things. Here's how to talk about them in French.

Une journée typique — A typical day

se lever	*to get up*	prendre le petit-déjeuner	*to eat breakfast*
se laver	*to wash (yourself)*	faire le lit	*to make the bed*
se doucher	*to shower*	se brosser les dents	*to brush your teeth*
s'habiller	*to get dressed*	se coucher	*to go to bed*

Question	**Simple Answer**	**Extended Answer**
Qu'est-ce que tu fais le matin?	Je quitte la maison à sept heures après avoir rangé la cuisine.	Je me lave, m'habille et prends mon petit-déjeuner en moins d'une heure. Mais l'année prochaine, j'aurai plus de temps car j'irai au lycée qui est plus proche.
What do you do in the morning?	*I leave home at seven after having tidied the kitchen.*	*I wash, get dressed and eat breakfast in less than an hour. But next year, I'll have more time because I will go to sixth form college which is closer.*

Grammar — reflexive

The 'se' part of reflexive verbs has to change:

Je	*me*
Tu	*te*
Il / elle / on	*se*
Nous	*nous*
Vous	*vous*
Ils / elles	*se*

See p.133 for more on this.

Gagner de l'argent de poche — To earn pocket money

les tâches (f) ménagères	*household tasks / chores*	faire du jardinage	*to do some gardening*
faire la lessive	*to do the laundry*	faire du bricolage	*to do some DIY*
faire la vaisselle	*to do the washing-up*	laver la voiture	*to wash the car*
mettre la table	*to lay the table*	garder des enfants	*to look after children / to babysit*

Je mets la table et je fais la vaisselle plusieurs fois par semaine. En plus, je range la cuisine le samedi.	*I lay the table and I do the washing up several times a week. In addition, I tidy the kitchen on Saturdays.*
Mes parents font les courses et la lessive en rentrant du travail.	*My parents do the shopping and the laundry once they get back from work.*
Parfois, j'aide ma mère à faire du jardinage ou du bricolage le week-end.	*Sometimes, I help my mum do some gardening or DIY at the weekend.*
Je n'achète rien avec mon argent de poche car je veux l'économiser.	*I don't buy anything with my pocket money because I want to save it.*

I vacuum — je passe l'aspirateur

I clean — je nettoie (from nettoyer)

cook — cuisiner
bake (cakes etc.) — faire des pâtisseries

And now for another chore — learn the phrases on this page...

Translate this blog entry about household chores **into English**. *[7 marks]*

Je reçois dix euros d'argent de poche par semaine. Mais je dois travailler pour gagner cet argent. Je participe tous les jours aux tâches ménagères pour aider mes parents. En plus, samedi dernier, j'ai gardé des enfants. J'achète beaucoup de musique en ligne, mais je vais essayer de faire des économies parce que j'aimerais partir en vacances avec mes copains.

There are some top tips for tackling translation questions on page 147.

Food

Food... my favourite topic. There's lots of vocab to learn — very useful for avoiding shocks in restaurants...

Qu'est-ce qu'on mange ce soir? — What are we eating tonight?

les légumes (m)	*vegetables*	les fruits (m)	*fruit*	le goût	*taste*
le chou-fleur	*cauliflower*	la pomme	*apple*	dégoûtant(e)	*disgusting*
le chou	*cabbage*	la poire	*pear*	épicé(e)	*spicy*
les haricots (m) verts	*green beans*	la framboise	*raspberry*	salé(e)	*salty*
le champignon	*mushroom*	la fraise	*strawberry*	sucré(e)	*sweet*
la pomme de terre	*potato*	les raisins (m)	*grapes*	amer / amère	*bitter*
les petits pois (m)	*peas*	l'ananas (m)	*pineapple*	bien cuit(e)	*well cooked*

le pain	*bread*	le lait	*milk*	la viande	*meat*	la saucisse	*sausage*
le riz	*rice*	le fromage	*cheese*	le poulet	*chicken*	le poisson	*fish*
les pâtes (f)	*pasta*	le beurre	*butter*	le bœuf	*beef*	le saumon	*salmon*
les frites (f)	*chips*	l'œuf (m)	*egg*	le jambon	*ham*	les fruits (m) de mer	*seafood*

Question	**Simple Answer**	**Extended Answer**
Quel est ton plat préféré?	Mon plat préféré c'est le steak frites, mais j'aime le potage aussi.	Je préfère manger du poisson plutôt que de la viande. Le poisson est meilleur pour la santé et plus nourrissant.
What's your favourite dish?	*My favourite dish is steak and chips, but I like soup too.*	*I prefer eating fish rather than meat. Fish is better for your health and more nourishing.*

Grammar — giving opinions

Use 'j'aime' (*I like*), 'je préfère' (*I prefer*) and 'je déteste' (*I hate*) to give a range of opinions.

Je préfère l'artichaut aux épinards.	***I prefer** artichoke to spinach.*
Je déteste l'agneau mais **j'aime** la dinde.	***I hate** lamb but **I like** turkey.*

For more food vocabulary, see the lists on p.185-186 and p.191.

Je mange... — I eat...

Get ready to talk about what you eat, what you think of it and why.

Je mange du saumon fumé — j'aime le goût.	*I eat smoked salmon — I like the taste.*
Je ne mange pas de plats cuisinés. Je préfère la cuisine faite maison car c'est plus sain.	*I don't eat ready meals. I prefer homemade food because it's healthier.*
Je devrais manger moins de nourriture sucrée parce que cela serait meilleur pour ma santé.	*I should eat less sugary food because that would be better for my health.*

tuna — du thon (m)
duck — du canard (m)
chocolate — chocolat (m)
cheese — fromage (m)

There's a lot of vocab here — you need to know all of it...

TRACK LISTENING 09

Listen to Selina, Ahmed and Élodie. Choose the correct answer to complete each statement.

e.g. Selina never eats... **A.** lamb **B.** fish **C.** pork   C

1 a. Ahmed particularly likes... **A.** raspberries   **B.** mushrooms   **C.** cauliflower   *[1]*

   b. Élodie's sister eats... **A.** sweet food   **B.** spicy food   **C.** healthy food   *[1]*

   c. Ahmed doesn't eat... **A.** ham   **B.** peas   **C.** vegetables   *[1]*

   d. Selina hates... **A.** bananas   **B.** pineapple   **C.** strawberries   *[1]*

Shopping

Whether you love fashion or you hate shopping, here's some stuff to help you talk about it in the exam.

Faire les magasins — To go shopping

'Faire les magasins' and 'faire des courses' refer to shopping in general. 'Faire les courses' refers to food shopping.

les vêtements (m)	clothes
la marque	brand
la mode	fashion
la carte bancaire	bank card
en espèces	with cash
la taille	size
le pantalon	trousers
la chemise	shirt
les chaussures (f)	shoes
en solde	in the sale
en vitrine	in the window
le ticket de caisse	receipt
l'étiquette (f)	label
rembourser	to refund
faire la queue	to queue

See p.186 for more clothes.

Question

Qu'est-ce que tu as acheté?
What did you buy?

Simple Answer

J'ai acheté un pull rouge et un T-shirt qui était en solde.
I bought a red jumper and a T-shirt that was in the sales.

Extended Answer

J'ai acheté une robe. Elle était chère, donc j'ai dû payer par carte bancaire. J'ai voulu acheter un pantalon aussi, mais il ne m'allait pas.
I bought a dress. It was expensive, so I had to pay by card. I wanted to buy some trousers too, but they didn't suit me.

Grammar — aller à (to suit)

'Ça me va' means 'it suits me'. The indirect object pronoun 'me' (see p.112) shows who it suits. The pronoun usually goes directly before the verb.

Je voudrais... — I would like...

Here are some useful phrases to use when you're shopping.

Autre chose?	Anything else?
Avec ça?	Anything else?
Ce sera tout?	Is that everything?
Ce sera tout.	That's all.
J'aimerais bien...	I would like...
Je regarde	I'm browsing

Grammar — rembourser (to refund)

'Rembourser' means 'to refund'.
Je vous rembourse. *I refund you.*
'Se faire rembourser' means 'to get a refund'.
Je me fais rembourser. *I get a refund.*
'Faire' doesn't agree in the perfect when followed by an infinitive: 'Elle s'est fait rembourser' *(She got a refund).*

J'adore l'écharpe en vitrine. Je peux l'essayer?	*I love the scarf in the window. Can I try it on?*	the jeans — le jean
Je voudrais savoir si ce pull est en solde.	*I would like to know if this jumper is in the sale.*	the raincoat — l'imperméable (m)
Je voudrais acheter cette chemise, mais il n'y a aucune étiquette. C'est combien s'il vous plaît?	*I'd like to buy this shirt, but there's no label. How much is it please?*	this hoodie — ce pull à capuche / this jacket — cette veste
Et l'avez-vous de taille moyenne?	*And do you have it in a medium size?*	in a large size — dans une grande taille
Est-ce que vous avez cette robe en vert?	*Do you have this dress in green?*	in a small size — dans une petite taille
Je cherche un jean blanc.	*I'm looking for white jeans.*	pyjamas — un pyjama
Je voudrais échanger ce pull contre un chapeau.	*I would like to exchange this jumper for a hat.*	some gloves — des gants (m)

Shopping

If you're interested in shopping, you're in luck — here's some stuff on quantities and online shopping...

Au magasin — At the shop

les courses (f)	*shopping*	la moitié	*half*
une tranche	*a slice*	le quart	*quarter*
tranché(e)	*sliced*	peser	*to weigh*
un morceau	*a piece*	un gramme	*a gram*
une portion	*a portion*	un kilogramme	*a kilogram*
une boîte	*a box / tin*	un paquet	*a packet*

Grammar — encore de (more)

'De' doesn't change with the gender or number of the noun after quantifiers. (See p.110.)
'Encore de' is an exception — it's followed by 'de' and the definite article (du, de la, de l', des).
Je voudrais encore du pain. *I'd like more bread.*

Je voudrais une tranche de pain. — *I would like a slice of bread.*

half of this tart — la moitié de cette tarte

Nous voudrions une petite portion de flan. — *We would like a small portion of flan.*

a piece of — un morceau de
more — encore du

Je pourrais avoir un demi-kilogramme de fromage, s'il vous plaît? — *Could I have half a kilogram of cheese, please?*

Voulez-vous un litre de lait? — *Do you want a litre of milk?*

half a litre — un demi-litre

Faire des courses en ligne — To shop online

Question	Simple Answer	Extended Answer
Est-ce que vous préférez faire des courses en ligne? *Do you prefer shopping online?*	Oui, je trouve ça très pratique. On sait qu'on pourra trouver ce qu'on veut. *Yes, I find it very convenient. You know you will be able to find what you want.*	Je ne suis pas sûr. C'est vraiment pratique et les prix sont souvent moins chers en ligne. Mais j'aime pouvoir toucher et voir ce que j'achète. En plus, dans les magasins, on peut demander conseil aux vendeurs. *I'm not sure. It's really convenient and prices are often cheaper online. But I like being able to touch and see what I'm buying. In addition, in shops, you can ask for advice from the shop assistants.*

J'ai acheté des légumes en ligne mais ils étaient abîmés. — *I bought some vegetables online but they were damaged.*

Je préfère acheter les vêtements en ligne parce qu'ils sont livrés vite et les prix sont souvent réduits. — *I prefer to buy clothes online because they're delivered quickly and the prices are often reduced.*

Mais c'est difficile car on ne sait pas si on a choisi la bonne taille. — *But it's difficult because you don't know if you've chosen the right size.*

TRACK LISTENING 10

Don't forget to use polite phrases like 's'il vous plaît'...

Listen to Sara and Pierre discussing the advantages and disadvantages of online shopping. Answer the following questions **in English**.

e.g. What does Sara think is the advantage of online shopping? **It's easier than going to the shops.**

1 a. Which disadvantage of online shopping does Sara mention? *[1]*

   b. What does Pierre find positive about online shopping? Give **two** details. *[2]*

   c. According to Pierre, what can't you be sure of when shopping online? *[1]*

Technology

Technology is a hot topic nowadays — it's difficult to imagine life without it. The examiners love asking questions that delve into its advantages and disadvantages, so it's worth going over these pages carefully.

Accro à mon ordinateur — Addicted to my computer

l'ordinateur (m) portable	*laptop*		le mail / le courrier	
la tablette	*tablet*		électronique	*email*
le portable	*(mobile) phone*		le mot de passe	*password*
le texto	*text message*		l'écran (m) tactile	*touch screen*

envoyer	*to send*	télécharger	*to download*
recevoir	*to receive*	faire des achats (en ligne)	*to shop (online)*
tchatter	*to talk online*	être accro à	*to be addicted to*

Grammar — pouvoir / vouloir / devoir / il faut + infinitive

Some verbs can be followed directly by an <u>infinitive</u> (see p.124):

Je <u>peux acheter</u> de la musique en ligne.
I <u>can buy</u> music online.

Je <u>veux avoir</u> la dernière technologie.
I <u>want to have</u> the latest technology.

Les jeunes <u>doivent être</u> prudents en ligne.
Young people <u>must be</u> careful online.

Il <u>faut faire</u> attention sur les forums.
You <u>must be</u> careful on chat rooms.

Question	**Simple Answer**	**Extended Answer**
Utilises-tu souvent la technologie dans ta vie quotidienne?	Oui, j'utilise mon portable tous les jours et j'ai un ordinateur portable.	Oui, je suis accro à mon portable et j'envoie des messages à mes amis tout le temps. Par contre, je n'ai pas d'ordinateur portable.
Do you often use technology in your everyday life?	*Yes, I use my mobile phone every day and I have a laptop.*	*Yes, I'm addicted to my mobile phone and I send messages to my friends all the time. On the other hand, I don't have a laptop.*

Jamais sans mon portable — Never without my mobile phone

J'ai eu mon premier portable à dix ans.	*I got my first mobile phone at age ten.*
J'envoie et je reçois des dizaines de textos par jour.	*I send and receive dozens of texts a day.*
Je ne pourrais pas vivre sans mon portable.	*I couldn't live without my mobile phone.*

Dans la vie quotidienne, les textos ont remplacé la conversation.	*In everyday life, text messages have replaced conversation.* ←	*we're constantly in contact with others* — on est toujours en contact avec d'autres
On passe trop de temps sur nos portables.	*We spend too much time on our mobile phones.* ←	*lots of* — beaucoup de *little* — peu de
Si je suis en retard, mes parents peuvent me téléphoner pour savoir où je suis. Je me sens en sécurité.	*If I'm late, my parents can phone me to find out where I am. I feel safe.* ←	*They find it very useful.* — Ils le trouvent très utile.

Technology

Of course, technology isn't just about phones — the Internet practically runs the world, so it probably deserves a mention. It could come up in any one of your French exams, so learn it well.

Parlons d'Internet — Let's talk about the Internet

Views about the <u>Internet</u> vary massively, so it's worth considering its <u>advantages</u> and <u>disadvantages</u>.

Je peux faire des recherches pour mes projets scolaires en ligne. Les sites web factuels sont très utiles.	*I can do research for my school projects online. Factual websites are very useful.*
On peut trouver toutes les informations que l'on recherche rapidement.	*You can find all the pieces of information that you're looking for quickly.*
Je peux jouer à des jeux en ligne avec mes copains sans sortir de ma chambre.	*I can play online games with my friends without leaving my bedroom.*
Mon frère achète des billets de concert et de cinéma en ligne. C'est plus facile et pratique que de faire la queue au guichet.	*My brother buys concert and cinema tickets online. It's easier and more convenient than queuing at the box office.*

my family abroad — ma famille à l'étranger

Grammar — direct object pronouns (me, te, le, la, nous, vous, les)

A <u>direct object</u> is the <u>person or thing</u> (noun) that an action is <u>being done to</u>.

Elle joue <u>le jeu</u> en ligne.   ***She plays <u>the game</u> online.***

<u>Direct object pronouns</u> (see p.114) <u>replace</u> that noun. In French, they come <u>before</u> the verb and are used to <u>avoid repetition</u>.

Elle <u>le</u> joue en ligne. *She plays <u>it</u> online.*

The direct object pronouns 'me', 'te', 'le' and 'la' drop their final letter and replace it with an apostrophe when they come directly before a word beginning with a vowel. E.g. 'Je peux t'aider.' (I can help you.)

Question	**Simple Answer**	**Extended Answer**
Selon vous, quels sont les dangers d'Internet?	Il faut faire attention à ce qu'on écrit sur Internet, surtout quand on met ses détails personnels en ligne.	Le problème principal, c'est de rester en sécurité. Il ne faut pas mettre de photos en ligne, ni afficher de détails personnels car tout le monde peut les voir. De plus, il faut faire attention en faisant des achats en ligne car il y a de la fraude. Il faut protéger tes détails personnels avec un mot de passe.
In your opinion, what are the dangers associated with the Internet?	*You need to be careful with what you write on the Internet, especially when you put personal details online.*	*The main problem is staying safe. You mustn't put photos online, nor post personal details because everyone can see them.*
		*Furthermore, you need to be careful when shopping online because of fraud. You must protect your personal details with a password.*

 ## Use 'on' to talk about what people do in general...

Traduis le passage suivant **en français**. *[12 marks]*

I got a new mobile phone for my birthday. My mum bought it for me. It's very useful because I can contact my parents and my friends when I want. I can also download music and games from the Internet. Tomorrow, I will use it to buy a book online.

Make sure you think about whether the nouns are masculine or feminine — you'll get marks for accurate grammar.

Social Media

And on to social media... chances are you know a fair bit about social media, so hopefully revising this page will be nice and straightforward. You just need to learn the terminology in French, and off you go...

Les réseaux sociaux — Social networks

le jeu	*game*
cliquer	*to click*
taper	*to type*
mettre en ligne	*to upload*
naviguer (sur)	*to browse*
l'écran (m)	*screen*
le forum	*chat room*

Grammar — irregular verb — 'envoyer' (to send)

'Envoyer' is an irregular verb. Learn how to <u>conjugate</u> it properly — it's useful for talking about <u>online communication</u>.

j'envoie	*I send*	nous envoyons	*we send*
tu envoies	*you send* (informal, singular)	vous envoyez	*you send* (formal, plural)
il / elle / on envoie	*he / she / one sends*	ils / elles envoient	*they send*

Question

Utilises-tu souvent les réseaux sociaux?

Do you often use social networks?

Simple Answer

Oui, j'utilise les réseaux sociaux chaque jour.

Yes, I use social networks every day.

deux fois par semaine	*twice a week*
de temps en temps	*from time to time*
tous les soirs	*every night*

Extended Answer

Oui, je suis un bloggeur. J'aime partager mes recettes et photos. Je passe en moyenne deux heures par jour sur les réseaux sociaux.

Yes, I am a blogger. I love to share my recipes and photos. On average, I spend two hours a day on social networks.

Je l'utilise parce que... — I use it because...

It's worth thinking about the different ways that people use social media and learning how to discuss them.

J'aime bien mettre mes vidéos en ligne pour les montrer à mes amis.	*I like uploading my videos to show them to my friends.*	my photos — mes photos / my blog posts — mes articles de blog
J'utilise les réseaux sociaux pour rencontrer ceux qui partagent les mêmes intérêts que moi.	*I use social networks to meet those who share the same interests as me.*	organise social events — organiser des événements sociaux
Les sites sociaux me permettent d'être à jour avec des nouvelles importantes.	*Social media sites allow me to keep up to date with important news.*	to stay in contact with my family — de rester en contact avec ma famille

Learn how to conjugate 'envoyer' — it's a bit tricky...

Lis les commentaires d'Anaïs, puis réponds aux questions **en français**.

En tout, je passe au moins trois heures par jour sur les réseaux sociaux. Je tchatte avec mes amis sur les sites sociaux **tout en faisant**[1] mes devoirs.

Je pense que, de nos jours, les réseaux sociaux sont indispensables. Par exemple, ils me permettent de savoir ce que fait mon cousin qui voyage en Amérique du Sud. Il met ses photos en ligne et je peux les regarder sur mon ordinateur.   [1]*while doing*

e.g. Combien de temps par jour passe Anaïs sur les réseaux sociaux ?
au moins trois heures

1. Qu'est-ce qu'Anaïs fait pendant qu'elle complète ses devoirs ? [1]

2. Qu'est-ce qu'Anaïs pense des réseaux sociaux ? [1]

3. Comment est-ce que les sites sociaux l'aident à savoir ce que fait son cousin ? [1]

The Problems with Social Media

Of course, social media does have its drawbacks — even if you think it's great, you still need to be able to talk about its disadvantages and give a balanced argument in the exam. Use this page to get some ideas.

Les inconvénients — Disadvantages

l'avantage (m)	*advantage*
l'inconvénient (m)	*disadvantage / drawback*
la cyber-intimidation	*cyber-bullying*
la vie privée	*private life*
à cause de	*as a result of*
au lieu de	*instead of*
grâce à	*thanks to*

Grammar — de (preposition)

à cause de and au lieu de both use the preposition '<u>de</u>'. Remember, if 'de' is followed by '<u>le</u>' or '<u>les</u>', they combine:

de + le = du   **de + les = des**

À cause <u>des</u> réseaux sociaux...

As a result <u>of</u> social networks...

À mon avis — In my opinion

You might have to discuss the <u>advantages</u> and <u>disadvantages</u> of social media.

Moi, j'adore utiliser les réseaux sociaux — grâce à eux, je sais ce que font mes amis, même quand on ne s'est pas vu depuis longtemps.

I love using social networks — thanks to them, I know what my friends are doing, even when we haven't seen each other for a long time.

Cependant, je reconnais qu'il y a aussi des inconvénients. Par exemple, la vie privée n'est plus privée du tout — dès qu'on a mis une photo en ligne, tout le monde peut la voir.

However, I recognise that there are also drawbacks. For example, your private life is no longer private at all — as soon as you've put a photo online, everybody can see it.

De plus, la cyber-intimidation est un grand problème. Il y a des personnes qui écrivent des choses fausses et méchantes sur les sites sociaux.

Furthermore, cyber-bullying is a big problem. There are people who write fake and cruel things on social media sites.

Giving a balanced opinion will really impress the examiner...

Have a look at Paul's answer to this question.

À ton avis, quels sont les avantages et inconvénients des réseaux sociaux ?

À mon avis, l'avantage le plus important des réseaux sociaux est que **n'importe qui**[1] peut être **écrivain**[2]. Moi, j'aimerais être journaliste un jour, et avec mon blog, j'ai l'opportunité d'écrire pour mes deux cents **abonnés**[3] — et c'est complètement gratuit !

Néanmoins[4], je les trouve parfois effrayants. De nos jours on est préoccupé des **centaines**[5] d'amis sur Internet, donc on abandonne souvent les rapports réels.

Grade 6-7

[1]anybody
[2]author
[3]subscribers
[4]nevertheless / however
[5]hundreds

Tick list:
✓ tenses: present, conditional
✓ superlative

To improve:
+ complex structures, e.g. pour + inf.
+ use quantifiers e.g. 'très' or 'vraiment'
+ more tenses: perfect, imperfect, future

Now answer the following questions.
Try to speak for about two minutes. [12 marks]

- *Comment utilises-tu les réseaux sociaux ?*
- *À ton avis, quels sont les avantages des réseaux sociaux ?*
- *À ton avis, quels sont les inconvénients des réseaux sociaux ?*

Knowing a range of conjunctions will come in handy when giving both sides of an argument:

pourtant	*however*
néanmoins	*nevertheless*
par contre	*on the other hand*

Listening Questions

We're on a roll with these practice questions — get to it, and have a crack at the next four pages.

1 Some shoppers were interviewed as part of a competition in a shopping centre. Answer the questions **in English**.

LISTENING TRACK 11

Example: What does Abdoul say he prefers to do?

window-shopping .... *[1 mark]*

(i) Which two extra items did Frédéric buy?

1. ....

2. .... *[2 marks]*

(ii) Why didn't Manon buy anything?

.... *[1 mark]*

2 Écoute ces interviews au sujet des réseaux sociaux. Pour chaque question, mets une croix dans chacune des **deux** cases correctes.

LISTENING TRACK 12

Example: Cho:

A	Elle n'utilise jamais les réseaux sociaux.	
B	Elle dit qu'on devrait être prudent concernant ce qu'on partage.	X
C	Elle connaît quelqu'un qui a eu des problèmes graves.	
D	Elle croit que les réseaux sociaux peuvent être dangereux.	X

(i) Jules:

A	Il préfère que ses vidéos restent privées.	
B	Il aime montrer à tout le monde qu'il s'amuse.	
C	Il envoie des messages constamment.	
D	Il aime voir ce que font les autres.	

[2 marks]

(ii) Clara:

A	Elle met toujours toutes ses photos en ligne.	
B	Elle demande la permission avant de partager des photos.	
C	Tout le monde peut voir les photos qu'on poste.	
D	Il est facile de supprimer les choses qu'on a mises en ligne.	

[2 marks]

Speaking Question

Candidate's Role

- Your teacher will play the role of your French friend's grandparent. They will speak first.

- You must use *vous* to address your friend's grandparent.

- – ! – means you will have to respond to something you have not prepared.

- – ? – means you will have to ask your friend's grandparent a question.

> Vous parlez de la technologie avec le grand-père / la grand-mère de votre ami(e) français(e).
>
> - Les smartphones — les avantages
>
> - S'en servir — comment
>
> - !
>
> - ? Utiliser souvent un smartphone.
>
> - ? Les réseaux sociaux — opinion

Teacher's Role

- You begin the role play using the introductory text below.

- You should address the candidate as *vous*.

- Do not supply the candidate with key vocabulary.

- You must ask the questions below exactly as they are written.

> Introductory text: *Vous parlez de la technologie avec le grand-père / la grand-mère de votre ami(e) français(e). Moi, je suis le grand-père / la grand-mère.*
>
> - Quels sont les avantage des smartphones ?
>
> - Comment vous vous en servez ?
>
> - ! Est-ce que vous pensez que c'est facile d'apprendre à utiliser les technologies modernes ?
>
> - ? Allow the candidate to ask you if you often use a smartphone.
>
> - ? Allow the candidate to ask you your opinion of social networks.

Reading Questions

1 Lis ces annonces et réponds aux questions. Mets une croix dans la case correcte.

> Étudiant honnête cherche du travail. Je peux vous aider à passer l'aspirateur, à nettoyer les salles de bain et la cuisine ou à laver la voiture: tous les travaux domestiques que vous détestez ! Je suis libre le lundi, le mardi et le samedi.

a Qu'est-ce que cet étudiant peut faire pour t'aider à la maison ?

A	faire la vaisselle	
B	laver la douche et le bain	
C	ranger les chambres	

[1 mark]

> Avez-vous besoin de quelqu'un qui peut prendre soin de votre pelouse et de vos fleurs, et qui est aussi capable de réparer une fenêtre ? Je peux vous aider et rendre votre vie plus facile. Appelez-moi, Marie Duris, au 06 78 93 02 12.

b Marie Duris vous offre de l'aide avec quelle tâche ?

A	le soin des enfants	
B	la cuisine	
C	le jardinage	

[1 mark]

2 Translate the following passage **into English**.

> Je dois utiliser les réseaux sociaux pour mon travail. Je les trouve pratiques pour organiser ma vie. Pourtant, je crois qu'il est important d'être responsable parce que les autres peuvent voir ce qu'on met en ligne. J'écris un blog de mode mais je ne partagerais jamais d'informations personnelles.

....

....

....

....

....

[7 marks]

Writing Questions

1 Le journal scolaire cherche des articles sur les dangers des réseaux sociaux.
Écrivez un article.

Vous **devez** faire référence aux points suivants :

• les problèmes concernant les réseaux sociaux

• si vous avez déjà été victime de la cyber-intimidation

• ce qu'il faut faire pour se protéger des risques en ligne

• vos idées pour une initiative au collège dans le but d'informer les élèves.

Justifiez vos idées et vos opinions.
Écrivez 130-150 mots environ **en français**. *[28 marks]*

2 Traduis le passage suivant **en français** :

> Marie must buy a present for her girlfriend because it is her birthday this week.
> Yesterday she went to the department store. She found a pretty dress but it was not the
> right size. She also saw a hat, but it was too expensive. Marie does not like shopping.

....

....

....

....

....

....

....

[12 marks]

Revision Summary for Section Three

These questions really do check what you know and what you don't know, so they're pretty handy as far as revision goes. If you need to flick back through and revise a couple of things, don't forget to come back to these questions and have another go — after all, practice makes perfect...

Everyday Life (p.30) ☑

1) What's the French for...?
   a) to get up   b) to shower   c) to brush your teeth   d) to go to bed   ☑

2) Qu'est-ce que tu fais pour aider tes parents à la maison?   ☑

3) Nadim is putting up some shelves this weekend. Which of these phrases best describes his plans?
   a) Il va faire du bricolage.   b) Il va faire du jardinage.   c) Il va faire la lessive.   ☑

Food (p.31) ☑

4) In French, write down five items you might buy at the supermarket to make a meal.   ☑

5) 'Quel est ton plat préféré?' Translate this question into English and then answer it in French.   ☑

6) Lionel tells you: 'Je préfère l'agneau au poulet et je déteste les fruits de mer.' What has he said?   ☑

Shopping (p.32-33) ☑

7) Renée wants to buy: some socks, some trousers, a jumper and a dress. Translate her shopping list into French.   ☑

8) You're talking to an assistant in a clothes shop. In French, say to them: 'I would like to know if these shoes are in the sale. Can I try them on?'   ☑

9) Your friend is telling you about his weekend. He says: 'Samedi, j'ai acheté un jean mais le vendeur ne m'a pas donné la bonne taille. J'ai perdu le ticket de caisse donc c'est impossible de me faire rembourser. Quel désastre!' What happened? Answer in English.   ☑

10) Est-ce que tu fais des courses en ligne? Pourquoi / Pourquoi pas?   ☑

Technology (p.34-35) ☑

11) Your bag has been stolen whilst you're on holiday in Belgium, and the police want a list of any valuables that were inside it. How would you say the following phrases in French?
    a) my laptop   b) my tablet   c) my mobile phone   ☑

12) Utilises-tu souvent ton portable dans la vie quotidienne? Réponds en français.   ☑

13) Aurélie says: 'Il n'est pas du tout nécessaire d'avoir un portable avant l'âge de onze ans. Quand on est petit, il suffit de voir les amis à l'école.' What does this mean in English?   ☑

14) In French, write down two advantages and two disadvantages of having a mobile phone.   ☑

15) 'Qu'est-ce que tu fais sur Internet en général?' Réponds en français.   ☑

Social Media (p.36-37) ☑

16) Do you use social networks? Why / Why not? Give at least three reasons (in French).   ☑

17) À ton avis, est-ce que c'est possible de devenir accro aux réseaux sociaux? Réponds en français. Utilise des phrases complètes.   ☑

18) Say in French that you have a blog and you like to share your opinions on important events.   ☑

19) Marie is giving her views on social media sites: 'À cause des sites sociaux, la vie privée n'existe plus.' Translate her sentence into English.   ☑

20) Qu'est-ce que c'est le cyber-intimidation?   ☑

Books and Reading

Whether or not electronic books will ever completely replace paper ones is a good topic for debate. Have a think about where you stand on this issue and make sure you can justify your opinions.

Est-ce que tu aimes lire? — Do you like reading?

la lecture	*reading*
le livre	*book*
le roman	*novel*
la bande dessinée (BD)	*comic book*
le magazine / la revue	*magazine*
le journal	*newspaper*
la liseuse électronique	*e-reader*
le livre électronique	*e-book*

Grammar — 'donc' vs. 'comme'

'Donc' (*therefore / so*) expresses a consequence.

J'adore lire, donc j'ai acheté une liseuse électronique.
I love to read, so I bought an e-reader.

'Comme' (*as*) expresses a reason for something.

Comme elle est légère, je peux l'emmener partout.
As it's light, I can take it everywhere.

J'adore lire des romans policiers, car les intrigues sont toujours très passionnantes.

I love reading crime novels, because the plots are always very exciting.

On peut s'immerger dans un autre monde en lisant des romans fantastiques.

You can immerse yourself in another world by reading fantasy novels.

Les livres ne m'intéressent pas. Je préfère regarder les films, car on voit de l'action.

Books don't interest me. I prefer to watch films, because you see the action.

Question

Que penses-tu des livres électroniques?

What do you think of e-books?

Simple Answer

À mon avis, ils sont très pratiques.

In my opinion, they are very practical.

Extended Answer

Ils sont géniaux. J'ai une liseuse électronique et je l'adore car il est très facile de télécharger des livres. En plus, il y a beaucoup de choix. Je crois qu'un jour, les livres électroniques remplaceront les livres en papier.

They are great. I have an e-reader and I love it because it is very easy to download books. In addition, there is a lot of choice. I believe that one day, e-books will replace paper books.

You can talk about things you read online too...

Here's an example role play — Nasreen is talking to her teacher about reading.

Teacher: Est-ce que tu aimes lire ?

Nasreen: Oui, je lis tout le temps, surtout les romans.

Teacher: Quel est ton opinion des livres électroniques ?

Nasreen: Je ne les aime pas car je préfère tenir un vrai livre en main. Mais **j'avoue**[1] qu'ils sont plus pratiques.

Teacher: Qu'est-ce que tu as lu récemment ?

Nasreen: Ce week-end, j'ai lu un roman historique, c'était super car je m'intéresse à l'histoire. Qu'est-ce que vous aimez lire ?

Teacher: Moi, j'aime lire des biographies.   [1] I admit

Nasreen: Avez-vous une liseuse électronique ?

Teacher: Oui, j'en ai une. Je l'utilise souvent.

Grade 8-9

Tick list:
✓ tenses: present, imperfect, perfect
✓ correctly-formed questions

To improve:
+ use different conjunctions to link phrases

Prepare the role play card below. Use 'vous' and speak for about two minutes. [10 marks]

Tu parles de la lecture avec ton professeur.
- *si tu aimes lire*
- *livres électroniques — opinion*
- *!*
- *? genre de livres préféré*
- *? liseuse électronique*

Celebrations and Festivals

Some of these festivals are similar to British ones, but it's important that you learn about the differences too.

Les fêtes françaises — French festivals

la fête	*festival / party*	la Saint-Sylvestre	*New Year's Eve*
fêter / célébrer	*to celebrate*	le Jour de l'An	*New Year's Day*
le jour férié	*bank holiday*	la fête des rois	*Epiphany / Twelfth Night*
le cadeau	*present*	la fête des mères / pères	*Mother's / Father's Day*
le défilé	*procession*	la Saint Valentin	*Valentine's Day*
la fête du travail	*May Day*	les feux (m) d'artifice	*fireworks*
la fête nationale	*Bastille Day*	Bon anniversaire!	*Happy birthday!*
le poisson d'avril	*April Fools' Day*	Bonne année!	*Happy New Year!*

Les écoles sont fermées les jours fériés.	*Schools are closed on bank holidays.*
On fête le Nouvel An à minuit et on prend des bonnes résolutions.	*People celebrate the New Year at midnight and make resolutions.*

La fête nationale — Bastille Day

Many events are held on <u>Bastille Day</u> to commemorate the <u>French Revolution</u>. It's the French <u>national day</u>.

Le quatorze juillet est le jour de la fête nationale. Il y a beaucoup d'événements pour la célébrer.	*14th July is Bastille Day. There are many events to celebrate it.*
Le quatorze juillet, beaucoup de gens s'habillent aux couleurs tricolores.	*On 14th July, lots of people dress in the colours of the French flag.*
J'aime regarder les feux d'artifice parce qu'ils sont toujours magnifiques.	*I like watching the fireworks because they're always amazing.*
J'aime la fête nationale parce qu'on peut la célébrer avec toute la famille.	*I like Bastille Day because you can celebrate it with the whole family.*

the processions — les défilés (m)
the dances — les danses (f)
impressive — impressionnant(e)s
it's an historical event — c'est un événement historique

Joyeux Noël! — Merry Christmas!

Nous mettons des cadeaux sous le sapin de Noël. Nous les ouvrons soit après la messe de minuit soit le jour de Noël.	*We put presents under the Christmas tree. We open them either after midnight mass or on Christmas Day.*
'Le réveillon' est le dîner qu'on mange après minuit la veille de Noël. Nous mangeons de l'oie pour le réveillon.	*'Le réveillon' is the dinner we eat after midnight on Christmas Eve. We eat goose for 'le réveillon'.*
Je pense que Noël est devenu trop commercial. Je préfère le fêter de façon traditionelle.	*I think that Christmas has become too commercial. I prefer to celebrate it in a traditional way.*
Le jour de Noël, j'aime regarder des films.	*On Christmas Day, I like to watch films.*

turkey — de la dinde
Christmas loaf — du pain calendal
yule log — de la bûche de Noël
to visit my family — rendre visite à ma famille
to eat a lot — beaucoup manger

Celebrations and Festivals

Even if you don't celebrate a particular festival, you can still talk about it, so here's some useful vocab.

La fête des rois — Epiphany

le roi	*king*
la reine	*queen*
la fève	*charm*
la couronne	*crown*
la galette des rois	*cake for Epiphany*
le gâteau des rois	*cake for Epiphany*

Dans une grande partie de la France on mange une 'galette des rois', qui est un type de gâteau rond.

In most of France people eat a 'galette des rois', which is a type of round cake.

On cache une fève dans la galette. La personne qui la trouve devient le roi / la reine.

A charm is hidden in the cake. The person who finds it becomes the king / the queen.

Question	**Simple Answer**	**Extended Answer**
Qu'est-ce que tu as fait pour la fête des rois?	J'ai fait une galette des rois pour ma famille.	Toute ma famille élargie était chez nous. Nous avons beaucoup mangé. J'ai trouvé la fève donc je suis devenu(e) le roi / la reine.
What did you do for Epiphany?	*I made a 'galette des rois' for my family.*	*All my extended family were at our house. We ate a lot. I found the charm so I became king / queen.*

D'autres fêtes religieuses — Other religious festivals

religieux / religieuse	*religious*	athée	*atheist*	le Pâques	*Easter*
juif / juive	*Jewish*	la Hanoukka	*Hanukkah*	la Carême	*Lent*
musulman(e)	*Muslim*	le ramadan	*Ramadan*	le vendredi Saint	*Good Friday*
chrétien(ne)	*Christian*	l'Aïd (f) al-Fitr	*Eid al-Fitr*	le Lundi de Pâques	*Easter Monday*

La Hanoukka est une fête juive. On allume des bougies et on prie ensemble.

Hanukkah is a Jewish festival. People light candles and pray together.

Au cours du Ramadan, les musulmans ne devraient ni manger ni boire de l'aube au coucher du soleil.

During Ramadan, Muslims should neither eat nor drink from dawn until sunset.

celebrate it for eight days — on la fête pendant huit jours

exchange gifts — on échange des cadeaux

Grammar — ne...ni...ni (neither...nor)

To say 'neither this nor that', use this structure: ne before the verb + ni ... ni ... .
Je ne fête ni Noël ni Pâques. *I celebrate neither Christmas nor Easter.*

Learn the French words for religions and their festivals...

Youssou is describing his birthday celebrations. Choose the correct option to finish each sentence.

e.g. Youssou is... *C*
- **A.** six years old.
- **B.** seventeen years old.
- **C.** sixteen years old.

b. His sister made him...
- **A.** his favourite meal.
- **B.** a cake.
- **C.** some biscuits. *[1]*

1 a. He opened his gifts in the evening because...
- **A.** he didn't want to get up early to do it.
- **B.** he starts school early in the morning.
- **C.** he didn't want to do it at school. *[1]*

c. There were fireworks...
- **A.** because it was Bastille Day.
- **B.** because it was May Day.
- **C.** to celebrate Youssou's birthday. *[1]*

Music

Free-time activities are a common topic in the exam. Music's a good one to talk about, but there's lots of vocabulary to get your head around, so take your time learning the stuff on this page.

La musique — Music

jouer	to play
(d'un instrument)	(an instrument)
la chanson	song
le musicien / la musicienne	musician
le chanteur / la chanteuse	singer
le genre	genre
le concert	concert
apprendre à	to learn to
faire partie de	to be part of
le groupe	band
la chorale	choir
l'orchestre (m)	orchestra
répéter	to rehearse

Grammar — jouer de

'jouer' is followed by 'de', 'du', 'de la' or 'des' when you're talking about playing a musical instrument.
For more on how 'de' changes see p.100.
Je joue du violon et de la flûte.
I play the violin and the flute.

Grammar — imperfect tense

To talk about what you 'used to' do, use the imperfect tense. See p.129 for more.
Je chantais. I used to sing.

Question	Simple Answer	Extended Answer
Est-ce que tu joues d'un instrument de musique?	Oui, je joue de la guitare et du piano.	Oui, maintenant je joue de la batterie. Quand j'étais petit(e), je jouais de la trompette et je chantais dans une chorale.
Do you play a musical instrument?	*Yes, I play the guitar and the piano.*	*Yes, now I play the drums. When I was younger, I used to play the trumpet and sing in a choir.*

Écouter de la musique — To listen to music

It's worth thinking about how to express your opinions about music.

Je préfère le rap à la musique classique.	*I prefer rap to classical music.*
Mon grand-père détestait écouter de la musique classique quand il avait mon âge, mais maintenant c'est son genre de musique préféré.	*My grandad hated listening to classical music when he was my age, but now it is his favourite music genre.*
À mon avis, les chansons techno sont quelquefois trop bizarres.	*In my opinion, techno songs are sometimes too weird.*

dance music — la dance
rock music — la musique rock
pop music — la musique pop

See p.8-9 for more on opinions.

Practice makes perfect — try this exam question...

TRACK LISTENING 14

Écoute cette interview avec le musicien Joël Lejoueur. Complète les phrases en choisissant un mot ou des mots dans la case. Il y a des mots que tu n'utiliseras pas.

1(i) a. L'instrument préféré de Joël est .... [1]

b. Il n'aimait pas .... [1]

(ii) a. Joël préfère jouer .... [1]

b. Selon Joël, pour devenir un bon musicien, il faut .... [1]

être doué
la guitare
collège
en groupe
répéter
son collège
seul
le violon
son professeur

Film and TV

Everyone loves a good film or TV show — and they're great to talk about in the exam. Make sure you know the names for different types of film and programme and that you can give and justify your opinions.

Allons au cinéma — Let's go to the cinema

See p.187-188 for more film vocab.

le film d'action / d'aventure	action film	les sous-titres (m)	subtitles
le film d'horreur / d'épouvante	horror film	les effets (m) spéciaux	special effects
le film d'amour / romantique	romantic film	la bande-annonce	trailer
le film d'animation	animated film	le billet de cinéma	cinema ticket

J'aime aller au cinéma pour voir des films sur grand écran, surtout les films comiques. Pourtant, les bandes-annonces m'énervent.

I like going to the cinema to see films on the big screen, especially comedies. However, the trailers annoy me.

Si le film est ennuyeux et les acteurs ne sont pas bons, je m'endors avant la fin.

If the film is boring and the actors aren't good, I fall asleep before the end.

Je n'ai pas aimé le film. L'intrigue n'était pas croyable et les personnages étaient agaçants.

I didn't like the film. The plot wasn't believable and the characters were annoying.

the tickets are expensive — les billets sont chers

the special effects — les effets spéciaux

Qu'est-ce qu'il y a à la télé? — What's on TV?

'On' is usually translated as 'sur' in French, but remember, you say 'à la télé'.

à la télé	on TV	l'émission (f)	programme	le documentaire	documentary
la publicité	advert	le feuilleton	soap opera	le jeu télévisé	game show
regarder	to watch	la télé réalité	reality TV	la chaîne de télé	TV channel
diffuser	to broadcast	les informations (f)	the news	célèbre	famous

Question

Qu'est-ce que tu as regardé à la télé hier soir?

What did you watch on TV last night?

Simple Answer

J'ai regardé un jeu télévisé et un feuilleton.

I watched a game show and a soap.

Extended Answer

J'ai regardé une émission de télé-réalité. Je trouve ce genre d'émission intéressant parce qu'on peut suivre la vie quotidienne des personnes célèbres. L'épisode que j'ai regardé hier était très divertissant.

I watched a reality TV show. I find this type of programme interesting because you can follow celebrities' daily lives. The episode that I watched yesterday was very entertaining.

Grammar — 'qui' and 'que'

'Qui' refers to the subject of the sentence. 'Que' refers to the object. See p.115 for more.

La personne qui regarde la télévision. *The person who watches television.*
La télévision que la personne regarde. *The television that the person watches.*

Vary your language — don't just use 'j'aime' all the time...

Traduis le passage suivant **en français**. *[12 marks]*

My friend and I went to the cinema last weekend. We watched a horror film. I wasn't scared, but my friend screamed during the film. I like going to the cinema. It is always entertaining. Next month, I will go to see the new action film.

Read each sentence fully before you decide which tense you need.

Sport

Whether you like sport or not, you need to be able to give your opinion on it. On your marks... get set... GO!

Faire du sport — To do sport

le foot / football	*football*	le hockey	*hockey*	l'aviron (m)	*rowing*
le rugby	*rugby*	le netball	*netball*	pratiquer un sport	*to do a sport*
le tennis	*tennis*	le basket	*basketball*	faire une randonnée	*to go on a walk*
l'équitation (f)	*horse riding*	la natation	*swimming*	faire du vélo	*to cycle*

Je joue au badminton deux fois par semaine, et parfois je fais de la voile aussi.

I play badminton twice a week, and sometimes I also go sailing.

on Mondays — le lundi

J'aime faire des randonnées avec mes parents et je voudrais essayer le tir à l'arc.

I like going on walks with my parents and I would like to try archery.

fencing — l'escrime (f)
scuba diving — la plongée sous-marine

Question

Est-ce que tu pratiques un sport régulièrement?

Do you do a sport on a regular basis?

Simple Answer

Oui, j'aime le sport et je joue au rugby le mercredi. Je regarde des matchs de tennis à la télé aussi.

Yes, I like sport and I play rugby on Wednesdays. I watch tennis matches on TV as well.

Extended Answer

Oui, je suis très sportif / sportive. Je fais partie d'une équipe de football et nous nous entraînons trois fois par semaine. La semaine dernière, nous avons perdu le match, mais j'ai marqué un but.

Yes, I'm very sporty. I'm part of a football team and we train three times a week. Last week, we lost the game, but I scored a goal.

Mon sport préféré c'est... — My favourite sport is...

le terrain de sport	*sports field*
s'entraîner	*to train*
le centre sportif	*sports centre*
le stade	*stadium*
la course	*race*
le tournoi	*tournament*
fana de	*a fan of*
à l'intérieur	*inside*
à l'extérieur	*outside*

Je préfère les sports individuels aux sports d'équipe. Ils sont plus compétitifs parce qu'on joue seulement pour soi-même.

Moi, je joue au tennis. Cependant, je préfère m'entraîner avec d'autres personnes donc je fais de l'aviron aussi.

I prefer individual sports to team sports. They're more competitive because you're playing just for yourself.

I play tennis. However, I prefer to train with other people so I do rowing as well.

READING — Don't just say which sport you do — add in when, where, why...

Read the advert. What does it tell us? Choose the three correct letters from the list. *[3 marks]*

Le nouveau centre sportif est ouvert tous les jours, sauf le dimanche. On peut jouer au tennis et nager dehors dans la piscine chauffée. En plus, il y a des terrains de sport à l'extérieur, où on peut pratiquer des sports en équipe. Il y a aussi trois terrains de badminton. Le centre organise des tournois régulièrement — hier, il y a eu un tournoi de tennis de table. Si vous aimez courir, venez participer à la course qui aura lieu ici vendredi prochain.

A. The centre is open every day.
B. You can go swimming outdoors.
C. You can't play any raquet sports.
D. There are weekly table tennis tournaments.
E. You can take part in competitions.
F. There's going to be a race at the centre.
G. It's not possible to do team sports there.

Listening Questions

Another section, another set of exam-style questions. Don't be tempted to flick past these pages — practising the skills you'll need in the exams is time well spent.

1   Listen to this podcast about Eid. What does the speaker talk about?
     Put a cross in each of the **three** correct boxes.

A	what time everyone gets up	
B	the clothes people wear to the mosque	
C	what Muslims eat in France	
D	what the guests do at the party	
E	the songs people sing	
F	the presents given to the children	
G	the games the children play	

[3 marks]

2   Listen to this radio report about the Lumière brothers.
     Answer the questions **in English**.

a   What does the cinematograph device do?

     .... *[1 mark]*

b   How long was the Lumière brothers' first film?

     .... *[1 mark]*

c   Give **two** details about the first paying public film screening.

     1. ....

     2. .... *[2 marks]*

Speaking Question

Candidate's Material

- Spend a couple of minutes looking at the photo and the prompts below it.

- You can make notes on a separate piece of paper.

© iStock.com/monkeybusinessimages

Regarde la photo et prépare des réponses sur les points suivants :

- la description de la photo

- les aspects positifs des fêtes

- un festival que tu as fêté cette année

- tes projets pour fêter ton prochain anniversaire

- !

Teacher's Material

- Allow the student to develop his / her answers as much as possible.

- You need to ask the student the following questions **in order**:

- Décris-moi la photo.

- Quels sont les aspects positifs des fêtes ?

- Parle-moi d'un festival que tu as fêté cette année.

- Quels sont tes projets pour fêter ton prochain anniversaire ?

- Tu préfères rester à la maison ou partir à l'étranger pendant les vacances de Noël ?

Reading Questions

1   Read the article about a reading group.

> Le premier jeudi du mois, des habitants du petit village de Millome se retrouvent au club de lecture pour discuter et pour débattre. C'est une initiative du professeur Carole Chemin, qui a remarqué que ses élèves ne s'intéressaient plus à la lecture. Elle voulait leur faire comprendre que la lecture, ce n'est pas que la littérature.
>
> Toutefois, le club n'est pas réservé aux jeunes. Bien au contraire, tout le monde y est le bienvenu, et les membres ont tous le droit de proposer des textes à lire. Il s'agit parfois de textes factuels ou d'articles Internet, mais on discute aussi de romans et d'histoires traditionnelles. Le club est devenu un grand succès, et cela fait plaisir aux générations différentes du village de faire quelque chose ensemble.

What does the article tell us? Put a cross next to the **three** correct statements.

A	The group meets once a week.	
B	Carole Chemin's students used to find reading boring.	
C	Carole wanted to make her students enthusiastic about literature.	
D	The group is only for young people.	
E	Everyone in the group can suggest things to read.	
F	Sometimes the group discusses texts found online.	
G	The residents of the village want to do more activities together.	

[3 marks]

2   Read these responses to an online questionnaire about TV.

Qu'est-ce que tu aimes regarder à la télé?			
Annabelle 	J'aime regarder les émissions informatives comme les documentaires et les actualités, mais je ne peux pas supporter les jeux télévisés.	Bastien	Je suis très sportif et j'adore regarder les émissions de sport. Je regarde un match de football tous les soirs, même si ce n'est pas mon équipe préférée.

Est-ce que tu penses qu'on regarde trop de télé?			
Annabelle 	Je pense qu'il y a beaucoup d'émissions intéressantes à la télé, et on peut profiter de toute cette variété. Pourtant je trouve qu'il y a trop de publicités.	Bastien	Selon moi, ce qui est important, c'est la qualité de ce qu'on regarde. La télévision peut nous aider à comprendre les gens. Même les feuilletons peuvent nous faire apprendre quelque chose de la vie.

Who says what about TV? Enter either **Annabelle** or **Bastien** in the gaps below.

a   .... says that some programmes are not worth watching.   *[1 mark]*

b   .... says that there is too much advertising on TV.   *[1 mark]*

c   .... says that TV can help us understand other people.   *[1 mark]*

Writing Questions

1   Vous aimeriez encourager plus de jeunes à jouer d'un instrument.
    Écrivez un article pour un magazine de musique.

    Vous **devez** faire référence aux points suivants :

    • l'instrument dont vous jouez

    • les raisons pour lesquelles vous avez commencé à jouer d'un instrument

    • les avantages de jouer d'un instrument

    • l'instrument dont vous voudriez apprendre à jouer.

    Justifiez vos idées et vos opinions.
    Écrivez 130-150 mots environ **en français**.   *[28 marks]*

2   Traduis le passage suivant **en français** :

    > The 14th July is Bastille Day in France. Lots of tourists go to Paris to see the processions.
    > This year, I went to a park near the Eiffel Tower to watch the fireworks. It was a great
    > experience. My friends would like to visit Paris next year, so we will celebrate together.

    ....

    ....

    ....

    ....

    ....

    ....

    ....

                                                                      [12 marks]

Revision Summary for Section Four

Now you've been through the section, it's time to bring all those fun free-time activities together — you could say it's the most enjoyable page in the book... Make sure you have a go at all of the questions, and don't forget to use the tick boxes to help you keep track of your progress.

Books and Reading (p.43) ☑

1) Est-ce que tu aimes lire? Pourquoi / pourquoi pas? Réponds en français. ☑

2) In French, write down one advantage and one disadvantage of e-readers. ☑

3) Brian tells you: 'Je préfère les bandes dessinées car j'aime regarder les images. En plus, je trouve les romans fantastiques passionnants.' What does he like to read and why? Answer in English. ☑

Celebrations and Festivals (p.44-45) ☑

4) Jot down the French for:
   a) Bastille Day   b) April Fools' Day   c) New Year's Eve   d) New Year's Day   e) Epiphany ☑

5) Qu'est-ce que tu fais normalement pour fêter ton anniversaire? ☑

6) Your French pen friend tells you: 'Moi, j'adore la fête nationale. Je regarde les feux d'artifice avec ma famille et chaque année nous prenons part aux défilés.' What is she saying? ☑

7) What's the French for...?
   a) Easter   b) Christmas   c) Ramadan   d) religious   e) church   f) mosque ☑

8) Kassim says: 'De nos jours, Noël est devenu trop commercial. Il ne s'agit que des cadeaux et du chocolat.' What is Kassim saying? Answer in English. ☑

9) Farid describes what he does during Ramadan. He says: 'During Ramadan, I don't eat or drink during the day, even when I'm at school.' Say this in French. ☑

Music (p.46) ☑

10) 'Est-ce que tu joues d'un instrument de musique?' Réponds en français. ☑

11) A French musician has given an interview: 'Je joue de plusieurs instruments de musique, mais j'adore surtout la flûte. Dans l'avenir, je veux apprendre à jouer de la batterie pour que je puisse jouer dans un groupe de rock.' What's he saying? ☑

12) You love pop music, but when you were little you liked dance music. Say this in French. ☑

Film and TV (p.47) ☑

13) Quels genres de film aimez-vous? Pourquoi? Répondez en français. ☑

14) Your friend tells you about a film she saw last week: 'Les effets spéciaux étaient mal faits et j'avais du mal à comprendre ce qui s'était passé.' Did she like it? Why / Why not? Answer in English. ☑

15) Think about the last film you watched. Did you enjoy it? Why / Why not? Answer in French. ☑

16) 'La télé-réalité est ennuyeuse et elle encourage les jeunes à avoir une perception fausse de la vie normale.' Do you agree with this statement? Explain your answer in French. ☑

Sport (p.48) ☑

17) Write three sentences about your favourite sport (make it up if you don't like sport). Think about why you like it and when / how regularly you play it. ☑

18) Olivier tells you: 'Je fais de l'aviron régulièrement et j'ai un tournoi la semaine prochaine. Si je gagne toutes mes courses, je ferai partie de l'équipe nationale.' Translate this into English. ☑

19) Est-ce que tu préfères les sports individuels ou d'équipe? Pourquoi ? Réponds en français. ☑

Talking About Where You Live

Whether it's in the middle of nowhere or the inner city, you need to be able to describe where you live...

Où habites-tu? — Where do you live?

le centre-ville	town centre	les transports (m)	
le marché	market	en commun	public transport
la poste	post office	la gare (routière)	(bus) station
le tabac	newsagent's	la zone piétonne	pedestrian zone
la boulangerie	bakery	la circulation	traffic
la boucherie	butcher's	l'embouteillage (m)	traffic jam
la bibliothèque	library	la piste cyclable	cycle path
la campagne	countryside	l'usine (f)	factory

Grammar —
noun endings

Most nouns ending in '-ie' are feminine, e.g. la bijouterie (the jeweller's). Have a look at p.99 for a list of common masculine and feminine endings.

J'habite dans une ville à la campagne.   *I live in a town in the countryside.*

Je préfère habiter dans une ville.   *I prefer living in a town.*

by the sea — au bord de la mer

in the mountains — à la montagne

a city — une grande ville

Parle-moi de ta ville — Tell me about your town

Le système des transports en commun marche bien. Il aide à réduire la circulation en ville.   *The public transport system works well. It helps to reduce the traffic in the town.*

Il n'y a pas beaucoup à faire dans ma ville. Il n'y a aucun cinéma, par exemple.   *There isn't a lot to do in my town. There's no cinema, for example.*

Dans ma ville, il y a un grand centre-ville et de nombreux magasins.   *In my town, there's a big town centre and numerous shops.*

Ma ville est pittoresque. Dans mon quartier, il y a une grande place avec des fountaines.   *My town is picturesque. In my area, there is a big square with fountains.*

the noise — le bruit

theatre — théâtre (m)

supermarket — supermarché (m)

shopping centre — centre commercial (m)

READING

Think of interesting ways to describe your town to gain marks...

Read this extract from 'Les Misérables' by Victor Hugo, and answer the questions **in English**. It describes how père Madeleine prospered in the black jet industry after moving to Montreuil-sur-mer.

Montreuil-sur-mer était devenu **un centre d'affaires**[1] considérable. L'Espagne, qui consomme beaucoup de **jais noir**[2], y commandait chaque année des grands achats. [...] L'argent que père Madeleine a gagné était tel que, dès la deuxième année, il avait pu construire une grande usine dans laquelle il y avait deux vastes **ateliers**[3], l'un pour les hommes, l'autre pour les femmes. N'importe qui avait faim pouvait s'y présenter, et était sûr de trouver là de l'emploi et du pain. [...] Le chômage et la **misère**[4] étaient inconnus.

[1] a centre of trade
[2] black jet (a gemstone)
[3] workshops
[4] poverty

e.g. Which country bought a large amount of black jet?   **Spain**

1. When had père Madeleine earned enough money to build a factory?   [1]
2. Why did père Madeleine build two workshops?   [1]
3. How did père Madeleine help people who were hungry? Give **two** details.   [2]
4. Name **two** things which were unheard of in Montreuil-sur-mer.   [2]

The Home

Home sweet home... this page will help you describe where you live using some super French sentences.

La maison — The home

le quartier	*area*	l'immeuble (m)	*block of flats*	la salle de bains	*bathroom*
la maison...	*...house*	la pièce	*room*	les meubles (m)	*furniture*
individuelle	*detached*	le salon	*living room*	le lit	*bed*
jumelée	*semi-detached*	la cuisine	*kitchen*	le placard	*cupboard*
mitoyenne	*terraced*	la chambre	*bedroom*	l'armoire (f)	*wardrobe*

J'habite dans une maison mitoyenne. Nous avons six pièces.   *I live in a terraced house. We have six rooms.*

Dans ma chambre, il y a une chaise bleue, un lit et un bureau.   *In my bedroom, there's a blue chair, a bed and a desk.*

Grammar — adjectives

Most adjectives go <u>after</u> the noun, but some go <u>in front</u>:
un <u>beau</u> quartier *a <u>beautiful</u> area*
See p.102 for more.

C'est comment chez toi? — What's your home like?

You need to vary which <u>adjectives</u> you use and learn some <u>descriptive phrases</u>.

J'habite dans un appartement.   *I live in a flat.*

J'aime habiter dans une maison jumelée.   *I like living in a semi-detached house.*

La cuisine est au rez-de-chaussée.   *The kitchen is on the ground floor.*

Nous avons un canapé confortable qui est dans le salon.   *We have a comfortable sofa which is in the living room.*

in a council house — dans une habitation à loyer modéré (une HLM)
on a farm — dans une ferme
on the first floor — au premier étage

 WRITING

Use adjectives to make your descriptions more detailed...

Mahmoud has written a letter to his British exchange partner about his new flat.

Mon appartement a cinq pièces et se situe dans un immeuble **tout neuf**[1]. J'ai **emménagé**[2] il y a dix jours — j'habitais à la campagne avant cela. Ma chambre n'est pas très grande, donc la semaine prochaine j'achèterai des meubles plus petits. La cuisine est **carrément**[3] géniale. Il y a une grande **baie vitrée**[4] alors on y voit le soleil et la mer. J'aime beaucoup le bureau aussi. J'y fais mes devoirs car il y a une bibliothèque pour ranger mes livres. Et comme c'est à côté de la cuisine, c'est l'idéal pour **grignoter**[5]. Cependant, si la cuisine était plus loin, ce serait plus facile de manger moins de chocolat !

Grade 8-9

[1] brand new
[2] moved in
[3] absolutely
[4] bay window
[5] snacking

Tick list:
✓ tenses: present, perfect, imperfect, future, conditional
✓ correct pronoun position
✓ complex vocabulary
✓ use of 'si' clause

To improve:
+ use more exciting adjectives

Vous écrivez un blog sur votre maison / votre appartement pour un site Internet français.
*Vous **devez** faire référence aux points suivants:*

- *une description de votre maison / de votre appartement*
- *ce que vous pensez de votre quartier*
- *où vous habitiez dans le passé*
- *où vous aimeriez habiter à l'avenir.*

*Justifiez vos idées et vos opinions. Écrivez **130-150** mots environ **en français**.*   [28 marks]

Weather

British people are famous for moaning about the weather. Now you even get to do it in a different language...

Le temps — The weather

'Pleuvoir' and 'neiger' are impersonal verbs that can only be used with 'il' — see p.140.

le climat	*climate*	**Il fait...**	*It is...*	pleuvoir	*to rain*
Il y a...	*It is...*	beau	*fine*	neiger	*to snow*
du vent	*windy*	mauvais	*bad*	ensoleillé(e)	*sunny*
du soleil	*sunny*	chaud	*hot*	nuageux / nuageuse	*cloudy*
du brouillard	*foggy*	froid	*cold*	sec / sèche	*dry*

Il pleut.	*It's raining.*
Le climat là est doux.	*The climate there is mild.*
C'est nuageux et il pleut beaucoup.	*It's cloudy and it's raining a lot.*

It's snowing. — Il neige.
It's hailing. — Il grêle.

stormy — orageux
misty — brumeux

Grammar — il y a

'Il y a' *(there is)* is often used to discuss the weather. 'Il y aura' is the future form and 'il y avait' is the imperfect — both are useful for talking about weather.

La météo — The weather forecast

Question	**Simple Answer**	**Extended Answer**
Quel temps fera-t-il demain?	Il va faire beau et chaud, mais il va pleuvoir le soir.	Il fera beau le matin, mais au cours de la journée le temps deviendra plus nuageux et orageux. Il pleuvra en fin d'après-midi. Il restera couvert le soir. La température moyenne sera de 16 degrés.
What will the weather be like tomorrow?	*It will be fine and hot, but it will rain in the evening.*	*It will be fine in the morning, but during the day the weather will become more cloudy and stormy. It will rain late in the afternoon. It will remain overcast in the evening. The average temperature will be 16°C.*

Demain, le temps sera variable.	*Tomorrow, it's going to be changeable.*	lightning — des éclairs (m)
Le week-end, il y aura **des éclaircies**.	*At the weekend, there will be bright spells.*	thunder — du tonnerre
Ce sera orageux et il va neiger.	*It will be stormy and it will snow.*	freeze — geler
Il fera mauvais et froid. Il y aura des orages dans le sud.	*The weather will be bad and cold. There will be storms in the south.*	showers — des averses (f)

READING

To describe the weather, use 'il fait' or 'il y a' to say 'it is'...

Read the weather forecast and decide whether each sentence is true or false.

[1]remains turbulent   [2]a sky

- Voici les provisions météo. Ce matin, le temps **reste agité**[1] dans le sud-est, et il y aura des nuages orageux. Pourtant, cet après-midi, il fera plus beau et sec.

- Un peu de neige est attendue sur les Pyrénées au-dessus de 2000 m. Des averses orageuses et des coups de tonnerres se produiront dans le sud-ouest.

- En revanche, pour les régions au nord de Bordeaux, il y aura du brouillard le matin, et **un ciel**[2] ensoleillé l'après-midi.

e.g. In the south-east, it will be cloudy and stormy all day. **false**

1. It will snow in the Pyrenees above 2000 m. [1]

2. There will be showers and thunder in the south-west. [1]

3. It will be foggy all day in the regions north of Bordeaux. [1]

Listening Questions

Time to home in on some exam practice. Remember that doing practice questions is
a great way to revise — you're less likely to get caught out if you keep going over everything.

1 Listen to this person describing her home.
Choose the correct answer for each question and put a cross in the box.

TRACK LISTENING 17

a Where is the flat?

A	near the shops	
B	on the third floor	
C	on the first street on the left	
D	on the ground floor	

[1 mark]

b How many people live there?

A	one	
B	two	
C	three	
D	four	

[1 mark]

c Why does she like the kitchen?

A	It smells of coffee.	
B	It's nice and big.	
C	It has a balcony.	
D	It's small and cosy.	

[1 mark]

2 Écoute ces gens qui parlent des villes où ils habitent. Pour chaque personne,
choisis l'expression qui décrit leur ville. Écris la bonne lettre dans la case.

TRACK LISTENING 18

A	à la campagne
B	à la montagne
C	au bord de la mer
D	une ville de production
E	dans une région isolée

a Yvette

[1 mark]

b Thomas

[1 mark]

Section Five — Where You Live

Speaking Question

Candidate's Material

- Spend a couple of minutes looking at the photo and the prompts below it.

- You can make notes on a separate piece of paper.

© iStock.com/johnnorth

Regarde la photo et prépare des réponses sur les points suivants :

- la description de la photo

- si tu préfères le temps froid ou chaud

- le temps qu'il a fait hier

- ce que tu feras s'il fait beau ce week-end

- !

Teacher's Material

- Allow the student to develop his / her answers as much as possible.

- You need to ask the student the following questions **in order**:

  - Décris-moi la photo.

  - Préfères-tu le temps froid ou chaud ? Pourquoi ?

  - Quel temps a-t-il fait hier ?

  - Que feras-tu s'il fait beau ce week-end ?

  - Est-ce que tu regardes la météo ? Pourquoi / pourquoi pas ?

Reading Questions

1 Lis ce que Jean a écrit sur sa ville. Réponds aux questions **en français**.

> J'habite à Bruxelles. Bruxelles a une population d'environ deux cent mille habitants. C'est une ville très notable parce que c'est la capitale de la Belgique et que la plupart des institutions de l'Union européenne y sont situées. C'est aussi une très belle ville, avec un grand nombre de bâtiments anciens et intéressants au cœur de la ville. Il y a beaucoup de touristes qui viennent visiter la ville — quelquefois ça m'énerve mais généralement j'aime habiter ici.

a Bruxelles est une ville importante pour quelles raisons ? Donne **deux** raisons.

1. ....

2. .... *[2 marks]*

b Qu'est-ce qu'il y a au centre ville ?

.... *[1 mark]*

c Qu'est-ce que Jean pense des touristes ?

.... *[1 mark]*

2 Read Rose's online review of her family holiday in London.

> Le matin du départ, il faisait mauvais et notre vol était retardé parce qu'il y avait des vents forts. Quand finalement nous sommes arrivés à Londres, il faisait très froid et il pleuvait. En fait, il a plu toute la semaine, sauf notre dernier jour quand il a neigé ! Nous n'avons pas pu visiter les parcs à cause de la pluie — nous ne voulions pas être trempés. Pour couronner le tout, le jour de notre départ il y avait des orages, du tonnerre et des éclairs. J'avais vraiment peur et je ne voulais pas sortir de l'hôtel. J'irai en Espagne l'année prochaine !

What does the review tell us? Put a cross next to the **three** correct statements.

A	The flight was delayed because of heavy rain.	
B	It was very cold when they arrived in London.	
C	It rained every day.	
D	The weather stopped the family going out.	
E	There was a storm on their last day.	
F	Rose was angry about the weather.	
G	Rose enjoyed staying in the hotel.	

[3 marks]

Writing Questions

1 Georges, ton correspondant québécois, aimerait en savoir plus sur ta ville.

Écris un email à Georges pour lui décrire l'endroit où tu habites.

Tu **dois** faire référence aux points suivants :

• une description de ta ville

• si tu aimes y habiter et pourquoi

• une activité que tu as faite récemment en ville

• où tu aimerais habiter à l'avenir.

Écris 80-90 mots environ **en français**.   *[20 marks]*

2 Traduis le passage suivant **en français** :

> Today it is sunny and very hot in the south of France. In the north of France, it is cloudy. Tomorrow it will be windy in the south, but the weather will be fine. However, in the north, it will rain and it will be quite cold, but there will be bright spells in the afternoon.

....

....

....

....

....

[12 marks]

Revision Summary for Section Five

Another section, another revision summary. Don't worry if some of the stuff in this section passed you by — once you've finished, just revisit anything you struggled with.

Talking About Where You Live (p.54) ☑

1) You've arrived in Boulogne and are writing to your penfriend Matthieu about the town. Tell him: 'In the town centre, there's a post office, a newsagent's, a library, a bakery and a bus station.' ☑

2) A friendly policeman warns you about "un embouteillage". What is he warning you about? ☑

3) In French, give three reasons why you like your town, then list three things you don't like about it. ☑

4) What could you buy if you were...?   a) au tabac   b) à la boucherie   c) au marché
In French, give two examples for each. ☑

5) On holiday in France, you read the following council advertisement in the local paper: 'Aidez-nous à réduire la circulation en ville en utilisant notre système de transports en commun. Laissez votre voiture chez vous et prenez le bus. Merci d'avance !' What does the council advise you to do? ☑

6) Your French friend Giselle tells you: 'À l'avenir, je voudrais habiter à la campagne car il y a trop de bruit au centre-ville.' What does she want to do and why? ☑

The Home (p.55) ☑

7) Choose a room in your house and describe it in detail in French. ☑

8) Leyla says: 'J'habite dans une habitation à loyer modéré, et ma chambre est au premier étage. Je préférerais habiter dans une maison à la campagne, mais ce serait trop cher.' What's she saying? ☑

9) Est-ce que tu aimes habiter dans ta région? Pourquoi / Pourquoi pas ? ☑

10) If you live 'dans une maison jumelée', where do you live? ☑

11) Hatsue is describing her bedroom. She tells you: 'J'aime ma chambre car elle est assez grande et je peux inviter mes amies chez moi. Cependant, les meubles sont très vieux et je n'ai pas le droit d'avoir une télé dans ma chambre, ce qui m'énerve.' What does she like / dislike about her bedroom? Answer in English. ☑

Weather (p.56) ☑

12) What is 'la météo'? ☑

13) In French, say: 'It's rainy, but tomorrow it's going to be fine.' ☑

14) 'Demain, au cours de la journée, le temps deviendra orageux.' What's the best way to describe this weather?   a) cold   b) stormy   c) windy ☑

15) Comment est le temps dans ta région en général ? Réponds en français. ☑

16) You hear the weather forecast for France. 'Dans le nord du pays, il y aura du brouillard et il y a un risque de visibilité réduite. Dans le sud, il y aura des averses et il fera froid. What will the weather be like...?   a) in the north   b) in the south ☑

17) Est-ce que tu préfères passer tes vacances dans des pays chauds ou dans des pays froids ? Justifie tes opinions. ☑

Where To Go

We're all going on a summer holiday... This page is all about different countries and places you can go to.

Les pays (m) du monde — The countries of the world

l'Angleterre (f)	England	l'Inde (f)	India
la Grande-Bretagne	Great Britain	l'Amérique (f)	America
les États-Unis (m)	United States	l'Afrique (f)	Africa
l'Allemagne (f)	Germany	l'Asie (f)	Asia
la Chine	China	l'Europe (f)	Europe
l'Espagne (f)	Spain	à l'étranger	abroad
la Russie	Russia	la mer	sea
la Belgique	Belgium	la plage	beach
la Suisse	Switzerland	la Méditerranée	
le Pays de Galles	Wales		the Mediterranean

Grammar — to go to...

To say you're going to a <u>country</u>, you need the correct form of '<u>aller</u>' *(to go)* and the correct <u>preposition</u>. Use:

- <u>au</u> for masc. sing. countries starting with a consonant.
- <u>aux</u> for plural countries.
- <u>en</u> for masc. sing. countries starting with a vowel and all <u>fem. sing.</u> countries.

If you're going to a <u>town</u>, you just need '<u>à</u>'.

Les vacances (f) — Holidays

la Bourgogne	*Burgundy*	la Picardie	*Picardy*	la Guyane	*French Guiana*
la Normandie	*Normandy*	la Corse	*Corsica*	la Réunion	*Reunion*

These are all <u>administrative regions</u> of France.

Je vais aller en Bretagne, et après ça, j'irai en Écosse pour trois jours.	*I'm going to go to Brittany, and after that, I will go to Scotland for three days.*
J'ai passé les vacances au bord de la mer.	*I spent the holidays at the seaside.*

to Paris — à Paris
to India — en Inde
to the Netherlands — aux Pays-Bas (m)

Question	**Simple Answer**	**Extended Answer**
Quels sont vos projets pour les vacances?	Je vais passer deux semaines en Algérie.	À la fin d'août, j'irai dans le sud de l'Inde pour trois semaines avec deux amis. Nous visiterons des sites historiques.
What are your plans for the holidays?	*I'm going to spend two weeks in Algeria.*	*At the end of August, I will go to the south of India for three weeks with two friends. We'll visit historical sites.*

READING

Make sure you use the right version of 'au' or 'en' with places...

Lis l'email de Françoise qui parle de ses vacances. Réponds aux questions **en français**.

Salut Marc,

Les grandes vacances sont arrivées enfin ! Mais je ne suis pas contente : ma famile n'a pas de projets pour les vacances. Nous ne pouvons pas arriver à une décision. Moi, je voudrais aller en Angleterre parce que j'ai envie de voir un match de football anglais. Ma sœur pense que nous devrions passer les vacances au bord de la mer. Elle veut aller chaque jour à la plage. Ma mère préférerait aller à Berlin car elle s'intéresse aux musées. Cependant, mon père dit que nous allons tous rester en France. Il croit que nous devrions faire du camping car il adore la vie en plein air. Et toi, où vas-tu passer les vacances ?

Françoise

1.   Comment veut-elle passer les vacances ? Donne **deux** détails.   [2]
2.   Qu'est-ce qu'elle dit au sujet de sa sœur ? Donne **deux** détails.   [2]
3.   Que veut faire son père ? Donne **deux** détails.   [2]

Accommodation

I know it's hard thinking about holidays while you're revising, but here's some stuff on accommodation.

Le logement — Accommodation

loger	*to stay*	faire du camping	*to go camping*
l'hôtel (m)	*hotel*	l'auberge (f) de jeunesse	*youth hostel*
le camping	*campsite*	la chambre d'hôte	*bed and breakfast*
la tente	*tent*	la colonie de vacances	*holiday camp*

Il cherche un hôtel au bord de la mer. *He's looking for a hotel at the seaside.*

Est-ce qu'il y a une auberge de jeunesse ici? *Is there a youth hostel here?*

in the town centre — au centre-ville
in Nice — à Nice

Où aimez-vous loger? — Where do you like to stay?

Question	**Simple Answer**	**Extended Answer**
Quel est votre type de logement préféré?	J'aime loger dans les hôtels car c'est plus pratique.	Je préfère faire du camping parce qu'il y a beaucoup de choses qu'on peut faire à la campagne. En plus, je trouve qu'on peut voir plus de choses de l'endroit qu'on visite.
What's your favourite type of accommodation?	*I like staying in hotels because it's more practical.*	*I prefer to go camping because there are many things you can do in the countryside. Also, I find that you can see more of the place you're visiting.*

Je préfère loger dans une auberge de jeunesse parce que c'est moins cher qu'un hôtel. *I prefer to stay in a youth hostel because it is less expensive than a hotel.*

I like getting to know other people — j'aime faire la connaissance de nouvelles personnes

J'aime faire du camping parce que j'adore la vie en plein air. *I like camping because I love life in the open air.*

nature — la nature
to explore the countryside — explorer la campagne

On peut se détendre plus si on loge dans un hôtel parce qu'on ne doit pas cuisiner. *You can relax more if you stay in a hotel because you don't have to cook.*

because the rooms are already prepared — parce que les chambres sont déjà préparées

 READING

Avoid always using 'j'aime' — add in 'je préfère' and 'je trouve'...

Read this extract from 'Le tour du monde en quatre-vingts jours' by Jules Verne. Answer the questions **in English**.

Lorsque Passepartout est arrivé à International-Hôtel, il ne lui semblait pas qu'il avait quitté l'Angleterre. Le rez-de-chaussée de l'hôtel était occupé par un immense «bar», sorte de buffet ouvert gratis à tout passant. Viande sèche, soupe aux huîtres, des biscuits et du fromage, y sont apparus sans que le consommateur ait dû payer. Cela paraissait «très-américain» à Passepartout. Le restaurant de l'hôtel était confortable. Mr. Fogg et Mrs. Aouda s'installaient devant une table et étaient abondamment servis.

1. What surprised Passepartout when he arrived at the International-Hôtel? *[1]*
2. Where was the hotel bar? *[1]*
3. What was provided in the buffet? Give **two** details. *[2]*
4. What was positive about the hotel? Give **two** details. *[2]*

Getting Ready to Go

And the boring but necessary admin bit... This page is about booking your holiday and getting ready to go.

Les préparatifs (m) — Preparations

réserver	to book / to reserve
la valise	suitcase
les bagages (m)	luggage
la pièce d'identité	ID
le passeport	passport
l'agence (f) de voyages	travel agency
la climatisation	air conditioning
le sac de couchage	sleeping bag
l'emplacement (m)	pitch
la chambre	room
le lit à deux places	double bed
les lits (m) jumeaux	twin beds
donner sur	to overlook

Grammar — from...to...

To say 'from...to...' when booking something, use 'du...au...'.

Je voudrais réserver une chambre du 25 août au 27 août.
I'd like to reserve a room from the 25th August to the 27th August.

J'ai mis mon passeport et mes lunettes de soleil dans ma valise. | *I put my passport and my sunglasses in my suitcase.*

J'ai réservé une chambre du 5 mai au 12 mai. | *I booked a room from the 5th May to the 12th May.*

Faire une réservation — To make a reservation

Je voudrais réserver une chambre avec un lit à deux places. | *I would like to book a room with a double bed.*

Nous voudrions réserver un emplacement pour une tente du 13 juillet au 17 juillet. Nous sommes deux adultes et un enfant. | *We would like to reserve a pitch for one tent from the 13th July to the 17th July. We are two adults and one child.*

Je préfère avoir une chambre simple avec climatisation qui donne sur la mer. | *I prefer to have a single room with air conditioning which overlooks the sea.*

with twin beds — à lits jumeaux

with bunk beds — à lits superposés

a campervan — un camping-car

a caravan — une caravane

Hope you've got all that vocab packed and ready for the exam...

Jo is having a conversation with a French travel agent about booking a hotel.
Read her responses, then have a go at doing your own role play using the instructions below.

Tu parles avec un agent de voyage (AV).

Grade 8-9

AV : Bonjour. Je peux vous aider ?

Jo : Bonjour ! Je voudrais réserver une chambre dans un hôtel à Toulouse, s'il vous plaît.

AV : Pour combien de personnes et pour combien de nuits ?

Jo : Pour deux adultes, du 3 juin au 5 juin, s'il vous plaît.

AV : D'accord. Vous avez des préférences particulières ?

Jo : Je préférerais une chambre **climatisée**[1] parce qu'il fera chaud. Est-ce qu'il y a un hôtel avec une piscine ?

AV : Oui, il y en a plusieurs, par exemple l'Hôtel Ensoleillé.

Jo : Combien ça coûtera par nuit ?

AV : Ça coûte cent euros par nuit.

[1]air-conditioned

Tick list:
✓ tenses: present, future, conditional
✓ complex and relevant vocab

To improve:
+ more varied conjunctions

Address the travel agent as 'vous' and speak for about two minutes. [10 marks]

Tu parles avec un agent de voyage.
* *réservation*
* *!*
* *dernières vacances — où*
* *? climatisation*
* *? activités pour enfants*

How to Get There

A vital thing about going on holiday is getting there. The transport vocab will be useful in other contexts too.

Comment y aller — How to get there

l'arrivée (f)	arrival	la voiture	car	conduire	to drive
le départ	departure	l'autobus (m)	bus	l'autoroute (f)	motorway
manquer	to miss	le train	train	la route	way / road
la carte	map	l'avion (m)	plane	le vol	flight
l'horaire (m)	timetable	le bateau	boat	louer	to rent / to hire

Voyager — To travel

Je suis allé(e) en train. — *I went by train.*

Je préfère les voitures aux bus — les bus sont peu fiables. — *I prefer cars to buses — buses are not very reliable.*

Nous avons manqué le bateau. — *We missed the boat.*

Grammar — monter, descendre

Use 'monter dans' to say 'to get on'.
Je monte dans le train. *I get on the train.*
Use 'descendre de' to say 'to get off'.
Il descend du bus. *He gets off the bus.*

'TGV' stands for 'train à grande vitesse' (high-speed train). The French national rail company is called SNCF.

Nous allons louer une voiture. Puis, selon la carte, nous devons prendre l'autoroute. — *We're going to hire a car. Then, according to the map, we need to take the motorway.*

J'ai regardé l'horaire — le TGV devrait arriver à six heures. Mais il est en retard. — *I looked at the timetable — the TGV should arrive at six o'clock. But it's late.*

En avion — By plane

Il faut arriver à l'aéroport deux heures avant l'heure de départ. — *You must arrive at the airport two hours before the departure time.* ← check in — s'enregistrer

Le vol était retardé à cause d'un problème technique. — *The flight was delayed due to a technical problem.* ← to bad weather — du mauvais temps

Question	Simple Answer	Extended Answer
Est-ce que tu aimes voler? *Do you like flying?*	Oui, les avions sont le moyen de transport le plus sûr. *Yes, aeroplanes are the safest mode of transport.*	J'ai peur de voler parce que mon imagination me fait toujours envisager le pire. Mais les avions sont si pratiques et rapides! *I'm scared of flying because I always imagine the worst. But planes are so convenient and fast!*

Remember that 'aller' (to go) takes 'être' in the past tense...

Translate this social media post about English. *[7 marks]*

La semaine prochaine, je vais aller en vacances aux États-Unis. En particulier, je voudrais voir New York. J'y ai réservé un hôtel de luxe avec une grande piscine. Cependant, le voyage m'inquiète beaucoup. J'ai peur de voler, et je serai dans l'avion pendant sept heures.

What to Do

So you've chosen a destination, booked your accommodation and got there... now what do you do?

Le tourisme — Tourism

l'office (m) de tourisme	*tourist office*	la cathédrale	*cathedral*	le tour	*tour*
les renseignements (m)	*information*	le château	*castle*	le plan de ville	*town plan*
le site touristique	*tourist attraction*	le musée	*museum*	la carte postale	*postcard*
le parc d'attractions	*theme park*	la visite guidée	*guided tour*	se faire bronzer	*to sunbathe*

En vacances, j'ai visité... — On holiday, I visited...

Question	**Simple Answer**	**Extended Answer**
Qu'est-ce que tu as fait en vacances?	J'ai visité une cathédrale et je suis allé(e) à la plage.	J'ai décidé d'aller au musée pour apprendre autant que possible sur la région. Ça m'intéressait beaucoup.
What did you do on holiday?	*I visited a cathedral and I went to the beach.*	*I decided to go to the museum to learn as much as possible about the region. It was really interesting.*

L'un de mes plus grands plaisirs, c'est acheter des souvenirs.	*One of my greatest pleasures is buying souvenirs.*	going on a boat tour — faire un tour en bateau
J'adore me faire bronzer à la plage. Malheureusement, j'ai oublié ma crème solaire.	*I love sunbathing at the beach. Unfortunately, I forgot my suncream.*	my swimming costume — mon maillot de bain my sunglasses — mes lunettes (f) de soleil
La cathédrale m'a beaucoup plu.	*I liked the cathedral a lot.*	the zoo — le zoo

Grammar — plaire and pleuvoir

'Plaire' means *'to please'* and 'pleuvoir' means *'to rain'*. They both have the same past participle — 'plu'.

Il m'a beaucoup plu. *I liked it a lot. (It pleased me a lot.)* **Il a beaucoup plu.** *It rained a lot.*

Make sure you know how to spell the key vocab correctly...

Jack has written a blog about his plans for his holiday in France.

Cet été, je vais passer deux semaines à Cherbourg pour améliorer mon français. J'ai quelques projets pour réaliser ce **but**[1]. Je logerai avec une famille française, donc je parlerai français tous les jours. Je vais faire une visite guidée pour essayer de faire la connaissance de la ville et des gens français.

Je vais visiter les sites historiques car on peut y apprendre beaucoup. L'été dernier, je suis allé à Vienne et j'ai visité un château historique — les histoires des gens qui y ont vécu m'ont beaucoup intéressées.

J'irai sur la **côte**[2] aussi parce que je veux passer des jours relaxants à la plage.

[1] aim
[2] coast

Grade 8-9

Tick list:
✓ tenses: present, perfect, both futures
✓ correct use of 'y'

To improve:
+ use the conditional
+ give opinions using adjectives

Écrivez un article sur vos projets pour les vacances. Vous devez faire référence aux points suivants :

- *ce que vous aimez faire en vacances*
- *les vacances dernières*
- *vos projets pour cet été*
- *vos vacances de rêve.*

Justifiez vos idées et vos opinions. Écrivez **130-150** *mots environ* **en français**. *[28 marks]*

Eating Out

It would be a real waste to go to France and miss out on the delicious cuisine, so here's some useful vocab.

Qu'est-ce que vous voudriez? — What would you like?

There's more vocab. on p.191.

la boisson	*drink*	le hors d'œuvre	*starter*
la carte	*menu*	le plat principal	*main meal*
l'eau (f) plate / gazeuse	*still / fizzy water*	le dessert	*dessert*
le thé	*tea*	commander	*to order*
le café	*coffee*	végétarien(ne)	*vegetarian*
le vin	*wine*	fermé (le lundi)	*closed (on Mondays)*
la bière	*beer*	le serveur / la serveuse	*waiter / waitress*
la pression	*beer (from the pump)*	l'addition (f)	*the bill*

Je voudrais un verre de jus d'orange et une portion de frites, s'il vous plaît.	*I would like a glass of orange juice and a portion of chips, please.*

Allons au restaurant — Let's go to the restaurant

J'aime manger au restaurant parce qu'on peut goûter des plats qu'on ne cuisinerait jamais chez soi. J'ai essayé la cuisine chinoise, par exemple.	*I like eating in restaurants because you can try food that you would never cook at home. I tried Chinese food, for example.*	Indian — indienne Mexican — mexicaine
Je suis végétarien(ne) donc c'est difficile de trouver des restaurants où je peux manger.	*I'm vegetarian so it's hard to find restaurants where I can eat.*	vegan — végétalien(ne) allergic to... — allergique à...
J'ai commandé des escargots au restaurant français. Comme dessert, j'ai mangé une glace à la fraise.	*I ordered snails in the French restaurant. For dessert, I ate a strawberry ice cream.*	frogs' legs — des cuisses de grenouille the fixed price menu — le menu à prix fixe

---

SPEAKING

Use 'vous' when talking to the waiter or waitress...

Here's an example role play — Yann is talking to Fatima about a visit to a restaurant.

Fatima : Qu'est-ce que tu as commandé au restaurant ?

Grade 8-9

Yann : J'ai commandé du potage comme hors d'œuvre et du poulet avec des haricots comme plat principal.

Fatima : Tout s'est bien passé ?

Yann : **Je me suis plaint**[1] du poulet parce qu'il était froid.

Fatima : Qu'est-ce que tu as aimé le plus ?

Yann : J'ai aimé les haricots verts car ils étaient bien cuisinés.

Fatima : Quel est ton repas préféré ?

Yann : Le poulet avec les petits pois et les pommes de terre. Et toi, quel est ton répas préféré ?

Fatima : Mon répas préféré est les fruits de mer.

Yann : Qu'est-ce que tu mangeras ce soir ?

Fatima : Je mangerai des pâtes avec des petits pois et des champignons. J'aime manger ça avec du fromage.

Tick list:
- ✓ tenses: perfect, imperfect, present, future
- ✓ opinion phrases
- ✓ correctly formed question

To improve:
- + use adjectives, e.g. 'délicieux', to avoid repeating 'aimer'

Prepare the role play card below. Use 'tu' and speak for about two minutes. [10 marks]

[1] I complained

Tu parles avec ton ami(e) d'une visite au restaurant.
- *les plats commandés*
- *problème*
- *!*
- *? repas préféré*
- *? ce soir — restaurant*

68

Practical Stuff

It's always good to know how to get out of a spot of bother on holiday, so learn this page well.

J'ai perdu mon billet — I've lost my ticket

On public transport in France, you normally have to validate your ticket in a machine before you travel.

le bureau des objets trouvés	*lost property office*	le retard	*delay*
le commissariat	*police station*	le quai	*platform*
l'accueil (m)	*reception*	composter	*to validate (ticket)*
le portefeuille	*wallet*	laisser	*to leave (behind)*
le pneu	*tyre*	voler	*to steal*
les freins (m)	*brakes*	tomber en panne	*to break down*

Qu'est-ce qui t'est arrivé? — What happened to you?

Holiday <u>mishaps</u> are just waiting to happen — especially when another <u>language</u> is involved.

Grammar — 'se faire' + infinitive

The <u>perfect tense</u> (see p.127-128) of '<u>se faire</u>' followed by an <u>infinitive</u> is a way of saying that <u>something happened to you</u>. It's often used when we would say 'got' in English, e.g. 'they got stranded.' Remember — all reflexive verbs use '<u>être</u>' in the perfect tense.

Il s'est fait piquer par un moustique.   <u>He got bitten</u> by a mosquito.

Hier, je me suis fait voler mon portefeuille.   *Yesterday, my wallet <u>was stolen</u>.*

En faisant du ski aux Alpes, j'ai glissé et je suis tombé(e) sur mon bras. J'ai dû aller aux urgences.

Whilst skiing in the Alps, I slipped and I fell on my arm. I had to go to A&E.

> *I broke my leg* — je me suis cassé la jambe

Je suis allé(e) au Maroc en famille. Nous sommes tombés en panne dans les montagnes — c'était un cauchemar.

I went to Morocco with my family. We broke down in the mountains — it was a nightmare.

> *We got a flat tyre* — Nous avons eu un pneu crevé

> *I had to go to customer services* — j'ai dû aller au service client

L'année dérnière, j'ai rendu visite à un ami en France. J'ai oublié de composter mon billet de train, alors j'ai reçu une amende.

Last year, I visited a friend in France. I forgot to validate my train ticket, so I received a fine.

> *the ticket inspector was angry* — le contrôleur / la contrôleuse était en colère

This page could be your ticket out of a tricky situation...

Marc has written a report describing an incident that happened during a recent trip.

La semaine dernière, je suis allé à Paris. Après avoir pris le métro, je me suis rendu compte que je n'avais plus mon portefeuille ! Je suis allé au bureau des objets trouvés, mais c'était évident que quelqu'un l'avait volé. J'étais en colère, et je n'avais plus d'argent ; j'ai dû aller au commissariat pour déclarer le vol. Les policiers étaient compréhensifs et ils m'ont aidé à **remplir les formulaires**[1].

Grade 8-9

Tick list:
- ✓ tenses: perfect, imperfect, pluperfect
- ✓ perfect infinitive
- ✓ negative construction

[1]to fill out the forms

To improve:
- + use the present, conditional and future
- + more varied conjunctions

Un site Internet touristique cherche des articles sur les problèmes et les solutions en vacances. Écrivez **130-150** mots environ **en français**. Vous **devez** faire référence aux points suivants :

- où vous êtes allé(e) et ce que vous avez fait
- un problème qui vous est arrivé
- ce que vous avez fait pour résoudre le problème
- si vous reviendriez au même endroit.   [28 marks]

Section Six — Travel and Tourism

Giving and Asking for Directions

This page has all you need to know about getting to where you want to go. So get learning it...

Où est...? — Where is...?

situé(e)	*situated*	en face de	*opposite*	environ	*about*
se trouver	*to be situated*	juste à côté de	*right next to*	jusqu'à	*until*
traverser	*to cross*	ici	*here*	le nord	*north*
à gauche	*on / to the left*	là-bas	*over there*	le sud	*south*
à droite	*on / to the right*	loin de	*far from*	l'est (m)	*east*
tout droit	*straight ahead*	près de	*near*	l'ouest (m)	*west*

La poste est située en face de l'église. Allez tout droit pour environ deux minutes, puis prenez la première rue à droite.

The post office is situated opposite the church. Go straight ahead for about two minutes, then take the first street on the right.

Traversez la rue, puis tournez à gauche. La boulangerie est juste à côté de l'école.

Cross the street, then turn left. The bakery is right next to the school.

Le village est au sud-ouest de la ville. La ville est dans le sud du pays.

The village is south-west of the town. The town is in the south of the country.

> Remember, if you're talking to someone you don't know, use the 'vous' form of the verb.

C'est loin d'ici? — Is it far from here?

It's useful to use <u>landmarks</u> when describing how to get somewhere.

la rue	*street*	les feux (m) (de signalisation)	*(traffic) lights*
la place	*square*	le rond-point	*roundabout*
le pont	*bridge*	le carrefour	*crossroads*
le trottoir	*pavement*	le panneau	*sign*

Grammar — imperative

The <u>imperative</u> form is used to give <u>instructions</u>:
Traversez! *Cross!*
See p.136 for more.

Pour aller à la gare, continuez tout droit, et tournez à gauche au carrefour.

To go to the train station, keep going straight ahead, and turn left at the crossroads.

to the bank — à la banque
to the theatre — au théâtre
to the café — au café
to the hospital — à l'hôpital (m)

Suivez le panneau 'toutes directions', et allez jusqu'aux feux, mais ne traversez pas le pont.

Follow the sign for 'all directions', and go up to the lights, but don't cross the bridge.

La banque est située en face de l'épicerie, juste à côté de la mosquée.

The bank is opposite the grocer's, right next to the mosque.

on the other side of — de l'autre côté de

the town hall — l'hôtel (m) de ville

TRACK LISTENING 19

Practise giving directions in French — it's a tricky thing to do...

Your friend left a voicemail message. Choose the correct answers to complete the statements.

1 a. You should change bus at the... **A.** park **B.** cinema **C.** bus Station [1]

b. The Grand-Place is... **A.** by the market **B.** near the supermarket **C.** on the coast [1]

c. After turning left you should... **A.** go as far as the library **B.** pass the library **C.** walk 100 m [1]

d. Then, you should... **A.** turn right **B.** cross at the traffic lights **C.** keep going for 200 m [1]

Listening Questions

If at first you don't succeed, try and try again. You'll be working against the clock in the exam, so knowing what you're likely to come across is essential — the last thing you want to do is panic.

---

1 You telephone a hotel in France to book your summer holiday.
Listen to the answerphone message.

Example: Where is the hotel?

.... _Cannes_ ....

a Which option do you need for a summer holiday?
Write the correct number in the box. ☐

[1 mark]

b What would you find on the hotel website?

.... *[1 mark]*

c Which **three** details should you provide if you wish to speak to someone?

1. ....

2. ....

3. .... *[3 marks]*

---

2 Listen to this phone conversation about eating out.
Answer the questions **in English**.

(i) a What kind of food is particularly good at the restaurant?

.... *[1 mark]*

(ii) a What did Juliette used to like eating?

.... *[1 mark]*

b What **two** excuses does Juliette give for not going to eat pancakes with Leo?

1. ....

2. .... *[2 marks]*

Speaking Question

Candidate's Material

- Spend a couple of minutes looking at the photo and the prompts below it.

- You can make notes on a separate piece of paper.

© iStock.com/MauritsVink

Regarde la photo et prépare des réponses sur les points suivants :

- la description de la photo

- le moyen de transport que tu préfères — raison

- comment tu as passé les vacances l'été dernier

- le pays que tu aimerais visiter le plus

- !

Teacher's Material

- Allow the student to develop his / her answers as much as possible.

- You need to ask the student the following questions **in order**:

  - Décris-moi la photo.

  - Quel moyen de transport préfères-tu ? Pourquoi ?

  - Comment as-tu passé tes vacances l'été dernier ?

  - Quel pays aimerais-tu visiter le plus ? Pourquoi ?

  - Où préfères-tu loger en vacances ? Pourquoi ?

Reading Questions

1 Read the directions for getting to the Hôtel Magnifique.
Answer the questions **in English**.

> Quand vous arriverez à la gare, suivez les panneaux 'Place de la Concorde' et sortez à cet endroit. Prenez ensuite la rue de la Gloire et allez tout droit jusqu'au <u>commissariat.</u> Tournez à droite et puis traversez la rue. L'église de Saint Michel sera à votre gauche. Prenez la rue à côté de l'église et allez tout droit. Vous passerez devant le parc. Prenez la première rue à gauche après le parc et l'Hôtel Magnifique se trouvera au bout de la rue, en face de la poste.

a What should you do when you get to the police station?

.... *[1 mark]*

b What should you do once you've got to the church?

.... *[1 mark]*

c Where is the post office?

.... *[1 mark]*

2 Lis ce blog de Flora.

> Je suis ici à Zenica en Bosnie-Herzégovine depuis seulement trois jours et je suis déjà tombée amoureuse du pays ! Une fois arrivée à l'auberge de jeunesse, j'ai commencé tout de suite à m'amuser. Tout le monde a des histoires rigolotes à raconter.
>
> Quant au pays, la Bosnie a un passé tragique et on peut le découvrir dans les nombreux musées. Les gens ici sont très aimables et j'ai déjà goûté des spécialités nationales. Demain je prendrai le train au petit matin pour aller à Sarajevo.

Complète les phrases en choisissant un mot ou des mots dans la case.
Il y a des mots que tu n'utiliseras pas.

> le passé   partir   drôles   l'histoire du pays   sympathiques
>
> se reposer   l'hospitalité   rentrer   bruyantes

a Flora pense que les autres jeunes sont _drôles_ . *[1 mark]*

b Elle s'intéresse à _l'histoire du pays_ *[1 mark]*

c Elle trouve que .... du pays est impressionnante. *[1 mark]*

d Flora a l'intention de .... le lendemain. *[1 mark]*

Writing Questions

1 Tu veux recommander la destination de tes vacances récentes.
Écris un article sur ton blog pour encourager les autres à y aller.

Tu **dois** faire référence aux points suivants :

• la destination et comment tu y es allé(e)

• où tu es resté(e)

• les lieux que tu as visités

• pourquoi tu recommanderais cette destination.

Écris 80-90 mots environ **en français**.   *[20 marks]*

2 Traduis le passage suivant **en français** :

> Last year my family stayed in a small hotel in England. What a disaster! Our room was very small. The bathroom was really dirty, it was disgusting. The food in the restaurant was terrible and the waiter was rude. Next year we will go to China and visit a theme park.

....

....

....

....

....

....

[12 marks]

Revision Summary for Section Six

Here's another delightful revision summary. You know the drill by now — go through the questions and make a note of which ones you struggle with.

Where to Go (p.62) ☑

1) A friend says to you: 'I went to Brazil, China, France and Russia.' Say this in French. ☑
2) Tell your friend that you're going to go to Nottingham next weekend. ☑
3) Où es-tu allé(e) en vacances l'année dernière ? ☑

Accommodation and Getting Ready to Go (p.63-64) ☑

4) In French, write down as many different types of accommodation as you can. ☑
5) Describe a holiday you've been on in French. Include who you went with and where you stayed. ☑
6) You're going to Paris. Imagine you're on the phone to the tourist information office. In French, say that you would like to stay in a youth hostel that isn't too expensive. ☑
7) You're ringing a hotel. Say that you'd like to reserve a room with a double bed from the 12th July to the 26th July. ☑
8) 'C'était un désastre. Les lits superposés se sont cassés, donc j'ai dû dormir par terre. De plus, la climatisation ne marchait pas.' In English, say why Jean-Luc was dissatisfied with his hotel room. ☑
9) Write down the French for... a) suitcase b) luggage c) sleeping bag d) travel agency ☑

How to Get There (p.65) ☑

10) Tell your French friend that you're going to miss your flight. ☑
11) An advert in the departures lounge says: 'Les transports en commun ne sont pas toujours fiables. Pour profiter de vos vacances, louez une voiture pendant votre séjour.' What is it advertising? Answer in English. ☑
12) 'If I had the money, I would go on holiday to Asia. I would travel by train and get to know other people.' How would you say this in French? ☑

What to Do and Eating Out (p.66-67) ☑

13) You're on holiday in Brittany. Ask a local where the museum is. ☑
14) Victoire is telling you about her holiday. 'Nous sommes allés à la plage tous les jours et à la fin de la semaine nous avons fait un tour en bateau. Mon père a organisé une visite guidée du château, mais je l'ai trouvée ennuyeuse.' Translate her sentences into English. ☑
15) Qu'est-ce que tu aimes faire en vacances? ☑
16) You're at a restaurant in France. Say that you'd like to see the menu, and order a glass of fizzy water. ☑
17) You're a vegetarian. Which of these dishes are you able to eat?
   a) le bœuf bourguignon b) le poulet rôti c) le potage aux légumes d) la tourte à la viande ☑

Practical Stuff and Directions (p.68-69) ☑

18) Phara tells you, 'J'ai laissé mon portefeuille dans le train et j'ai oublié de composter mon billet. Puis, j'ai perdu mon passeport.' What problems did she have? ☑
19) In French, say that someone has stolen your bike and say what colour it is. ☑
20) In French, how would you say...? a) on the left b) on the right c) opposite d) over there ☑
21) A tourist comes up to you and asks: 'Excusez-moi, où est l'église?' What does she want to know? ☑
22) In French, tell the tourist: 'It's right next to the swimming pool. Go straight ahead for about 5 minutes, then turn left.' ☑

School Subjects

Talking about subjects is pretty straightforward — plus, you're probably bursting to say that you adore all things French-related. Explaining your opinion will get you more marks, so use this page to prepare properly.

Les matières (f) — Subjects

For more school subjects, see p.191-192.

For how to pronounce the letters of the French alphabet, look at p.16.

l'allemand (m)	*German*	la matière obligatoire	*compulsory subject*
l'espagnol (m)	*Spanish*	la littérature anglaise	*English literature*
le français	*French*	le dessin	*art*
la biologie	*biology*	l'EPS (éducation physique	
la chimie	*chemistry*	et sportive) (f)	*PE (physical education)*
la physique	*physics*	l'informatique (f)	*IT (information technology)*

Ma matière préférée c'est... — My favourite subject is...

Moi, j'adore l'EPS. C'est chouette parce que je ne dois pas me concentrer et les cours sont détendus.

I love PE. It's great because I don't have to concentrate and the lessons are relaxed.

À mon avis, la physique est affreuse. C'est trop compliqué et je n'aime pas faire les expériences.

In my opinion, physics is awful. It's too complicated and I don't like doing the experiments.

my teacher is funny — mon / ma professeur est amusant(e)

I love doing exercise — j'adore faire de l'exercice

is boring — est ennuyeuse

is useless — ne sert à rien

Question	**Simple Answer**	**Extended Answer**
Quelle est ta matière préférée?	J'aime assez les maths. *I quite like maths.*	J'aime assez les maths car c'est logique, cependant, je préfère la littérature anglaise. C'est fascinant et je m'intéresse aux histoires des autres.
What's your favourite subject?	j'aime bien *I really like* j'adore *I love*	*I quite like maths because it's logical, however, I prefer English literature. It's fascinating and I'm interested in other people's stories.*

Always explain your opinions — it'll gain you marks...

Cho a envoyé un email à sa copine pour lui parler de ses matières préférées.

Au lycée, ma matière préférée c'est le français parce que c'est tellement intéressant. J'aime assez le dessin et la technologie, mais je les trouve difficiles car je n'ai pas de **côté artistique**[1]. L'année dernière, j'ai étudié l'espagnol, et je m'intéressais beaucoup à cette matière. Malheureusement, le professeur d'espagnol a quitté le lycée, et j'ai dû **laisser tomber**[2] cette matière.

Je déteste l'allemand — pour moi c'est vraiment une langue affreuse. C'est dommage car j'aime apprendre les langues. Je voudrais étudier d'autres langues dans l'avenir et, si j'ai de la chance, peut être je pourrais devenir **traductrice**[3].

Grade 8-9

Tick list:
- ✓ tenses: present, perfect, imperfect, conditional, future
- ✓ si clause
- ✓ good use of conjunctions

[1]artistic side
[2]to drop
[3]translator

To improve:
+ include more varied sentence structures, e.g. 'pour' + infinitive

Écris un email à un(e) copain / copine pour donner ton avis sur les matières scolaires.
*Tu **dois** faire référence aux points suivants :*

- *les matières que tu aimes / n'aimes pas au collège et pourquoi*
- *les matières que tu as trouvées difficiles cette année*

- *pourquoi tu penses que les matières que tu étudies sont utiles (ou pas)*
- *les matières que tu voudrais faire dans l'avenir.*

*Écris **80-90** mots environ **en français**.* [20 marks]

School Routine

You probably know your school routine off by heart — now it's time to learn how to speak about it in French...

Aller à l'école — To go to school

For more modes of transport, see p.65.

la salle de classe	*classroom*
le cours	*lesson*
l'emploi (m) du temps	*timetable*
la récré(ation)	*break*
les vacances (f)	*holidays*
le trimestre	*term*
la semaine	*week*
la rentrée	*return to school (after the summer)*
en retard	*late*
de bonne heure	*early*
tous les jours	*every day*
aller à pied	*to go on foot*

Question

Comment vas-tu à l'école?
How do you get to school?

Simple Answer

J'y vais à pied.
I walk there.

Grammar — 'y' (there)

'Y' is a pronoun — it means 'there'. It can replace nouns that are locations. It normally goes before the verb — see p.113-114.

J'y vais ce week-end.
I'm going there this weekend.

Extended Answer

Normalement, j'y vais à pied parce que j'habite près du lycée. Par contre, quand il pleut, ma mère m'emmène en voiture.

Normally, I walk there because I live close to college. However, when it's raining, my mum takes me in the car.

Une journée typique — A typical day

See p.2 for more about stating the time.

La journée scolaire commence à neuf heures, et elle finit à quinze heures trente. Il y a deux récrés de vingt minutes, et on prend le déjeuner à midi.

The school day starts at nine o'clock, and it finishes at three thirty pm. There are two twenty-minute breaks, and we have lunch at midday.

J'ai un cours de maths chaque jour. Par contre, je ne fais qu'une heure d'EPS par semaine.

I have a maths lesson every day. On the other hand, I only do one hour of PE a week.

C'est une journée fatigante. Si j'avais le choix, je commencerais les cours plus tard.

It's a tiring day. If I had the choice, I would start lessons later.

Pendant la récré — During break

Je fais partie de l'équipe scolaire de natation, donc je m'entraîne souvent pendant la récré.

I'm part of the school swimming team, so I often train during break.

the holidays — les vacances

the term — le trimestre

Normalement, je reste dehors avec mes amis et nous jouons au football. Mais parfois nous allons à la cantine.

Normally, I stay outside with my friends and we play football. But sometimes we go to the canteen.

Make sure you go over this again and again and again...

Nicolas parle de son emploi du temps. Complète les phrases en choisissant des mots dans la case.

son frère	libres	le mardi	~~la chimie~~	stressés	d'EPS	la voiture	le soir	fatigués

e.g. Nicolas adore .... *la chimie* ....

1 a. Nicolas dit qu'il arrive à l'école en retard à cause de .... *[1]*

  b. Nicolas se sent très fatigué après les cours .... *[1]*

  c. Le mercredi, les élèves sont .... *[1]*

School Life

The French system is a little different to ours, and you need to understand it in case it pops up in your exams.

La vie scolaire — School life

bien équipé(e)	*well equipped*	l'élève (m / f)	*pupil*	apprendre	*to learn*
mal équipé(e)	*badly equipped*	l'internat (m)	*boarding school*	être en seconde	*to be in year 11*

Où vas-tu à l'école? — Where do you go to school?

Grammar — present tense + 'depuis'

To say you've been doing something since a certain age, use the <u>present tense</u> with '<u>depuis</u>' (*since*). See p.124 for more on this.

**J'étudie le français <u>depuis</u> l'âge de six ans.
*I've been studying French <u>since</u> the age of six.***

(2 - 6 years)	la maternelle	*nursery school*
(6 - 11 years)	l'école (f) primaire	*primary school*
(11 - 15 years)	le collège	*secondary school*
(15 - 18 years)	le lycée	*sixth form college*
(15 - 18 years)	le lycée professionnel	*technical college*

Je vais au collège près de chez moi. Je l'aime bien, et mes professeurs ont un bon sens de l'humour.

I go to the secondary school close to my home. I really like it, and my teachers have a good sense of humour.

are very engaging — sont très passionnants

Mon école est un internat. J'y vais depuis l'âge de onze ans.

My school is a boarding school. I've been going there since the age of eleven.

a state / private / religious school — une école publique / privée / confessionnelle

Décris ton école — Describe your school

Mon collège est très vieux, mais c'est génial à l'intérieur. Les couloirs sont vifs et pleins de couleur.

My school is very old, but it's great inside. The corridors are lively and full of colour.

it's modern — c'est moderne

the atmosphere is very different — l'ambiance (f) est très différente

Au total, il y a environ trois cents élèves. Il y a deux terrains de sport.

In total, there are around three hundred pupils. There are two sports pitches.

sports halls — gymnases (m)

It's useful to know how the French school system works...

Read these forum comments about school life, then answer the questions below.

Karine : Je vais au lycée à Paris et je suis en seconde. Les cours de sciences me fascinent car nos laboratoires sont très bien équipés : on peut faire plein d'expériences.

Alain : Je vais au lycée professionnel, et je prends des cours pour devenir mécanicien. Malheureusement, il faut que tout le monde étudie les maths. Je les déteste : le prof est vraiment ennuyeux, donc je n'arrive pas à m'intéresser aux cours.

Vusi : Je vais au collège. Il y a une piscine, donc je peux faire de l'exercice après les cours, ce qui m'aide à me relaxer.

Who says what about school life? Choose either Karine, Alain or Vusi.

1. .... says that sport is relaxing. [1]
2. .... says that having good resources encourages learning. [1]
3. .... says that the teacher's personality makes a big difference. [1]

School Pressures

School can be pretty stressful — you're trying to study and get the grades you need whilst maintaining a social life and doing your hobbies. Here's how to talk about it in French — let all that stress out...

Le règlement — School rules

la pression	*pressure*	le bulletin scolaire	*school report*
les devoirs (m)	*homework*	la retenue	*detention*
la note	*mark*	permettre	*to allow*
les résultats (m)	*results*	passer un examen	*to sit an exam*
l'examen (m)	*examination*	échouer	*to fail*
l'erreur (f)	*error / mistake*	réussir un examen	*to pass an exam*
les incivilités (f)	*rudeness*	redoubler	*to resit the year*

Watch out — 'passer un examen' doesn't mean 'to pass an exam', it means 'to take an exam'.

L'uniforme scolaire aide à rendre tous les élèves égaux.	*School uniform helps to make all pupils equal.*
Il est interdit de courir dans les couloirs.	*It is forbidden to run in the corridors.*
Si on enfreint le règlement, on sera en retenue.	*If you break the school rules, you'll be in detention.*

prevents students from being individual — empêche les élèves d'être individuels

to wear make-up at school — de se maquiller à l'école

to be rude to the teachers — d'être impoli(e) envers les professeurs

If you forget your homework — Si on oublie ses devoirs

If you're late — Si on est en retard

Être sous pression — To be under pressure

If you're asked for your <u>views on school</u>, this is a great chance to <u>add detail</u> to your answer.

Il y a beaucoup de pression à l'école à obtenir de bonnes notes.	*There's a lot of pressure at school to get good marks.*
J'ai étudié dur cette année donc j'espère réussir mes examens.	*I studied hard this year so I hope to pass my exams.*
Je me sens sous forte pression car j'ai peur de devoir redoubler.	*I feel under lots of pressure because I'm scared of having to repeat the year.*

to be fashionable — d'être à la mode

to get a good school report — obtenir un bon bulletin scolaire

my older brother is very gifted — mon frère aîné est très doué

Keep learning this vocab if you want to get great 'résultats'...

Read the example then have a go at the photo question below. Talk for about three minutes.

Es-tu sous pression dans ta vie scolaire ?

Moi, je me sens sous assez de pression. Il y a des devoirs chaque semaine pour l'anglais, les mathématiques et les sciences ; d'ailleurs, si nous n'obtenons pas de bonnes notes, les profs nous en donnent plus. Je voudrais aller à l'université, donc je dois réussir tous mes examens. Pourtant, il est difficile de trouver assez de temps pour étudier et aussi de passer du temps avec ses amis.

Grade 8-9

Tick list:
✓ tenses: present, conditional
✓ pronouns ('nous', 'en')
✓ reflexive verb

To improve:
+ talk about the past
+ include intensifiers, e.g. 'très'

Regarde la photo et prépare des réponses sur les points suivants :

- *la description de la photo*
- *ton opinion sur le règlement scolaire*
- *comment était ton école primaire*

- *comment tu changerais la vie scolaire si tu avais le choix*
- *!*

[24 marks]

School Events

Being able to talk about school events is pretty handy — we all love a good moan about parents' evening...

Faire un échange — To do an exchange

participer à	to take part
l'échange (m) (scolaire)	(school) exchange
l'excursion (f) scolaire	school trip
à l'étranger	abroad
le car de ramassage	school bus
un(e) correspondant(e)	penfriend
la remise des prix	prize giving
la réunion	meeting
la rencontre parents-professeurs	parents' evening

Grammar — perfect infinitive

The perfect infinitive (see p.138) is formed by 'après avoir' + past participle. It means 'after having done' something.

Après avoir écrit à mon / ma correspondant(e)...
After having written to my penfriend...

If the verb takes 'être' instead of 'avoir' in the perfect tense, use 'après être' + past participle.

Après être rentré(e)(s) chez moi...
After having returned home...

Question

As-tu participé à un échange scolaire?

Have you taken part in a school exchange?

Simple Answer

Oui, j'ai fait un échange scolaire cette année.

Yes, I did a school exchange this year.

Grammar — 'Il y a' + period of time

'Il y a' followed by a period of time means 'ago'.

Il y a deux ans. *Two years ago.*

Extended Answer

Oui, j'ai participé à un échange il y a six mois. J'ai une correspondante française qui s'appelle Anna, et je suis resté(e) chez elle pendant une semaine. Après avoir fait cet échange, j'ai vraiment envie de passer plus de temps à l'étranger.

Yes, I took part in a school exchange 6 months ago. I have a French pen pal who's called Anna, and I stayed at her house for one week. After having done that exchange, I really want to spend more time abroad.

Des événements scolaires — School events

L'année dernière, je suis allé(e) au musée avec ma classe d'histoire. Pendant la visite guidée, nous avons pris des notes pour faire une rédaction.

Last year, I went to the museum with my history class. During the guided tour, we took some notes to write an essay.

À la fin de l'année scolaire, j'assisterai à une remise des prix. J'ai eu les meilleures notes de la classe pendant toute l'année, et ma prof m'a attribué(e) le prix d'excellence.

At the end of the school year, I will attend a prize giving. I have had the best marks in the class all year, and my teacher has awarded me the top prize.

I went on a school trip — je suis parti(e) en excursion scolaire

Use 'il y a' to say how long ago something happened...

Listen to Marie talk about her French exchange, and then answer the questions below.

e.g. Marie's exchange...

    A. happened last year.   **B.** happened this year.   **C.** will happen next year. **A**

1. (i) Before the exchange, Marie...

  A. wrote to Marc once.
  B. wrote to Marc every two weeks.
  C. had never written to Marc.
  D. wrote to Marc often.   *[1]*

(ii) During the exchange, Marie...

  A. improved her French.
  B. offended Marc's family.
  C. never watched the TV.
  D. went to the zoo.   *[1]*

Education Post-16

It's more than likely you've given this a lot of thought already, so you've already done the hardest part. All that's left is to work out how to say it in French — here's a little something to help you on your way...

L'enseignement postscolaire — Further education

You might have to discuss your plans for <u>future studies</u>, so it's important to know some <u>key vocabulary</u>.

laisser tomber	*to drop*
former	*to train*
en première	*in year 12*
en terminale	*in year 13*
le conseiller d'orientation / la conseillère d'orientation	*careers adviser*
le bac(calauréat)	*A-levels*
l'apprentissage (m)	*apprenticeship*
l'apprenti(e) (m / f)	*apprentice*
la licence	*degree*
l'université (f), la faculté	*university*
l'année (f) sabbatique	*gap year*

'Collège' means 'secondary school' in French. The French equivalent of technical college is a 'lycée professionnel'. For more about the school system, see p.77.

Grammar — 'avoir' constructions + infinitive

'<u>Avoir envie de</u>' means '<u>to want</u>' to do something. '<u>Avoir l'intention de</u>' means '<u>to intend</u>' to do something.

Both of these constructions are followed by an infinitive (see p.124).

J'ai envie d'<u>aller</u> à l'université.
I want <u>to go</u> to university.

Elle a l'intention de <u>faire</u> un apprentissage.
She intends <u>to do</u> an apprenticeship.

Mes études à l'avenir — My future studies

Question	Simple Answer	Extended Answer
Pourquoi as-tu choisi de passer / ne pas passer le bac? *Why have you chosen to do / not to do A-levels?*	J'ai besoin du bac pour faire mon métier préféré. *I need A-levels to do my preferred job.* Je préférerais faire une formation. *I'd prefer to do some training.*	Pour moi, ce n'est pas un choix. Il faut avoir une licence pour faire mon métier préféré, et pour faire ça, j'ai besoin du bac. *For me, it isn't a choice. You have to have a degree to do my preferred job, and to do that, I need A-levels.* Pour moi, il s'agit de l'argent. Je voudrais trouver un emploi et gagner de l'argent dès que possible. j'ai parlé au conseiller d'orientation et il m'a conseillé de faire un apprentissage. *For me, it's about money. I would like to find a job and earn money as soon as possible. I've spoken to the careers adviser and he advised me to do an apprenticeship.*

J'ai l'intention d'aller au lycée l'année prochaine pour passer le bac.

I plan to go to sixth form next year to do A-levels.

to study history, maths and French — pour étudier l'histoire, les maths et le français

Avant d'aller à l'université, j'aimerais prendre une année sabbatique pour découvrir le monde.

Before going to university, I would like to take a gap year to discover the world.

do some voluntary work — faire du travail bénévole

'Future plans' is a common topic, so prepare your answers now...

Traduis le passage suivant **en français**. *[12 marks]*

To celebrate the end of the exams, I watched films with my friends. We are very happy because it is the holidays. Next September, I will go to the sixth form college to do A-levels and I would like to get good results. However, my best friend wants to do an apprenticeship.

Career Choices and Ambitions

Deciding what to do with your life isn't exactly plain sailing, but don't worry about having to reveal your grand plans to the world in French. If you're uncertain, don't let it stop you — just make something up.

Le monde du travail — The world of work

le petit job	*part-time job*
le boulot	*job (informal)*
l'emploi (m)	*job (formal)*
l'employé(e) (m / f)	*employee*
l'employeur (m) / l'employeuse (f)	*employer*
le débouché	*job opportunity / prospect*
le / la patron(ne)	*boss*
le salaire	*salary*
l'ingénieur (m / f)	*engineer*
l'avocat(e) (m / f)	*lawyer*
l'infirmier (m) / l'infirmière (f)	*nurse*

See the vocab list on p.193 for more jobs.

Grammar — articles with jobs / professions

In French, you <u>don't need</u> an indefinite article ('<u>un</u>' / '<u>une</u>') when you describe someone's job.

Ma mère <u>est avocate</u>. *My mother's <u>a lawyer</u>.*
Je veux <u>être infirmier</u>. *I want <u>to be a nurse</u>.*

Grammar — venir + de + infinitive

'<u>Venir + de + infinitive</u>' means '<u>to have just done something</u>'. Don't forget that 'venir' (*to come*) is an <u>irregular</u> verb.

Je <u>viens d'aller</u> à un entretien.
I <u>have just been</u> to an interview.

Mon père <u>vient de prendre</u> sa retraite.
My dad <u>has just taken</u> his retirement.

Don't forget that 'venir' (to come) is an irregular verb.

Ton métier idéal — Your ideal job

Question	**Simple Answer**	**Extended Answer**
Quel est ton métier idéal? Pourquoi?	Je rêve d'être médecin afin de soigner les malades.	Je crois qu'être vétérinaire serait idéal pour moi car c'est un métier enrichissant. Pour moi, c'est important de trouver de la satisfaction dans mon travail.
What is your ideal job? Why?	*I dream of being a doctor so that I can care for sick people.*	*I believe that to be a vet would be ideal for me because it's an enriching job. For me, it's important to find job satisfaction.*

As-tu un petit-job? — Do you have a part-time job?

Je suis vendeur / vendeuse. Je travaille le week-end pour gagner de l'argent.

I'm a shop assistant. I work at the weekend to earn money.

Je travaille dans un café. Mon salaire n'est pas très bon, mais je travaille dur.

I work in a café. My salary isn't very good, but I work hard.

Je fais du travail bénévole. C'est gratifiant d'aider les autres.

I do voluntary work. It's rewarding to help others.

I babysit — Je fais du babysitting
I work at a hairdresser's — Je travaille dans un salon de coiffure
I like working there — j'aime y travailler
an interesting challenge — un défi intéressant

Remember you don't need 'un(e)' to talk about someone's job...

Your French pen pal sends you this message. Translate it **into English**. *[7 marks]*

Quand j'étais plus jeune, j'avais envie d'être boulanger parce que j'adorais faire des gâteaux. Aujourd'hui, je m'intéresse toujours à la cuisine, et j'aimerais être chef quand je quitterai l'école. J'ai un petit job dans la cuisine d'un restaurant. Je ne gagne pas beaucoup d'argent, mais j'espère que l'expérience sera utile dans l'avenir.

Languages for the Future

Learning a language isn't just about getting a qualification — it's meant to create opportunities. Knowing the local lingo could get you an amazing holiday deal, or even land you with the love of your life.

Apprendre une langue étrangère — To learn a foreign language

It's worth thinking about <u>the importance</u> of foreign languages — try to give a <u>balanced view</u>.

rencontrer quelqu'un	*to meet someone*
discuter	*to talk*
s'exprimer	*to express oneself*
obtenir un métier	*to get a job*
parcourir le monde	*to travel the world*
communiquer	*to communicate*
parler couramment	*to speak fluently*
les vacances (f) scolaires	*school holidays*
l'assistant(e) (m / f) de langue	*language assistant*
les langues (f) étrangères	*foreign languages*
les possibilités (f) d'avancement	*promotion prospects*

Question

Devrait-on apprendre une langue étrangère?

Should you learn a foreign language?

Simple Answer

Oui, car tout le monde ne parle pas couramment l'anglais.

Yes, because not everyone speaks English fluently.

Extended Answer

Oui, absolument. Le monde se compose de langues différentes, et elles sont toutes importantes.

Yes, absolutely. The world is made up of different languages, and they are all important.

Non, je pense qu'apprendre une autre langue est une perte de temps. Tout le monde parle anglais donc c'est déjà facile de communiquer.

No, I think that learning another language is a waste of time. Everyone speaks English so it's already easy to communicate.

Grammar — 'si' + imperfect + conditional

If you use '<u>si</u>' (*if*) with the <u>imperfect tense</u> (see p.129-130), the next verb should be in the <u>conditional tense</u> (see p.135).
Si j'apprenais une autre langue, j'aurais plus de débouchés.
***If I learnt** another language, **I'd have** more job prospects.*

Pourquoi parler une autre langue? — Why speak another language?

Si on parle une deuxième langue, c'est plus facile de trouver un emploi: les entreprises s'intéressent au marché mondial.

If you speak a second language, it's easier to get a job: businesses are interested in the global market.

Quand je vais en vacances, j'aime pouvoir comprendre ce que disent les gens du pays.

When I go on holiday, I like to be able to understand what the locals are saying.

Je veux apprendre des langues étrangères pour me faire des amis quand je ferai mon année sabbatique.

I want to learn foreign languages to make friends when I take my gap year.

we live in a multicultural society — on vit dans une société multiculturelle

the signs — les panneaux (m)
the menus — les menus (m)

Learning a language can lead to interesting opportunities...

Read Hélène's blog post, then answer the questions below **in English**.

J'étudie deux langues au collège : l'anglais et l'allemand. Je pense que ce sera utile plus tard car je veux être **hôtesse de l'air**[1] et parcourir le monde. D'ailleurs, si je me marie avec un étranger, je voudrais que nous puissions nous parler dans leur **langue maternelle**[2]. À mon avis, pour comprendre la culture d'un pays il faut parler sa langue.

e.g. Which languages is Hélène learning? **English and German**

[1]air hostess [2]native language

1. Why would these languages be useful in her preferred job? *[1]*
2. Why does Hélène think that learning another language could be useful in her future personal life? *[1]*
3. According to Hélène, what does speaking a language help you to understand? *[1]*

Applying for Jobs

Applying for jobs isn't always fun, but at least when you're pretending there's a little less pressure...

Poser sa candidature — To apply for a job

postuler	*to apply*
faire un stage	*to do work experience*
remplir un formulaire	*to fill in a form*
le poste	*position*
l'offre (f) d'emploi	*job offer*
l'annonce (f) de recrutement	*job advertisement*
la lettre de motivation	*application letter*
le salaire	*salary*
l'entretien (m)	*(job) interview*
les conditions (f) d'emploi	*terms of employment*
à temps plein	*full-time*
à temps partiel	*part-time*
au chômage	*unemployed*

Question

Quelles qualités faut-il pour trouver un emploi?
What qualities do you need to find a job?

Simple Answer

Il faut être motivé(e) et bien organisé(e).
You must be motivated and well organised.

Extended Answer

Il faut être ambitieux / ambitieuse et bien préparé(e) pour l'entretien. Il faut aussi avoir des diplômes.

You must be ambitious and well-prepared for the interview. You must also have qualifications.

Vous devez me recruter car... — You should hire me because...

Je suis la meilleure personne pour ce poste parce que je suis patient(e) et travailleur / travailleuse.

I'm the best person for this job because I'm patient and hardworking.

J'ai beaucoup d'expérience et de compétences.

I have lots of experience and skills. ← the required qualifications — les diplômes requis

J'ai fait un stage dans un hôpital l'été dernier. On m'a donné beaucoup de responsabilités.

I did work experience in a hospital last summer. I was given lots of responsibilities.

Learn this page and you'll be well-qualified for the exam...

Read the sample role play. Mehul is talking to an employee at the job centre.

Employé : Où est-ce que vous aimeriez travailler ?

Mehul : Je voudrais devenir éditeur, donc j'aimerais travailler pour une **maison d'édition**[1].

Employé : Pourquoi vous y intéressez-vous ?

Mehul : Je pense que ce serait un métier varié et enrichissant. En plus, j'adore écrire.

Employé : Avez-vous de l'expérience dans ce domaine ?

Mehul : Oui, en effet. L'été dernier, j'ai fait un stage au journal local. J'y ai beaucoup appris, c'était très intéressant. Est-ce qu'il y a des postes à Paris ?

Employé : Oui, il y a un poste chez «Curiosité», une maison d'édition.

Mehul : Quelles sont les conditions d'emploi ?

Employé : Le salaire est de €2100 par mois. Vous aurez vingt-cinq **jours de congés**[2] par an.

Grade 8-9

Tick list:
✓ tenses: present, imperfect, perfect, conditional
✓ correctly-formed questions
✓ opinion phrases

To improve:
+ use different conjunctions to link phrases

Prepare the role-play card below. Use 'vous' and speak for about two minutes. [10 marks]

Tu passes un entretien pour un emploi d'été dans une colonie de vacances.

- *travailler pendant les vacances — raison*
- *travail — ton expérience*
- *!*
- *? heures de travail*
- *? commencer — quand*

[1]publishing house   [2]days' leave

Listening Questions

Here come the next four pages of exam practice — give them your best shot. Don't forget that there's also a full practice exam at the end of this book — it's fantastic preparation for the real thing.

1   Écoute ces jeunes qui parlent de leurs études.
     Mets une croix dans la case pour compléter les phrases.

(i) a Pour Karine...

A	les langues ne sont pas faciles.	
B	la chimie est difficile.	
C	c'est très utile de savoir parler une autre langue.	

[1 mark]

(ii) a Nadia pense que c'est essentiel de...

A	parler avec les autres.	
B	ne pas perdre son temps devant un écran.	
C	savoir bien utiliser un ordinateur.	

[1 mark]

b Salim pense que...

A	les jeunes utilisent trop les ordinateurs.	
B	c'est toujours nécessaire d'utiliser un ordinateur.	
C	les ordinateurs aident à étudier les maths.	

[1 mark]

2   Listen to this phone call about a job advert and answer the questions **in English**.

a   What should the successful applicant be like? Give **two** details.

.... *[2 marks]*

b   What is essential for the job?

.... *[1 mark]*

c   What does Annette need to do to apply? Give **two** details.

1. ....

2. .... *[2 marks]*

Speaking Question

Candidate's Role

- Your teacher will play the role of your French friend. They will speak first.

- You must use *tu* to address your friend.

- – ! – means you will have to respond to something you have not prepared.

- – ? – means you will have to ask your friend a question.

> Tu parles de ta routine scolaire avec ton ami(e) français(e).
>
> - Transport au collège
>
> - !
>
> - Les devoirs — opinion
>
> - ? Matières étudiées
>
> - ? Activités extrascolaires

Teacher's Role

- You begin the role play using the introductory text below.

- You should address the candidate as *tu*.

- Do not supply the candidate with key vocabulary.

- You must ask the questions below exactly as they are written.

> Introductory text: *Tu parles de ta routine scolaire avec ton ami(e) français(e). Moi, je suis ton ami(e).*
>
> - Comment vas-tu au collège ?
>
> - ! Qu'est-ce que tu as fait pendant la récré hier ?
>
> - Que penses-tu des devoirs ?
>
> - ? Allow the candidate to ask you which subjects you study.
>
> - ? Allow the candidate to ask you if you do any extra curricular activities.

Reading Questions

1 Lis ce blog. Réponds aux questions **en français**.

> Chaque été il y a une pièce de théâtre à mon collège. Cette fois, la pièce était l'histoire d'Anne Frank, une jeune fille juive qui a dû se cacher pendant la Seconde Guerre mondiale. Elle a écrit un journal intime et quand on l'a trouvé après la guerre, son auteuse est devenue célèbre.
>
> Tout le monde devait aider à produire la pièce — on a dû mettre des affiches, fabriquer des costumes et vendre des billets. J'ai eu le rôle principal, celui d'Anne Frank. C'était difficile de trouver assez de temps pour apprendre mon texte car je devais faire mes devoirs aussi. Toutefois, la pièce a été un grand succès.

a Comment l'histoire d'Anne Frank est-elle devenue célèbre ?

.... *[1 mark]*

b Que pouvait-on faire pour contribuer à la pièce ? Donne **un** détail.

.... *[1 mark]*

c Quelle difficulté l'actrice principale a-t-elle rencontrée ?

.... *[1 mark]*

2 Read these Internet posts about further education.

Yuki	Si on veut faire un travail manuel, c'est mieux de faire un apprentissage. En travaillant comme apprenti, on apprend un métier et on ne perd pas de temps.
Ankit	Je trouve que si on veut une carrière intéressante, il est essentiel de continuer ses études. Moi, je veux réussir mon bac et après ça, on verra.
Marc	C'est très important de réussir aux examens. Je vais continuer mes études parce que je sais ce que je veux faire plus tard et j'ai besoin de qualifications.
Lucie	Je pense qu'on peut étudier et travailler en même temps. On peut trouver un travail à temps partiel donc gagner de l'argent et avoir un diplôme.

Who says what about further education? Enter either **Yuki**, **Ankit**, **Marc** or **Lucie** in the gaps.

Example: ......Yuki...... says that he / she wants to learn on the job.

a .... says that he / she has already decided on a career path. *[1 mark]*

b .... says that it's sensible to have a part-time job while studying. *[1 mark]*

c .... says that he / she will make plans after doing A-levels. *[1 mark]*

Writing Questions

1 Ta correspondante luxembourgeoise, Nora, s'intéresse à tes projets pour l'avenir.
Écris un email à Nora pour lui décrire tes ambitions pour l'avenir.

Tu **dois** faire référence aux points suivants :

• ta carrière de rêve

• les matières que tu as étudiées l'année dernière

• l'expérience de travail dont tu as besoin

• tes projets pour une année sabbatique.

Écris 80-90 mots environ **en français**.   *[20 marks]*

2 Traduis le passage suivant **en français** :

> I have been learning French and Italian for five years. I will go to
> sixth form because I hope to study foreign languages at university.
> I would like to be an interpreter because I could travel around the
> world. This summer, I am going to go to Italy to practise my Italian.

....

....

....

....

....

....

[12 marks]

Revision Summary for Section Seven

What better way to round off a section on study and employment than with another revision summary? Use these questions to help you discover the gaps in your knowledge — then go back afterwards and plug those holes.

School Subjects and Routine (p.75-76) ☑

1) Say what your GCSE subjects are in French. ☑
2) What's your favourite subject? Which subject(s) don't you like? Answer in French. ☑
3) What's the French for...? a) lesson   b) timetable   c) holidays   d) term ☑
4) In French, describe a normal day at school. ☑
5) Say, in French, that you have five lessons every day and that each lesson lasts 50 minutes. ☑
6) Qu'est-ce que tu fais normalement pendant la récré? ☑

School Life and Pressures (p.77-78) ☑

7) Your French friend writes, 'Je suis en seconde et je vais au lycée en banlieue parisienne. C'est un internat de garçons et j'y vais depuis l'âge de quinze ans.' Translate this into English. ☑
8) Imagine the council has given you money to improve your school. What would you do with it? Answer in French, giving three suggestions. ☑
9) Translate these words and phrases into English:
   a) le règlement   b) échouer   c) la note   d) les devoirs   e) le bulletin scolaire ☑
10) In French, write down one advantage and one disadvantage of having a school uniform. ☑
11) Do you feel pressured at school? Why / Why not? Answer in French. ☑

School Events (p.79) ☑

12) List as many different kinds of school events as you can think of in French. ☑
13) En français, décris une excursion scolaire à laquelle tu as participé. ☑

Education Post-16 and Career Choices and Ambitions (p.80-81) ☑

14) Your French friend says: 'Je suis en terminale. J'étudie pour le bac car je veux aller à l'université pour faire une licence d'informatique.' What's she saying? ☑
15) Est-ce que tu vas continuer tes études après les examens? Pourquoi / Pourquoi pas? ☑
16) In French, say: 'I want to take a gap year and do some voluntary work.' ☑
17) What's the French for...? a) job   b) job opportunity   c) salary   d) interview ☑
18) Quel serait ton métier idéal? Pourquoi? ☑
19) In French, tell your friend: 'I've just started a new part-time job. I work in a supermarket at the weekend. I like working there, but it's tiring.' ☑

Languages for the Future (p.82) ☑

20) À ton avis, devrait-on apprendre une langue étrangère? Réponds en français. ☑
21) In French, say that you want to be able to communicate with the locals when you go abroad. ☑

Applying for Jobs (p.83) ☑

22) You see an advert for 'un poste à temps partiel'. What does this mean? ☑
23) You're applying for a job in a shop. In French, write down three reasons you'd be good at it. ☑

Problems in Society

Some of the issues in this section are quite controversial, so you need to be able to back up your opinions.

Les problèmes sociaux — Social problems

l'égalité (f)	*equality*	les SDF, les sans-abri (m / f)	*homeless people*
effrayant(e)	*frightening*	le chômage	*unemployment*
voler	*to steal*	la pauvreté	*poverty*
la guerre	*war*	mal nourri(e)	*malnourished*
mourir	*to die*	affamé(e)	*starving*

'SDF' stands for 'sans domicile fixe' *(without a permanent home).*

L'inégalité sociale — Social inequality

Le chômage est un problème grave dans les pays européens.

Unemployment is a serious problem in European countries.

Racism — Le racisme

Discrimination — La discrimination

Il faut lutter contre les mentalités racistes et sexistes.

We need to fight against racist and sexist mentalities.

combat — combattre

eradicate — éradiquer

Le problème principal est... — The main problem is...

Question

À ton avis, quels sont les problèmes principaux pour les SDF?

In your opinion, what are the main problems facing homeless people?

Simple Answer

Je crois que le plus grand problème est qu'ils ne peuvent pas trouver un emploi pour pouvoir payer un logement.

I think the biggest problem is that they cannot find a job to be able to afford accommodation.

Extended Answer

Je pense que les problèmes des SDF sont complexes. Si on est au chômage, on n'a pas les moyens de payer un logement. Cependant, il n'est pas possible de trouver un emploi sans domicile fixe. Il s'agit d'un cercle vicieux.

I think homeless people's problems are complicated. If people are unemployed, they can't afford to pay for accommodation. However, it is not possible to find a job without a permanent address. It's a vicious circle.

socialement exclu(e)	*socially excluded*
déprimé(e)	*depressed*
vulnérable	*vulnerable*

Grammar — on doit... / il faut...

Use 'on doit...' (from 'devoir') or 'il faut...' (from 'falloir') to say 'we must'. The verb which follows is in the infinitive.

On doit aider les pauvres.
We must help the poor.

Il faut empêcher les guerres.
We must prevent wars.

You can also use the verb 'devoir' to say that someone needs to do something.

Les politiciens doivent donner la priorité à la question de l'inégalité sociale.
Politicians must prioritise the issue of social inequality.

Make sure you can identify and talk about problems in society...

Translate this passage **into English**. *[7 marks]*

Il y a beaucoup de problèmes sociaux dans ma région, comme le chômage. En plus, il y a des gens qui vivent dans la rue. Hier, j'ai vu des SDF et ils étaient mal nourris. À mon avis, il faut faire quelque chose pour aider ces gens. On doit combattre l'inégalité.

Environmental Problems

That's right — it's time to start thinking about all things green, natural and... erm... polluted.

L'environnement (m) — The environment

l'effet (m) de serre	*the greenhouse effect*	le pétrole	*oil*
le réchauffement de la Terre	*global warming*	jeter	*to throw away*
la couche d'ozone	*ozone layer*	gaspiller	*to waste*
augmenter	*to increase*	les déchets (m) / les ordures (f)	*rubbish*
mondial(e)	*worldwide*	pollué(e)	*polluted*
le charbon	*coal*	le déboisement	*deforestation*
le gaz carbonique	*carbon dioxide*	détruire	*to destroy*
le gaz d'échappement	*exhaust fumes*	l'eau (f) douce	*fresh water*

Ce n'est pas écologique — It's not environmentally friendly

Les gens jettent souvent des choses recyclables dans la poubelle.

People often throw recyclable things in the bin.

paper — du papier
glass — du verre

Un sac en plastique peut prendre des années à se décomposer.

A plastic bag may take years to decompose.

an aluminium can — une boîte en aluminium

L'emballage est un gaspillage des ressources naturelles de la Terre.

Packaging is a waste of the Earth's natural resources.

of raw materials — des matières (f) premières

Nous gaspillons de l'eau dans la vie quotidienne.

We waste water in everyday life.

electricity — de l'électricité (f)

La pollution est un risque sanitaire — Pollution is a health hazard

La pollution est causée par les activités humaines.

Pollution is caused by human activity.

Parfois, les usines contaminent les lacs et les rivières avec des produits chimiques nocifs.

Sometimes, factories contaminate lakes and rivers with harmful chemicals.

Dans les grandes villes, la pollution de l'air peut provoquer des problèmes de santé.

In cities, air pollution may cause health problems.

La destruction des habitats — The destruction of habitats

Le déboisement contribue à l'effet de serre et mène à la perte des écosystèmes.

Deforestation contributes to the greenhouse effectand leads to the loss of ecosystems.

Certaines espèces sont menacées d'extinction. Elles ne survivraient pas les effets du réchauffement de la Terre.

Certain species are threatened by extinction. They would not survive the effects of global warming.

Environmental Problems

You might prefer hiding away in a darkened room to roaming the hills and basking in the glories of nature, but you still need to have an opinion about environmental problems, so listen up...

Les catastrophes naturelles — Natural disasters

l'incendie (m)	*fire*	l'ouragan (m)	*hurricane*
l'inondation (f)	*flood*	la sécheresse	*drought*
le tremblement de terre	*earthquake*	le désastre	*disaster*

Des milliers de personnes ont dû quitter leurs maisons après les inondations l'année dernière.

Thousands of people had to leave their homes after the floods last year.

Un incendie a ravagé le village.

A fire devastated the village.

Le gouvernement prend des mesures pour aider les victimes du tremblement de terre.

The government is taking measures to help the victims of the earthquake.

Il y a des problèmes graves — There are some serious problems

Question

À ton avis, quelles sont les plus grandes menaces pour l'environnement?

In your opinion, what are the biggest threats to the environment?

Simple Answer

Je crois que les plus grandes menaces sont le déboisement, le réchauffement de la Terre et la pollution de l'air.

I believe that the biggest threats are deforestation, global warming and air pollution.

Extended Answer

D'abord, il y a l'utilisation mondiale des énergies fossiles, comme le charbon, qui mène à une augmentation du gaz carbonique. Cela est responsable du réchauffement de la Terre.

En plus, je trouve qu'on a trop de déchets — une famille moyenne jette plus d'une tonne de déchets chaque année!

Enfin, il y a le gaspillage de l'eau. Malgré les 780 millions personnes dans le monde qui n'ont pas d'eau potable, ici on gaspille de l'eau chaque jour.

Firstly, there is the global use of fossil fuels, like coal, which leads to an increase in carbon dioxide. This is responsible for global warming.

Furthermore, I find that we have too much rubbish — an average family throws away more than a tonne of rubbish each year!

Lastly, there's water wastage. Despite the 780 million people in the world who don't have drinking water, we waste water each day here.

Grammar — adjective position

In French, adjectives usually come after the noun. However, this isn't always the case, e.g.

Il y a un grand problème.   There is a big problem.

Adjectives such as beau — *beautiful*, joli — *pretty*, jeune — *young*, gentil — *kind*, grand — *big*, petit — *small* usually come before the noun. See p.102 for more.

Le déboisement abîme le beau paysage.
Deforestation ruins the beautiful landscape.

Les petites actions peuvent avoir un grand effet.
Small actions can have a big impact.

Learning these pages will help you avoid problems in the exam...

Traduis le passage suivant **en français**. *[12 marks]*

Samit thinks that we must protect the planet. He believes that global warming has caused some serious problems, like droughts and hurricanes. In his opinion, people waste too many natural resources. He thinks that, in the future, we will have to use renewable energy instead of coal and oil.

Caring for the Environment

You might be feeling a bit down about the state of the world, but fear not — there's plenty you can do to make things better. Just don't go recycling this book before you've learnt it all...

Comment pouvons-nous aider? — How can we help?

éteindre	to switch off	l'énergie (f) renouvelable	renewable energy
le manque (de)	lack (of)	les produits (m) bio	green products
protéger	to protect	le centre de recyclage	recycling centre
faire du compost	to make compost	faire du recyclage / recycler	to recycle
l'énergie solaire (f)	solar power	être vert(e)	to be green
l'énergie éolienne (f)	wind power	l'organisation charitable (f)	charity
sauvegarder	to keep safe	le commerce équitable	fair trade

Pour conserver l'énergie, il faut se souvenir d'éteindre les lumières quand on quitte la maison.

To save energy, you must remember to switch off the lights when you leave the house.

Il faut privilégier les énergies renouvelables.

We must give priority to renewable energy.

Grammar — se souvenir de

'Se souvenir de' means 'to remember'. It's a <u>reflexive verb</u> so it needs a <u>reflexive pronoun</u> (p.133 has more about this).

Je me souviens toujours de trier mes déchets quand je fais du recyclage.
I always <u>remember</u> to sort my rubbish when I recycle.

Question

Que fais-tu pour protéger la planète?
What do you do to protect the planet?

Simple Answer

Je trie mes ordures et je fais du compost. En plus, je fais du recyclage.
I sort my rubbish and I make compost. Also, I recycle.

Extended Answer

Je fais autant que possible dans la vie quotidienne. Par exemple, je prends des mesures pour économiser l'eau, comme prendre une douche au lieu d'un bain. Cette année, je vais organiser un événement dans ma ville pour promouvoir les produits bio qui endommagent moins l'environnement.

I do as much as possible in my daily life. For example, I take action to save water, such as having a shower instead of a bath. This year, I am going to organise an event in my town to promote green products, which harm the environment less.

This is a great topic for using the conditional and future tenses...

Read the sample response, then answer the questions below. Talk for about three minutes.

Est-ce que tu fais du recyclage ? Pourquoi / pourquoi pas ?

À mon avis, protéger l'environnement, c'est très important. Je recycle autant que possible — le verre, le plastique et même mes vieux vêtements. En plus, j'ai mené une campagne à l'école pour encourager les élèves à faire du recyclage. Je pense que si chaque personne prenait une ou deux mesures pour combattre le gaspillage des ressources, nous pourrions sauver la planète.

Grade 6-7

Tick list:
✓ detailed answer
✓ tenses: perfect, imperfect, present, conditional

To improve:
+ more adjectives and adverbs
+ use 'il faut...' or 'on doit...'
+ add a future tense

Regarde la photo et prépare des réponses sur les points suivants :

- *la description de la photo*
- *si l'environnement est important pour toi*
- *une mesure que tu as prise récemment pour protéger la Terre*
- *ce que tu pourrais faire pour être plus vert(e)*
- *!* [24 marks]

© iStock.com/Jani Bryson

Global Events

The Global Events topic covers everything from sport to charity fundraising, so there's plenty to talk about.

Être spectateur / spectatrice — To be a spectator

assister à	to attend	l'événement (m)	event
fêter	to celebrate	le festival (de musique)	(music) festival
bénéficier	to benefit	les Jeux (m) olympiques	Olympic Games
collecter des fonds	to raise money	la coupe du monde	world cup

Question

As-tu déjà assisté à un événement international?

Have you already attended an international event?

Simple Answer

Oui, j'ai assisté à un concert de charité pour les victimes du tremblement de terre en Asie.

Yes, I attended a charity concert for the victims of the earthquake in Asia.

Extended Answer

Oui, je suis allé(e) voir le Tour de France, mais je n'ai pas encore assisté aux Jeux olympiques.

Yes, I've been to see the Tour de France, but I haven't attended the Olympic Games yet.

Grammar — 'déjà' (already)

'Déjà' (*already*) goes <u>before</u> the past participle when it's used with the perfect tense (see p.127-128).

J'ai <u>déjà</u> mangé.	*I've <u>already</u> eaten.*
Il est <u>déjà</u> parti.	*He has <u>already</u> left.*

It's used in front of <u>adjectives</u> and <u>adverbs</u>, too.

Il est <u>déjà</u> fatigué.	*He's <u>already</u> tired.*
Elle est <u>déjà</u> là.	*She's <u>already</u> there.*

Grammar — 'ne...pas encore' (not...yet)

'Ne...pas encore' means '<u>not...yet</u>'. Just like a normal negative, the 'ne' and 'pas' go <u>either side of the verb</u> (see p.134). In the <u>perfect tense</u>, they go around the bit of '<u>avoir</u>' or '<u>être</u>':

Je n'ai <u>pas encore</u> mangé.	*I've <u>not</u> eaten <u>yet</u>.*
Il n'est <u>pas encore</u> fatigué.	*He's <u>not</u> tired <u>yet</u>.*
Elle <u>n</u>'est <u>pas encore</u> là.	*She's <u>not</u> there <u>yet</u>.*

Les campagnes mondiales — Global campaigns

Je fête la Journée mondiale de l'enfance. Il y a trop d'enfants dans le monde qui doivent travailler et qui ne peuvent pas aller à l'école.	*I celebrate Universal Children's Day. There are too many children in the world who have to work and can't go to school.*
Consacrer des journées aux campagnes mondiales ne change pas le problème — je les trouve ridicules.	*Dedicating days to global campaigns doesn't change the problem — I find them ridiculous.*
Les campagnes mondiales rappellent aux gens les problèmes de société.	*Global campaigns remind people about problems in society.*
Je crois qu'on devrait avoir plus de publicité pour promouvoir les campagnes mondiales.	*I believe that we should have more advertising to promote global campaigns.*

doesn't benefit anybody — ne bénéficie à personne

good causes — les bonnes causes (f)

funding — d'aide (f) financière

Think about the pros and cons of global campaigns...

Traduis le passage suivant **en français**. *[12 marks]*

For his birthday, I gave my dad two tickets for a Rugby World Cup match. We're going to go to the match together. We like to watch sport. In 2012, we went to the Olympic Games and it was amazing. There was a pleasant atmosphere with people from many different countries.

Listening Questions

Nearly there... just four pages of exam practice, then this section is almost done and dusted.
Don't forget to keep coming back to any questions you're unsure about — practice makes perfect.

---

1   Écoute ces interviews avec des jeunes qui parlent de l'inégalité sociale.
     Complète les phrases en choisissant un mot ou des mots dans la case.

la discrimination   les opinions   la religion   sa nationalité   agace
énerver   sa peau   le racisme   sa famille   la violence

a   Certaines personnes traitent Henri différemment à cause de ....   *[1 mark]*

b   Ce traitement lui ....   *[1 mark]*

c   Mischa pense que .... n'est pas le seul problème grave.   *[1 mark]*

2   Listen to this local radio report about a charity fundraising event.
     Complete the sentences by putting a cross in the correct box.

a   People living in the town have just put on...

A	a week of sporting competitions.	
B	a charity sports day.	
C	an inter-school rugby tournament.	

[1 mark]

b   The mayor came up with the idea because...

A	her mother died from cancer.	
B	there is a cancer hospital in town.	
C	she is interested in medical research.	

[1 mark]

c   The events included...

A	a race around the town.	
B	a boxing tournament.	
C	a dressing up competition.	

[1 mark]

Speaking Question

Candidate's Material

- Spend a couple of minutes looking at the photo and the prompts below it.

- You can make notes on a separate piece of paper.

© iStock.com/sirichai_raksue

Regarde la photo et prépare des réponses sur les points suivants :

- la description de la photo

- les activités humaines qui contribuent à la pollution

- les solutions aux problèmes de pollution

- ton opinion sur le déboisement

- !

Teacher's Material

- Allow the student to develop his / her answers as much as possible.

- You need to ask the student the following questions **in order**:

- Décris-moi la photo.

- À ton avis, quelles activités humaines contribuent à la pollution ?

- Quelles sont les solutions aux problèmes de pollution ?

- Qu'est-ce que tu penses du déboisement ?

- Qu'est-ce que tu suggérerais pour protéger les espèces menacées d'extinction ?

Reading Questions

1   Read these forum comments about the environment.

Amir

Je m'intéresse beaucoup à l'environnement. Selon moi, il faut penser à l'avenir, et nous devrions sauvegarder l'environnement pour nos enfants. Les émissions générées par le monde développé sont la cause principale du réchauffement de la Terre. Nous devons tous changer notre mode de vie et utiliser des énergies renouvelables, comme l'énergie solaire, avant qu'il ne soit trop tard.

Blaise

Je ne m'inquiète pas du tout au sujet de l'environnement. Je ne me fais pas de soucis pour le futur de la Terre. Les gouvernements devraient trouver des solutions pour que nous puissions maintenir le style de vie auquel nous sommes habitués. Moi, je ne voudrais pas changer mes habitudes. En plus, il y a d'autres choses qui sont plus importantes, comme les problèmes sociaux.

Who says what about the environment? Enter either **Amir** or **Blaise** in the gaps below.

Example: ....Amir......... says that we should protect the environment for future generations.

a   .... says that the government is responsible for the environment.   *[1 mark]*

b   .... says that everyone should change their habits.   *[1 mark]*

c   .... says that the environment is not the biggest problem.   *[1 mark]*

2   Translate the following passage into **English**.

> La Coupe du monde aura lieu en juin. C'est une rencontre sportive que j'adore car il y a des joueurs célèbres qui viennent de tous les coins du monde. Malheureusement, je n'ai pas pu acheter de billets car ils étaient trop chers. J'espère que l'équipe française marquera beaucoup de buts.

....

....

....

....

....

[7 marks]

Writing Questions

1 Vous voulez poser votre candidature pour un travail bénévole dans une association charitable française.

Écrivez une lettre au chef de l'association charitable française au sujet de votre candidature.

Vous **devez** faire référence aux points suivants :

- votre motivation pour aider les gens

- le travail bénévole que vous avez déjà fait

- les problèmes sociaux que vous avez remarqués dans la société

- comment vous aideriez l'association à faire son travail.

Justifiez vos idées et vos opinions.

Écrivez 130-150 mots environ **en français**. *[28 marks]*

2 Traduis le passage suivant **en français** :

I think that it is very important to protect the environment. There is a lot that we could do at home. For example, in the winter I always switch off the central heating during the day. Yesterday, I took a shower instead of a bath because that uses less water.

....

....

....

....

....

....

....

[12 marks]

Revision Summary for Section Eight

Just before you tuck into the delights of French grammar, here's a page of revision questions for you to tackle. Try to answer all of the questions without cheating — make a note of any you find tricky and then go back through the section. Reward yourself with a big old tick when you can answer a question.

Problems in Society (p.89) ☑

1) What's the French for...?
   a) war   b) unemployment   c) poverty   d) inequality   e) homeless people ☑

2) 'À mon avis, la société n'est pas égalitaire.' What does this sentence mean in English? ☑

3) Penses-tu que le chômage soit un grand problème? Réponds en français. Utilise des phrases complètes. ☑

4) Saïd says: 'J'ai peur de ne pas trouver d'emploi.' What is Saïd afraid of? Answer in English. ☑

5) Your penfriend has written to you about what she does to help others: 'Je fais du travail bénévole pour une association charitable qui aide les sans-abri. Parfois c'est dur, mais cela en vaut la peine.' What does this mean in English? ☑

Environmental Problems (p.90-91) ☑

6) What do these words mean in English?
   a) le déboisement   b) l'effet de serre   c) le gaz carbonique   d) le gaz d'échappement ☑

7) 'Global warming is a worldwide problem.' Translate this sentence into French. ☑

8) You're listening to the news. You hear that: 'There has been an earthquake and a flood in Japan.' How would you say this in French? ☑

9) An environmental leaflet warns: 'La pollution commence à abîmer notre planète. Nos lacs et nos rivières sont devenus pollués, ce qui menace les écosystèmes qui existent depuis des millions d'années.' What is it saying? ☑

10) Est-ce qu'il y a des problèmes d'environnement dans ta région? Réponds en français. Utilise des phrases complètes. ☑

11) Danielle says: 'On gaspille des ressources tous les jours. On jette les déchets, sans faire du recyclage. Mais ce qui m'énerve le plus, c'est qu'on ne pense pas aux générations futures.' Does she think we do enough for the environment? Why / Why not? Answer in English. ☑

Caring for the Environment (p.92) ☑

12) Does caring for the environment matter to you? Answer in French, giving at least three reasons. ☑

13) 'J'aimerais être vert, mais les produits bios sont trop chers.' Translate this sentence into English. ☑

14) In French, write down three things you could do to help the environment. ☑

15) How would you say 'I always remember to recycle my rubbish' in French? ☑

16) Que penses-tu des énergies renouvelables? ☑

Global Events (p.93) ☑

17) Joelle tells you, 'C'est mon rêve d'assister un jour au Coupe du monde.' Which of these is she interested in? a) la musique   b) le sport   c) la technologie   d) la danse ☑

18) Emily tells you: 'Last summer I went to a charity concert, and next year I will go to the Olympic Games.' Translate this into French. ☑

19) In French, write down three possible benefits of global campaigns. ☑

Words for People and Objects | Nouns

Nouns are words for people and objects. This is important in French because all nouns have a gender.

Every noun in French is masculine or feminine

1) Whether a noun is <u>masculine</u> or <u>feminine</u> affects loads of things. The words for '<u>the</u>' and '<u>a</u>' are <u>different</u> and, if that wasn't enough, <u>adjectives</u> change to match the gender too.

2) '<u>Le</u>' in front of a noun means it's <u>masculine</u>. '<u>La</u>' in front means it's <u>feminine</u>.

> le livre (m) intéressant   *the interesting book*

> la matière (f) intéressante   *the interesting subject*

For more on how adjectives change to fit the gender, see p.101.

3) When you <u>learn</u> a <u>noun</u>, learn the <u>article</u> too — don't think 'chien = dog', think '<u>le</u> chien = the dog'.

Sometimes you can guess which gender a word is

If you have to <u>guess</u> whether a noun is <u>masculine</u> or <u>feminine</u>, use these <u>rules of thumb</u>:

It's probably <u>masculine</u> if... | ...*it ends in*: -age, -al, -er, -eau, -ing, -in, -ment, -ou, -ail, -ier, -et, -isme, -oir, -eil | ...<u>or</u> it's a | male person, language, day, month or season.

It's probably <u>feminine</u> if... | ...*it ends in*: -aine, -ée, -ense, -ie, -ise, -tion, -ance, -elle, -esse, -ière, -sion, -tude, -anse, -ence, -ette, -ine, -té, -ure | ...<u>or</u> it's a | female person.

These rules don't work every time — there are some exceptions.

Nouns can also be made plural

1) Nouns in French are <u>usually</u> made <u>plural</u> by adding an '<u>s</u>' — the <u>same</u> as in English.

> le chat *the cat* ⟹ les chats *the cats*

2) When you make a noun <u>plural</u>, instead of '<u>le</u>' or '<u>la</u>' to say '<u>the</u>', you have to use '<u>les</u>' — see p.100.

3) Some nouns can't be made plural by sticking an '<u>s</u>' on the end — they have <u>irregular plural forms</u>:

Noun ending	Example	Meaning	Irregular plural ending	Example
-ail	le travail	work	-aux	les travaux
-al	le journal	newspaper	-aux	les journaux
-eau	le bureau	office	-eaux	les bureaux
-eu	le jeu	game	-eux	les jeux
-ou	le chou	cabbage	-oux	les choux

Only a handful of nouns follow this rule — e.g. 'genou' (*knee*), 'bijou' (*jewel*) — most nouns ending in 'ou' are <u>regular</u>.

4) Some nouns <u>don't change</u> in the plural form. These are usually nouns that end in <u>-s</u>, <u>-x</u> or <u>-z</u>.

> la croix *the cross* ⟹ les croix *the crosses*

> la souris *the mouse* ⟹ les souris *the mice*

Using the correct gender will help boost your marks...

Add 'le' or 'la' to these words and then put the whole thing into its plural form.

1. cadeau *(present)*   **3.** citron *(lemon)*   **5.** voiture *(car)*

2. piscine *(swimming pool)*   **4.** cheval *(horse)*   **6.** pâtisserie *(cake shop)*

Articles — 'The', 'A' and 'Some'

'The' and 'a' are some of the most common words in a language, so it's a good idea to revise them well...

Un, une — A

The word for '<u>a</u>' depends on the <u>gender</u> of the <u>noun</u> (see p.99).

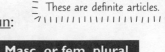
'Un' and 'une' are indefinite articles.

'<u>Un</u>' is used with masculine words...

| un café (m) | *a coffee* |

...and '<u>une</u>' is used with feminine ones.

| une tasse (f) | *a cup* |

Le, la, l', les — The

These are definite articles.

1) The word for '<u>the</u>' is <u>different</u> depending on the <u>gender</u> and <u>number</u> of the <u>noun</u>:

Masculine singular	Feminine singular	Before vowels / 'h' (sometimes)	Masc. or fem. plural
le	la	l'	les

2) For words starting with a <u>vowel</u>, 'le' or 'la' is shortened to '<u>l'</u>'. This makes them <u>easier</u> to say.

| l'avion (m) | *the aeroplane* |

| l'émission (f) | *the programme* |

3) Some words starting with an '<u>h</u>' also take '<u>l'</u>' <u>instead</u> of 'le' or 'la'. Sadly there's <u>no rule</u> for when this happens — you just have to <u>learn</u> it.

| l'homme (m) | *the man* |

'De' and 'à' change before 'le' and 'les'

1) '<u>De</u>' *(of / from)* and '<u>à</u>' *(to / at)* are <u>prepositions</u> (see p.119).

2) <u>Be careful</u> when you use them before a <u>definite article</u> (le/la/l'/les). They <u>combine</u> with 'le' and 'les' to make <u>new words</u>. ➡

	le	la	l'	les
à +	au	à la	à l'	aux
de +	du	de la	de l'	des

Je reste à	**+**	le collège.	➡	Je reste au collège.	*I'm staying at school.*
Je viens de	**+**	le Canada.	➡	Je viens du Canada.	*I come from Canada.*
Je vais à	**+**	les États-Unis.	➡	Je vais aux États-Unis.	*I'm going to the United States.*

Du, de la, de l', des — 'Some' or 'any'

1) If you want to say '<u>some</u>' or '<u>any</u>', use '<u>de</u>' with the correct <u>definite article</u> (see the table above). These are called <u>partitive articles</u>.

2) In <u>negative</u> sentences (see p.134), you <u>only</u> use '<u>de</u>', regardless of the gender or whether it's singular or plural.

| Je n'ai pas de pain. | *I haven't got any bread.* |

| Je n'ai pas de pantalon. | | *I haven't got any trousers.* |

3) You also just use '<u>de</u>' after most <u>quantities</u> — such as '<u>beaucoup de</u>' *(lots of)* or '<u>un peu de</u>' *(a bit of)*.

| J'ai un peu de fromage. | *I have a bit of cheese.* |

Knowing how to use French articles is crucial...

Fill in the gaps with the correct article.

1. L'homme a un peu ...... pain.

2. Les étudiants viennent ...... Maroc.

3. Je vais ...... pays de Galles.

4. Nous avons ...... bananes.

5. Ils n'ont pas ...... raisins.

6. Il va ...... bibliothèque.

Words to Describe Things

Adjectives are very useful, but they're a little bit tricky in French...

Adjectives describe things — here are some common ones

beau / belle	*beautiful*	affreux / affreuse	*awful*	nouveau / nouvelle	*new*
triste	*sad*	long(ue)	*long*	lent(e)	*slow*
normal(e)	*normal*	facile	*easy*	pratique	*practical*
intéressant(e)	*interesting*	difficile	*difficult*	amusant(e)	*funny*

French adjectives 'agree' with the thing they're describing

1) In English, adjectives don't <u>change form</u> — even when the word being described is plural, e.g. <u>big</u> boots.

2) In French, most adjectives <u>change</u> to match the <u>gender</u> and <u>number</u> of the word they're <u>describing</u>.

3) You often add an '-e' to the adjective if the word being described is <u>feminine</u> (see p.99). But <u>don't</u> do this if the word <u>already ends</u> in 'e'.

le livre intéressant	*the interesting book*	la vie intéressante	*the interesting life*

4) Add an '-s' to the adjective if the word being described is <u>plural</u> (see p.99). This means that with <u>feminine plurals</u>, you're adding '-es'.

les livres intéressants	*the interesting books*	les vies intéressantes	*the interesting lives*

Some adjectives don't follow these rules

Adjectives with <u>certain endings</u> follow <u>different</u> rules:

Ending	Important examples	Masculine singular	Feminine singular	Masculine plural	Feminine plural
-x	heureux *(happy)*, sérieux *(serious)*, ennuyeux *(boring)*, dangereux *(dangerous)*	heureux	heureuse	heureux	heureuses
-on, -en, -el, -il	bon *(good)*, mignon *(sweet)*, cruel *(cruel)*, gentil *(kind)*	bon	bonne	bons	bonnes
-er	premier *(first)*, dernier *(last)*, fier *(proud)*, cher *(expensive)*, étranger *(foreign)*	premier	première	premiers	premières
-f	sportif *(sporty)*, actif *(active)*, vif *(lively)*, négatif *(negative)*	sportif	sportive	sportifs	sportives
-c	blanc *(white)*, sec *(dry)*	blanc	blanche	blancs	blanches

These double the last letter + add 'e' in the feminine.

'Sèche' (f. sing.) and 'sèches' (f. pl.) have an accent added to them.

Adjectives — très sérieux, et un peu ennuyeux, mais utiles...

Translate these phrases into **French**, making sure the adjectives agree.

1. The proud mother.
2. A sad girl.
3. The slow cat.
4. A blue house.
5. The lively dogs.
6. The white cars.
7. A kind woman.
8. An expensive jacket.

Adjectives | Words to Describe Things

Adjectives add details to what you've written, which will get you those extra marks. So they're pretty useful...

Some adjectives don't follow the rules

1) These adjectives are <u>irregular</u>.

2) Some <u>change</u> before <u>masculine singular</u> nouns starting with a <u>vowel</u> because it's <u>easier</u> to say.

3) Some adjectives <u>never change</u>, e.g. '<u>marron</u>' *(brown)* and '<u>orange</u>' *(orange)*.

Masculine singular	Before a masc. sing. noun starting with a vowel	Fem. sing.	Masc. plural	Fem. plural
vieux *(old)*	vieil	vieille	vieux	vieilles
beau *(beautiful)*	bel	belle	beaux	belles
nouveau *(new)*	nouvel	nouvelle	nouveaux	nouvelles
fou *(mad)*	fol	folle	fous	folles
long *(long)*	long	longue	longs	longues
tout *(all)*	tout	toute	tous	toutes
rigolo *(funny)*	rigolo	rigolote	rigolos	rigolotes

Most adjectives go after the word they're describing...

1) In French, <u>most</u> adjectives follow the <u>noun</u> (the word they're describing).

> J'ai une voiture rapide.   *I have a fast car.*

Adjectives are always masculine singular after 'ce', e.g. 'c'est nouveau' (it's new).

2) You can also <u>use adjectives</u> in sentences with <u>verbs</u> such as '<u>être</u>' *(to be)* and '<u>devenir</u>' *(to become)*. The adjective still needs to <u>agree</u> with the noun though.

> Ils sont prêts maintenant.
> *They are ready now.*

> Elle devient grande.
> *She is becoming tall.*

...but there are some odd ones which go before

'Grand(e)' goes after the noun when it's describing a person.

1) These adjectives almost always go <u>before</u> the noun:

bon(ne)	*good*	nouveau / nouvel(le)	*new*	grand(e)	*big / tall*
mauvais(e)	*bad*	beau / bel(le)	*beautiful*	haut(e)	*high*
jeune	*young*	premier / première	*first*	joli(e)	*nice / pretty*
vieux / vieil(le)	*old*	petit(e)	*small / short*	faux / fausse	*false*

Adjectives have to agree regardless of whether they come before or after the noun.

> J'ai une petite maison, avec un joli jardin et une belle vue.
> *I have a small house, with a pretty garden and a beautiful view.*

2) Some adjectives <u>change meaning</u> depending on whether they go <u>before</u> or <u>after</u> a word. For example, 'propre' means '<u>own</u>' before a noun but '<u>clean</u>' after it. '<u>Ancien</u>' is another example:

> l'ancien château *the former castle*

> le château ancien *the old castle*

Learn which adjectives go where...

Without looking at the page above, pick the sentences that have the adjective(s) in the right place.

1. C'est un chien jeune.   **3.** Elle est une fille sportive.   **5.** J'ai une voiture rouge nouvelle.

2. Le long train est bleu.   **4.** Tu as lu un ennuyeux livre.   **6.** Vous avez la meilleure maison.

Words to Describe Things

They're no ordinary adjectives on this page — they're possessives, indefinites and demonstratives. Fancy.

Words like 'my' and 'your' show who an object belongs to

1) Possessive adjectives show that something belongs to someone. They go before the noun.

notre cousin   *our cousin*

	My	Your (inf. sing.)	His / her / its	Our	Your (formal, pl.)	Their
Masculine singular	mon	ton	son	notre	votre	leur
Feminine singular	ma	ta	sa	notre	votre	leur
Plural	mes	tes	ses	nos	vos	leurs

2) They match the thing being described — NOT the person it belongs to. The different forms are in this table.

3) So, for example, it's always 'mon père' *(my father)* even if a girl is talking.

Voici mon père et ma mère.
Here is my dad and my mum.

This means that 'son', 'sa' or 'ses' could all mean either 'his' or 'her'. You can usually tell which one it's meant to be by using the context.

4) Before vowels, or words starting with 'h' that take 'l'', you use the masculine possessive adjective — even if the noun is feminine. It's easier to say.

Mon amie s'appelle Ana.   *My friend's called Ana.*

Quelque, chaque — Some, each

'Quelque chose' is a fixed phrase that uses 'quelque'. It means 'something'.

1) 'Quelque' *(some)* and 'chaque' *(each)* are indefinite adjectives. They don't have a set of different forms for masculine, feminine or plural.

2) 'Quelque' doesn't have a feminine form, but it does add an '-s' when it changes from singular to plural.

J'ai acheté quelques bonbons au magasin qui est à quelque distance de chez moi.
I bought some sweets at the shop which is some distance from my house.

3) 'Chaque' never changes whether it's describing something masculine or feminine.

Je lis chaque nuit.   *I read every night.*

Ce, cet, cette, ces — This, these

1) To say 'this' or 'these', you need the right form of 'ce':

Masculine singular	Feminine singular	Masc. words that take 'l''	Masculine or feminine plural
ce	cette	cet	ces

Choose the one that matches the noun you're describing.

2) These are demonstrative adjectives — they're used when you use 'this' as a describing word.

Ce film est terrible.   *This film is terrible.*   Cet homme est grand.   *This man is tall.*

You need to be able to use all of these adjectives correctly...

Complete these sentences using the correct translation of the words in brackets.

1. ...... père n'aime pas ...... nouvelle voiture. (my, his)

2. ...... amis ne vont pas à ...... lycée. (your (sing. inf.), our)

3. ...... hôtel est grand. (this)

4. ...... cuisinière a ...... légumes. (this, some)

Words to Compare Things

When you're describing something, it's often useful to be able to compare it to something else. Doing this will also make your language more complex and gain you marks — hurrah! Here's how to do it...

Plus..., le plus... — More..., the most

You can do this with most adjectives.

1) In French you <u>couldn't</u> say, for example, 'weird<u>er</u>' or 'weird<u>est</u>' — you have to say 'more weird' or 'the <u>most weird</u>', using '<u>plus</u>' and '<u>le plus</u>'. Use '<u>que</u>' to say '<u>than</u>'.

Layla est bizarre. *Layla is weird.*	⇒	Rose est plus bizarre que moi. *Rose is weirder than me.*	⇒	Paul est le plus bizarre. *Paul is the weirdest.*

2) To say '<u>less</u>' or '<u>the least</u>', you use the word '<u>moins</u>' in the <u>same</u> way as '<u>plus</u>'.

fort *strong*	⇒	moins fort *less strong*	⇒	le moins fort *the least strong*

3) If you want to say something is the <u>same</u>, use '<u>aussi...que</u>' *(as...as)*.

Cette émission est aussi passionnante que l'autre.	*This programme is as exciting as the other one.*

4) '<u>Plus</u>', '<u>moins</u>' and '<u>aussi</u>' form <u>comparative adjectives</u>. '<u>Le plus</u>' and '<u>le moins</u>' form <u>superlative adjectives</u> — they're saying something is '<u>the most</u>', rather than directly <u>comparing</u> it to something else.

The adjectives still need to agree

1) If you're using <u>comparatives</u> or <u>superlatives</u>, the adjectives still need to <u>agree</u> with the <u>word</u> they're <u>describing</u>.

Elle est plus sportive.	*She is more sporty.*

2) If you're saying '<u>the most</u>' or '<u>the least</u>', you have to make '<u>the</u>' agree as well.

Jean et Françoise sont les plus jeunes. *Jean and Françoise are the youngest.*

There are some exceptions

1) There are some <u>odd ones out</u> when it comes to making <u>comparisons</u> — just like in English. Unfortunately, these tend to be words that come up a lot.

2) With these words, you <u>don't</u> use '<u>plus</u>' or '<u>moins</u>':

Adjective		Comparative		Superlative	
bon(ne)(s)	*good*	meilleur(e)(s) *better*	⇒	le/la/les meilleur(e)(s)	*the best*
mauvais(e)(s)	*bad*	pire(s) *worse*	⇒	le/la/les pire(s)	*the worst*

Ce livre est meilleur que le dernier. *This book is better than the last one.*	Les questions grammaticales sont les pires. *The grammar questions are the worst.*

Make sure you can use comparatives and superlatives accurately...

Translate these phrases into **French**. Remember those pesky adjective agreements...

1. Navid and Pauline are the strongest.
2. Your grandma is older than my grandad.
3. This shop is the least expensive.
4. Julie is as active as Thérèse.
5. His ideas are the worst.
6. French is the best.

Quick Questions

Knowing all this grammar is vital, so you need to make sure it sticks in your mind. Test what you've read with these quick questions — don't move on until you can answer them all correctly.

Quick Questions

1) Write down whether each of these words is masculine or feminine.
   a) chien
   b) lapin
   c) sœur
   d) souris
   e) vache
   f) frère
   g) chat
   h) père
   i) pomme
   j) oiseau
   k) mère
   l) orange
   m) maison
   n) hôpital
   o) école

2) For each of the following word endings, say whether words which end that way are usually masculine or feminine.
   a) -tion
   b) -ou
   c) -er
   d) -ière
   e) -ée
   f) -elle
   g) -ment
   h) -sion
   i) -isme
   j) -esse
   k) -ail
   l) -ise
   m) -té
   n) -ure
   o) -et

3) For each of these words, swap the indefinite article ('un' or 'une') for the definite article ('le', 'la' or 'l'').
   a) une maison
   b) un jardin
   c) un professeur
   d) une orange
   e) une robe
   f) un hôpital
   g) un abricot
   h) un hiver

4) Fill in the gaps in these sentences using the correct partitive article ('de', 'du', 'de la', 'de l'' or 'des').
   a) Sophia a .... oranges.
   b) Je n'ai pas .... poires.
   c) Ils ont gagné .... argent.
   d) Elle prend .... soupe.
   e) Il mange beaucoup .... chips.
   f) Richard n'a pas .... chaussettes.
   g) Il me donne .... chocolat.
   h) Je veux .... frites.

5) Underline all of the adjectives in the following sentences.
   a) L'examen était facile.
   b) Tes amis sont amusants et gentils.
   c) Thomas a un vieux chien.
   d) C'est une belle femme.
   e) Le film est triste.
   f) Alice habite dans une grande maison.
   g) J'ai une bonne idée.
   h) Le voyage sera long et ennuyeux.

6) Cross out the incorrect form of the adjectives in bold to complete the sentences.
   a) Alexandre a les yeux **bleu / bleus**.
   b) J'habite dans une maison **moderne / modernes**.
   c) La **premier / première** question est très **difficile / difficiles**.
   d) Susanna porte un chapeau **rouge / rouges** et des chaussures **orange / oranges**.
   e) Mes frères sont assez **sportif / sportifs**.
   f) Le cochon d'Inde est **heureux / heureuse** et **mignon / mignonne**.

7) Fill in the gaps with the correct form of the adjective chosen from the four options in **bold**.
   a) Ces rues sont très .... **long, longues, longue, longs**
   b) Clara a une .... souris. **nouvelles, nouvelle, nouveaux, nouvel**
   c) Je dors pendant .... la journée. **tout, tous, toute, toutes**
   d) Ton professeur est .... **rigolote, rigolotes, rigolos, rigolo**

Quick Questions

Quick Questions

8) Fill in the gaps in these sentences using the correct form of the adjectives in brackets.
   a) Elle porte une robe .... (blanc)
   b) En France, il y a beaucoup de gens .... (étranger)
   c) Florence et Charlotte sont les .... (dernier)
   d) Cette chemise est trop .... (cher)
   e) Mes chaussettes sont .... (sec)

9) Add the adjective in brackets to the correct gap in the sentences.
   a) J'ai une .... chemise .... (bleue)
   b) Nous sommes au .... étage .... (premier)
   c) Loïc habite dans un .... appartment .... (petit)
   d) Il chante des .... chansons .... (étrangères)
   e) C'est une .... peinture .... (bonne)

10) What's the French for...?
    a) my dog   c) your house   e) his shoes   g) our parents
    b) their car   d) my friend   f) her brother   h) your horse

11) Translate the following sentences into French.
    a) My bicycle is red.   d) Did you (formal) speak to your grandmother?
    b) Is your (sing.) coat blue?   e) They haven't done their homework.
    c) His mother lives in Ireland.   f) Have you (informal) seen her money?

12) Rewrite each of these sentences, replacing the English word in brackets with the correct
    form of 'chaque' or 'quelque.'
    a) Je joue au rugby (each) week-end.   c) (Each) élève doit faire ses devoirs.
    b) Eric a acheté (some) légumes.   d) Il a trouvé (some) livres intéressants.

13) Fill in the gaps in these sentences using the correct demonstrative adjective ('ce', 'cette' or 'ces').
    a) Je pense que .... travail est un peu ennuyeux.
    b) .... hôpital est merveilleux.
    c) Je ne me souviens pas de .... film.
    d) .... animaux sont malheureux.
    e) Les hommes vont aux États-Unis .... année.

14) Translate these sentences into French using 'le plus', 'la plus' or 'les plus'.
    a) This festival is the most exciting.
    b) I am strange, but he is the strangest.
    c) These trees are the greenest.

Words to Describe Actions

Words that describe actions are called adverbs. Like adjectives, they're useful for adding more detail to your French and gaining you marks. Nifty...

Adverbs describe how something's being done

1) In English, you don't say 'I run <u>slow</u>' — you add '<u>-ly</u>' on the end to say 'I run <u>slowly</u>'. '<u>Slowly</u>' is an <u>adverb</u>.

2) In French, you add '<u>-ment</u>' on the <u>end</u> of an <u>adjective</u> to make an <u>adverb</u>.
   But <u>first</u> you have to make sure it's in the <u>feminine form</u> (see p.101-102).

> adroit *(skilful)* ⟹ adroite (feminine form) **+** -ment ⟹ adroitement *(skilfully)*

3) Unlike adjectives, <u>adverbs</u> don't have to <u>agree</u> — they're <u>describing</u> an <u>action</u>, not the <u>person</u> doing it.

> Elle court adroitement.
> *She runs skilfully.*

> Nous courons adroitement.
> *We run skilfully.*

There are some small exceptions

1) Some adjectives <u>don't</u> follow the rules above.

2) If an adjective ends in '<u>-ant</u>' or '<u>-ent</u>', the '<u>nt</u>' is replaced with '<u>-mment</u>'.

> *'Présentement' and 'lentement' follow the normal rule and use their feminine adjective forms + '-ment'.*

> fréquent *(frequent)* ⟹ fréque- + -mment ⟹ fréquemment *(frequently)*
> récent *(recent)* ⟹ réce- + -mment ⟹ récemment *(recently)*

3) With <u>some</u> adjectives ending in '<u>-e</u>', the '<u>e</u>' changes to '<u>é</u>' when they become <u>adverbs</u>.

> énorme *(enormous)* énormément *(enormously)*

> précise *(precise)* précisément *(precisely)*

4) If an adjective's <u>masculine</u> form ends in a <u>vowel</u>, you can just add '<u>-ment</u>' to it to make an <u>adverb</u> — you <u>don't</u> need to use the <u>feminine</u> form.

> poli *(polite)* poliment

5) '<u>Gentiment</u>' *(gently, kindly)* is <u>completely irregular</u>. It comes from '<u>gentil</u>' *(gentle, kind)*.

Some adverbs don't use '-ment'

Some <u>adverbs</u> are quite <u>different</u> from their <u>adjectives</u>.

> bon(ne)   *good* ⟹ bien   *well*
> mauvais(e) *bad* ⟹ mal   *badly*
> rapide   *fast* ⟹ vite   *fast*

> Nous jouons bien au tennis.   *We play tennis well.*
> Elle écrit mal.   *She writes badly.*
> Tu parles vite.   *You talk fast.*

Remember, adverbs don't have to agree...

Turn these adjectives into adverbs.

1. triste *(sad)*   **3.** sérieux *(serious)*   **5.** absolu *(absolute)*   **7.** mauvais *(bad)*
2. négatif *(negative)* **4.** fier *(proud)*   **6.** lent *(slow)*   **8.** constant *(constant)*

Adverbs	# Words to Describe Actions

Adverbs don't just describe how something's being done — you can use them to specify the time and place it's happening as well. Read on for more...

Adverbs can describe when something's being done

1) <u>Adverbs of time</u> describe <u>when</u>, or <u>how frequently</u>, something happens.

tous les jours	*every day*	il y a...	*...ago*	immédiatement	*immediately*
normalement	*normally*	récemment	*recently*	en même temps	*at the same time*
souvent	*often*	avant	*before*	tôt	*early*
quelquefois	*sometimes*	déjà	*already*	tard	*late*
jamais	*never*	maintenant	*now*	bientôt	*soon*

2) You can also form <u>phrases</u> to describe the <u>day</u>, <u>month</u>, <u>season</u> or <u>year</u> something happens using the adjectives '<u>dernier</u>' *(last)* and '<u>prochain</u>' *(next)*. They can go at the <u>start</u> or <u>end</u> of a <u>sentence</u>.

> Je vais partir lundi prochain.
> *I'm going to leave next Monday.*

> L'année dernière, je suis allé(e) en Italie.
> *Last year, I went to Italy.*

See p.126 for more on the future tense and p.127-130 for more on the past tenses.

3) Words to describe <u>different days</u> can be used as adverbs.

hier	*yesterday*	avant-hier	*the day before yesterday*
aujourd'hui	*today*	après-demain	*the day after tomorrow*
demain	*tomorrow*		

Some adverbs describe location

<u>Adverbs of place</u> usually come <u>after</u> the <u>verb</u> in a phrase or sentence.

ici	*here*	Elle court partout.	*She runs everywhere.*
là	*there*		
là-bas	*over there*	Il marche loin chaque jour.	*He walks far every day.*
partout	*everywhere*		
quelque part	*somewhere*	Je fais mes devoirs ici.	*I do my homework here.*
loin	*far*		
près	*near*	Il gare sa voiture là-bas.	*He parks his car over there.*

If there's a direct object, e.g. 'les devoirs', the adverb always goes after it.

Phrases can be used as adverbs

Adverbial phrases are often really handy when you're giving your opinion on something.

You can use <u>adverbial phrases</u> in the <u>same</u> way as <u>adverbs</u>. They often come at the <u>beginning</u> of a <u>sentence</u>.

> En général, les lapins sont mignons.
> *In general, rabbits are cute.*

par conséquent	*consequently*	tout à fait	*absolutely*
en tout cas	*anyway*	de toute façon	*anyway*

Adverbs — learn them <u>well</u>, revise them <u>often</u> and you'll go <u>far</u>...

Translate these sentences into **French**. Make sure you use the right adverbs.

1. I play tennis over there.
2. You (sing.) sing every day.
3. I normally go to town by bus.
4. They're (fem.) going over there.
5. Consequently, I like my subjects.
6. I like this new teacher now.

Words to Compare Actions

You can also use adverbs to compare how people do things, or to say they're the best or worst at something.

Comparative adverbs compare actions

1) 'Plus' is used to say someone is doing something 'more...' than someone else. Use 'que' to say 'than'.

'Plus' comes before the adverb.

> Jean lit plus vite que Souad.   *Jean reads more quickly than Souad.*

2) You can use 'moins' to say 'less...' — use it in the same way as 'plus'.

> Souad lit moins souvent que Danielle.   *Souad reads less often than Danielle.*

3) There are two expressions for when something is done equally. Use 'aussi...que' to say 'as...as' and 'autant que' to say 'as much as'.

> Danielle lit aussi vite que Jacques.   *Danielle reads as fast as Jacques.*

> Danielle lit autant que Jacques.   *Danielle reads as much as Jacques.*

Le plus — The most

1) 'Le plus...' is a superlative adverb — you use it to say someone does something 'the most...'.

> Vivienne chante le plus musicalement.
> *Vivienne sings the most musically.*

2) You always use 'le' because adverbs don't have to agree with the person doing the action — they're describing the action itself. This is different from adjectives.

> Ils conduisent le plus dangereusement.
> *They drive the most dangerously.*

'Bien' and 'mal' are the odd ones out

1) 'Bien' *(well)* and 'mal' *(badly)* don't follow the rules. You just need to learn their comparative and superlative forms.

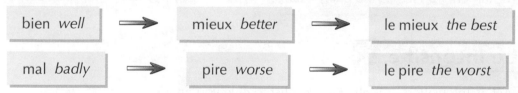

bien *well* ⟹ mieux *better* ⟹ le mieux *the best*

mal *badly* ⟹ pire *worse* ⟹ le pire *the worst*

2) 'Beaucoup' *(lots / a lot)* and 'peu' *(little)* are also irregular — they're a bit confusing because they change to 'plus' and 'moins'.

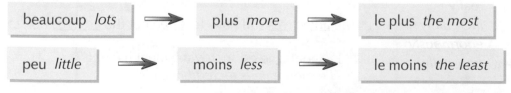

beaucoup *lots* ⟹ plus *more* ⟹ le plus *the most*

peu *little* ⟹ moins *less* ⟹ le moins *the least*

Use comparatives to make sure you write as well as possible...

Translate the words in brackets to fill in the gaps in these sentences.

1. Thomas joue du piano .... *(the best)*
2. François va à l'étranger .... *(the most frequently)*
3. Lucie court ...... Emmanuel. *(more than)*
4. Je regarde la télévision .... *(the least often)*
5. Tu ris ..... moi. *(as much as)*
6. Je chante ..... toi. *(worse than)*

Words to Say How Much

Intensifiers and quantifiers change the meaning of adjectives and adverbs slightly, so you can give more precise descriptions and impress the examiners.

Intensifiers strengthen what you're saying

1) Words such as '<u>trop</u>' *(too)* and '<u>assez</u>' *(quite)* can add <u>detail</u> to your sentences. They're called <u>intensifiers</u>.

trop	*too*	assez	*quite*
très	*very*	peu	*not very*

2) You can use them to <u>emphasise</u> an <u>adjective</u>, or to say <u>what</u> something's like or what you <u>think</u> of it.

3) <u>Intensifiers</u> can be used with <u>adjectives</u> — they always go <u>before</u> them.

> Camille est trop sérieuse.
> *Camille is too serious.*

> La géographie est peu intéressante.
> *Geography is not very interesting.*

4) You can use intensifiers with <u>adverbs</u>. They go <u>before</u> the adverb.

> J'écris très vite. *I write very fast.*

> Ils courent assez lentement. *They run quite slowly.*

Quantifiers help you say how many or how much

1) <u>Quantifiers</u> let you say roughly how much of something you have, without being specific, e.g. '<u>lots</u>' or '<u>not many</u>'.

trop de	*too many, too much*
beaucoup de	*lots of, many*
assez de	*enough*
peu de	*little, not much, not many*
un peu de	*a little, a little bit of*

2) Many are the <u>same</u> words as above, followed by '<u>de</u>'.

> J'ai assez de chaussures. *I have enough shoes.*

3) With <u>quantifiers</u>, '<u>de</u>' doesn't change to agree with the noun, but it changes to '<u>d'</u>' before a <u>vowel</u>.

> Nous avons peu d'argent. *We have little money.*

> Il a trop d'examens. *He has too many exams.*

Adverbs can be intensifiers

1) Some <u>adverbs</u> can act as <u>intensifiers</u> as well. Here's a <u>list</u> to give you an idea:

particulièrement	*particularly*
vraiment	*really*
incroyablement	*incredibly*
énormément	*enormously*
exceptionnellement	*unusually*

> Ce film est vraiment passionnant. *This film is really exciting.*

2) The <u>adjectives</u> still have to <u>agree</u> but the <u>adverbs</u> don't.

> La montagne est incroyablement haute.
> *The mountain is incredibly high.*

Intensifiers will make your French incredibly good...

Correct these sentences — find incorrectly written quantifiers / intensifiers and wrong genders / agreements.

1. Elle est trèse vive.
2. Ils ont une peu d'eau.
3. Le musicien est vraimment doué.
4. C'est assez d'intéressant.
5. Tu as beaucoup des chaussettes.
6. L'homme a trop chocolat.

Quick Questions

From time to time, I like to do some practice questions. Each question is based on the pages you've just read, so if there's something you're stuck on, go back and refresh your memory.

1) Turn each of these adjectives into adverbs.
   - a) facile
   - b) précis
   - c) heureux
   - d) évident
   - e) gentil
   - f) complet
   - g) clair
   - h) stupide
   - i) deuxième
   - j) calme
   - k) incroyable
   - l) honnête

2) Translate these sentences into French.
   - a) Zanna writes as much as Étienne.
   - b) The black dog is the oldest.
   - c) Chocolate cakes are the best.
   - d) I play tennis better than my sister.

3) Use the correct form of 'bien', 'mal', 'peu' and 'beaucoup' to fill the gaps in these sentences.
   - a) Julian joue du banjo .... que Claude.   (bien)
   - b) Ayesha nage le .... dans la mer.   (mal)
   - c) Lucie écrit le .... au collège.   (peu)
   - d) Matthieu cuisine .... à la maison que Charles.   (beaucoup)

4) Fill in the gaps in these sentences with the correct adverb from the list.
   - a) ...., nous sommes montées dans la tour.
   - b) Je vais .... au cinéma.
   - c) ...., il se douche à six heures.
   - d) Ils vont voyager ....
   - e) Ton cadeau est .... arrivé.

   demain
   déjà
   souvent
   normalement
   hier

5) Use a French adverb to fill the gap in each of these sentences and match the English translation.
   - a) Je l'ai vu ....   *I saw it over there.*
   - b) Elle a perdu son portable ....   *She has lost her mobile phone somewhere.*
   - c) Mon père a ses papiers ....   *My dad has his papers everywhere.*
   - d) L'aéroport est assez .... de la ville.   *The airport is quite far from the town.*
   - e) Venez ...., s'il vous plaît.   *Come here, please.*

6) Translate each of these adverbial phrases into English.
   - a) en général
   - b) tout à fait
   - c) de temps en temps
   - d) l'année prochaine
   - e) en retard
   - f) en tout cas
   - g) la semaine dernière
   - h) en même temps

7) Translate these quantifiers into English.
   - a) un peu de
   - b) assez de
   - c) trop de
   - d) peu de
   - e) beaucoup de

8) Now use the quantifiers to fill in these gaps, using the clues in brackets to help you.
   - a) Elles ont .... poissons.   (they don't need any more)
   - b) Elle a .... argent.   (more than she needs)
   - c) Mon ami a .... serpents.   (more than a few)
   - d) Le magicien a eu .... succès.   (not much)

Pronouns

I, Me, You, We, Them

I'm sure you're thrilled by the idea of learning lots of pronouns. They're useful words though — they'll help your French sound less repetitive. You use them all the time in English — probably without realising...

Subject pronouns replace the subject of the sentence

1) <u>Subject pronouns</u> are words like '<u>I</u>' and '<u>you</u>':

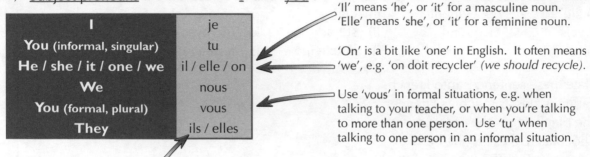

I	je
You (informal, singular)	tu
He / she / it / one / we	il / elle / on
We	nous
You (formal, plural)	vous
They	ils / elles

'Il' means 'he', or 'it' for a masculine noun.
'Elle' means 'she', or 'it' for a feminine noun.

'On' is a bit like 'one' in English. It often means 'we', e.g. 'on doit recycler' *(we should recycle)*.

Use 'vous' in formal situations, e.g. when talking to your teacher, or when you're talking to more than one person. Use 'tu' when talking to one person in an informal situation.

'Ils' is for a group of masculine nouns, or a mixture of masculine and feminine. 'Elles' is for a group of feminine nouns.

2) Subject pronouns can <u>replace</u> the <u>subject</u> (the person or thing <u>doing</u> the action in a sentence). Using them means you <u>don't</u> have to <u>keep saying</u> the same noun over and over again.

> Mon frère est musicien. Il est fana de musique rock.

> *My brother is a musician. He is a fan of rock music.*

'My brother' can be replaced with 'he' to sound less repetitive.

There are different pronouns for the direct object...

The <u>direct object</u> is the <u>person</u> or <u>thing</u> that the action is <u>being done to</u> — direct object pronouns <u>replace</u> the <u>noun</u> used as the direct object:

Remember, when 'le' or 'la' is followed by a word beginning with a vowel, it becomes 'l'.

Me	You (inf sing.)	Him / her / it	Us	You (formal, pl.)	Them
me	te	le / la	nous	vous	les

> Il voit son amie. $\longrightarrow$ Il la voit.
> *He sees his friend.* $\longrightarrow$ *He sees her.*

...and for the indirect object

<u>Indirect objects</u> are things that are <u>affected</u> by the <u>action</u> being done, but not <u>directly</u>. They often have '<u>to</u>' or '<u>for</u>' before them in English:

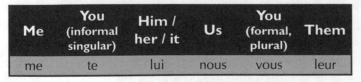

Me	You (informal singular)	Him / her / it	Us	You (formal, plural)	Them
me	te	lui	nous	vous	leur

> Il donne le cadeau à son amie.
> *He gives the present to his friend.*

> Il lui donne le cadeau.
> *He gives her the present.*

Pronouns are tricky, so make sure you learn this page...

Replace the words in bold with the correct pronoun from the brackets.

1. Hélène (lui / la / les) donne le livre **à son ami**.
2. **Emilie** (Elle / Tu / La) aime les chiens.
3. Tu peux (leur / elles / les) voir **les tortues**?
4. Avez-vous le livre? Non, elle (il / l' / le) a **le livre**.
5. **Moi et mon amie** (Nous / Elles / La) allons au cinéma.
6. Non, **les tortues** (les / elles / ils) ne sont pas ici.

Something, There, Any

There are even pronouns for unspecified things, e.g. 'everyone'. There are a couple of tricky little ones on this page too, so have a good read and then try the questions at the bottom of the page to test yourself.

Use indefinite pronouns for unspecified things

Indefinite pronouns refer to general, unspecific things, such as 'everyone' and 'something'.

quelqu'un	*someone*	plusieurs	*several*
tout le monde	*everyone*	tout	*all / everything*
quelque chose	*something*	chacun(e)	*each one*

> Tout le monde aime le chocolat.
> *Everyone likes chocolate.*

Y — There

1) '<u>Y</u>' can mean '<u>there</u>'. It replaces the <u>noun</u> for a <u>location</u> which has <u>already</u> been <u>mentioned</u>.

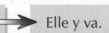

> Elle va à la banque.   *She's going to the bank.*   ➡   Elle y va.   *She's going there.*

> *This is often used to talk about weather. See p.56.*

2) It's also used in some <u>common expressions</u>.

> Allons-y! *Let's do it! / Let's go!*   Vas-y!   *Do it! / Go on!*   Il y a...   *There is / There are...*

3) It means '<u>it</u>' or '<u>them</u>' after <u>verbs followed</u> by '<u>à</u>'.

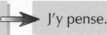

> Je pense à l'idée.   *I'm thinking about the idea.*   ⟹   J'y pense.   *I'm thinking about it.*

En — Of it, of them, some, any

1) '<u>En</u>' has a few meanings — depending on the <u>context</u>, it can mean '<u>of it</u>', '<u>of them</u>', '<u>some</u>' or '<u>any</u>'.

> As-tu peur des guêpes? Oui, j'en ai peur.   *Are you scared of wasps? Yes, I'm scared of them.*

> As-tu des oranges? Oui, j'en ai.   *Have you got any oranges? Yes, I have some.*

> As-tu des poires? Non, je n'en ai pas.   *Have you got any pears? No, I don't have any.*

2) It means '<u>it</u>' or '<u>them</u>' after <u>verbs followed</u> by '<u>de</u>'.

> Tu as besoin d'aide.   *You need help.*   ⟹   Tu en as besoin.   *You need it.*

Indefinite pronouns? J'en ai besoin.

Choose the correct sentences and have a go at rewriting the ones that are wrong.

1. Il y a une cuisine si vous en avez besoin.
2. Toutes le monde sait que c'est vrai.
3. A-t-elle des livres? Oui, elle y a.

4. J'y réfléchis.
5. Tu connais le château? J'en suis allé(e).
6. Il y en a plusieurs.

Pronouns | # Position and Order of Object Pronouns

To give you a break from learning pronouns, some of this page is about the order they go in instead...

Object pronouns always go before the verb

1) If there's <u>more than one pronoun</u>, they go in a <u>certain</u> order:

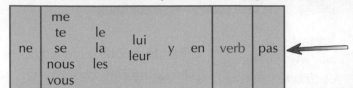

| ne | me
te
se
nous
vous | le
la
les | lui
leur | y | en | verb | pas |

In negative sentences, 'ne' goes before the object pronouns and 'pas' goes after the verb. See p.134 for more about negatives.

> Elle me le donne.
> *She gives it to me.*

2) With <u>compound</u> tenses, which use 'avoir' or 'être' before the main verb, the pronouns go <u>before both verbs</u>.

> Elle me l'a donné.   *She gave it to me.*

The perfect (p.127-128) and pluperfect (p.138) are compound tenses.

3) Certain verbs (vouloir, pouvoir, devoir) are often used with the <u>infinitive</u> of another verb. The <u>object pronouns</u> go <u>between</u> them.

> Je peux le lui donner.   *I can give it to him / to her.*

Use pronouns to emphasise who you're talking about

1) <u>Emphatic pronouns</u> make it really <u>clear</u> who you're talking about.

2) You need them...

Me	moi
You (informal singular)	toi
Him / her / one	lui / elle / soi
Us	nous
You (formal, plural)	vous
Them (m / f)	eux / elles

   - if the words are <u>on their own</u>, or <u>after 'c'est'</u>.

> Qui parle? Moi! C'est moi!   *Who's speaking? Me! It's me!*

   - to <u>compare</u> people or things — the emphatic pronoun goes after 'que' *(than)*.

> Il est plus petit que toi.   *He's smaller than you.*

   - for <u>giving instructions</u>. (See p.136 for more on how to do this.)

> Écoutez-moi!   *Listen to me!*

> Donne-lui ton portable!   *Give him your mobile!*

   - <u>after prepositions</u> such as '<u>for</u>' or '<u>with</u>'.

> Tu le fais pour elle.   *You do it for her.*

> Je suis allé avec eux.   *I went with them.*

3) You can add '<u>-même</u>' on the end of an <u>emphatic pronoun</u> to say '<u>-self</u>'. Add an '<u>s</u>' if it's <u>plural</u> ('<u>-mêmes</u>').

> On le fait soi-même.   *One does it oneself.*

Don't forget that by itself, 'même' means 'even', e.g. 'même si' (even if).

> Elles l'ont écrit elles-mêmes.   *They wrote it themselves.*

Getting your pronouns in the right order will impress the examiner...

Unscramble the words in these sentences and then translate them into English.

1. donne. lui Il le
2. ai l' qui C'est écouté. moi
3. l' toi- Tu as écrit même.
4. nous. êtes allés Vous y avec
5. t' Elle dit. a
6. vais en parler. Je lui

Relative and Interrogative Pronouns

These help link bits of a sentence together so you're not stuck with lots of short phrases. Read on for more...

'Qui' and 'que' are relative pronouns

1) Relative pronouns introduce extra information about something you've mentioned in your sentence.

2) 'Qui' is used if you're referring to the subject of the sentence — the person or thing doing the action.

> La femme qui a volé le portefeuille.   *The woman who stole the wallet.*

3) 'Que' is used to refer to the object of the sentence — the person or thing that something's being done to.

> Le portefeuille que la femme a volé.   *The wallet that the woman stole.*

You can use 'qui' and 'que' to ask questions

See p.4-5 on questions.

1) In questions, 'qui' and 'que' are interrogative pronouns. 'Qui' means 'who', and 'que' means 'what'.

2) They can be the subject of a question. 'Que' changes to 'qu'est-ce qui' when it's the subject.

> Qui parle?   *Who is speaking?*   Qu'est-ce qui se passe?   *What is happening?*

3) You can also use 'qui' and 'que' as the object of the question.

> Qui connaissez-vous?   *Who do you know?*   Que savez-vous?   *What do you know?*

4) 'Qui' and 'que' can be used after prepositions (words such as 'with' or 'for' — see p.119-120). 'Que' changes to 'quoi' after a preposition but 'qui' stays the same.

> Tu parles avec qui?   *Who are you talking to?*   De quoi parles-tu?   *What are you talking about?*

Dont — Of which, whose, about which...

You only need to recognise 'dont' — you don't have to use it.

'Dont' has several meanings and can be used in different ways:

- To replace 'de' when 'de' is used with a verb. For example, 'parler de' (to talk about).

> L'araignée dont on a parlé.   *The spider we talked about. (The spider about which we talked.)*

- To say 'whose'. 'Dont' replaces the 'de' used to show possession.

> La chef dont les repas sont délicieux.
> *The chef whose meals are delicious.*

Literally 'The chef of whom the meals are delicious'.

- To talk about something that's part of a group.

> J'ai trois films dont un est une comédie.   *I've got three films, of which one is a comedy.*

Make sure you learn the difference between 'qui' and 'que'...

Translate these sentences, making sure you're using the correct pronoun.

1. The man who is sporty.
2. The pizza that I like eating.
3. I've got five pencils which are red.
4. Who do you run with?
5. The car that she drives is slow.
6. What are you thinking about?

Pronouns — Possessive and Demonstrative Pronouns

There are pronouns for showing who owns something, as well as for saying 'this one' and 'that one'.

Possessive pronouns show something belongs to someone

1) Possessive pronouns replace a noun that belongs to someone — they're words like 'mine' and 'yours'. You need to be able to recognise them for the exam — but you don't have to use them.

> Le ballon rouge est ici. C'est le mien. *The red ball is here. It's mine.*

2) They agree with the gender and number of the noun being replaced — have a look at the table:

	Mine	Yours (informal singular)	His / her / its	Our	Yours (formal, plural)	Their
Masculine singular	le mien	le tien	le sien	le nôtre	le vôtre	le leur
Feminine singular	la mienne	la tienne	la sienne	la nôtre	la vôtre	la leur
Plural (m / f)	les miens / miennes	les tiens / tiennes	les siens / siennes	les nôtres	les vôtres	les leurs

> Il y a trois bananes — ce sont les miennes. *There are three bananas — they're mine.*

Celui, celle, ceux, celles — This, these, those

Don't worry — you don't have to use these, just know what they mean.

1) 'Celui', 'celle', 'ceux' and 'celles' are demonstrative pronouns. They mean 'this', 'this one' 'those' or 'the one(s)'.

Masculine singular	celui
Feminine singular	celle
Masculine plural	ceux
Feminine plural	celles

> J'aime ce gâteau, mais celui qu'on a mangé hier était meilleur. *I like this cake, but the one we ate yesterday was better.*

2) They're used with '-ci' on the end to mean 'this one' or 'this one here'. Adding '-là' on the end changes the meaning to 'that one' or 'that one there'.

> Il y a deux gâteaux. J'aime celui-ci, mais celui-là est meilleur. *There are two cakes. I like this one, but that one there is better.*

'Celui-ci' and 'celui-là' are used to point things out.

Ceci, cela, ça — This, that, that

1) 'Ceci', 'cela' and 'ça' are also demonstrative pronouns. They're used for more general things, not when you're pointing something out.

2) You need to be able to use these ones, so take a look at these examples:

> Ceci est intéressant. *This is interesting.*

> Cela n'est pas vrai! *That isn't true!*

> Je n'aime pas faire ça. *I don't like doing that.*

'Ça' is a more informal way to say 'that'.

Demonstrate your knowledge of pronouns in the task below...

Translate the words in brackets to fill in the gaps.

1. Le stylo là est .... *(yours, informal)*
2. Celle-là est .... *(hers)*
3. .... n'est pas drôle! *(that)*
4. Ces chiens sont .... *(ours)*
5. Où as-tu vu .... ? *(that)*
6. C'est .... *(yours, formal)*

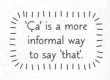

Quick Questions

Pronouns may seem tricky at first, but with practice, they'll be a doddle. Speaking of practice, here are some more quick questions to be getting on with. See if you can do them without cheating.

1) For each of these sentences replace the underlined subject with the correct subject pronoun.
   a) <u>Amy</u> aime le chocolat.
   b) <u>Le chien</u> a mangé mes chaussures.
   c) <u>Les garçons</u> détestent les filles.
   d) <u>Mark</u> joue au football.
   e) <u>La souris</u> est sous la table.
   f) <u>Emma et Sarah</u> sont allées au cinéma.

2) For each of these sentences, fill in the correct French direct object pronoun.
   a) Je regarde la télévision. — Je .... regarde.
   b) Paul lit le journal. — Paul .... lit.
   c) Je déteste les chats et les chiens. — Je .... déteste.

3) Translate these indefinite pronouns into French.
   a) something   b) someone   c) everyone   d) each one   e) several

4) Use 'y' or 'en' to fill in the gaps in these sentences.
   a) On .... va s'il fait beau.
   b) Est-ce que tu peux m' .... acheter?
   c) Je n' .... vais pas à cause des monstres.
   d) Les vacances, parlons-............ .
   e) Tu .... es déjà allée?
   f) On ne s' .... sortira jamais!

5) Rearrange the French words to make a complete sentence, making sure the pronouns are in the correct order.
   a) le Nous pouvons leur donner.
   b) attend. t' Mon y père
   c) en Vous achetez. lui
   d) Elle y rencontre. les
   e) la offerte. lui avais Je
   f) téléphoné leur a hier. Il

6) Fill in the gaps in these sentences with 'qui', 'que' or 'qu'.'
   a) Le lapin .... tu as tué était délicieux.
   b) C'est un homme .... aime le poulet.
   c) Les sandales .... il porte avec des chaussettes sont laides.
   d) Le gendarme .... a volé ma voiture était vieux.

7) Translate each of these sentences into English.
   a) Le fermier a une poule dont les œufs sont parfaits.
   b) Il avait trois gâteaux dont deux étaient pleins de fruits.
   c) La maladie dont elle souffre lui donne un nez bleu.

8) Write the correct possessive pronouns in the gaps to complete the following sentences.
   a) Donnez-nous le mouton d'or — c'est ....
   b) Cette carotte longue est à Anaïs — c'est ....
   c) Passe-moi les saucisses — ce sont ....
   d) La veste rouge est à Larry — c'est ....

9) Translate these sentences into English.
   a) Je n'aime pas cette robe. Je préfère celle-là.
   b) As-tu lu ces livres? Celui-ci est très bon, mais celui-là est ennuyeux.
   c) J'aime les chiens, mais ceux-là sont vraiment méchants.

Conjunctions

Joining Words

Conjunctions link words together. They help make your French sound more natural and more sophisticated, too — because nothing says sophistication like accurate French conjunctions...

Use conjunctions to make longer sentences

1) Here are some <u>common</u> conjunctions:

mais	*but*	ou bien	*or else*	ainsi	*therefore / so*
et	*and*	puis	*then*	ensuite	*then / next*
ou	*or*	donc	*therefore / so*	ni...ni	*neither...nor*

> A clause is a group of words that has a subject and a verb. For more on verbs, see p.122.

2) Some conjunctions <u>link</u> two <u>clauses</u> or <u>sentences</u> together. They make the sentences sound more <u>natural</u>.

J'ai un petit job.	**donc**	Je mets de l'argent de côté chaque mois.	→	J'ai un petit job, donc je mets de l'argent de côté chaque mois.
I have a part-time job.	**therefore**	*I save some money every month.*		*I have a part-time job, therefore I save some money every month.*

Les fleurs sont bleues claires et l'herbe est verte.	*The flowers are light blue and the grass is green.*

3) 'Ou' (*or*) is used to give <u>more than one</u> option.

Amélie veut être infirmière.	**ou**	Amélie veut être ingénieur.	→	Amélie veut être infirmière ou ingénieur.
Amélie wants to be a nurse.	**or**	*Amélie wants to be an engineer.*		*Amélie wants to be a nurse or an engineer.*

> Make sure you don't get mixed up between 'ou' (*or*) and 'où' (*where*).

Some conjunctions add extra information to a sentence

1) Some conjunctions can also add <u>extra detail</u> to a <u>sentence</u>.

2) Often these conjunctions introduce a <u>reason</u> for something happening, a <u>contradiction</u> or a <u>condition</u>.

parce que	*because*	pendant que	*while*	comme	*like*
puisque	*since*	par contre	*on the other hand*	y compris	*including*
quand	*when*	lorsque	*when / as soon as*	si	*if*
cependant	*however*	par exemple	*for example*	même si	*even if*

Je déteste le tabac parce que c'est mauvais pour la santé.	
I hate smoking because it's bad for your health.	

> Conjunctions can go at the beginning of sentences, too.

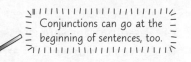

Même s'ils sont délicieux, je ne les veux pas.	*Even if they're delicious, I don't want them.*

Using conjunctions will make your sentences sound more natural...

Match the French conjunctions below with their English definitions.

1. therefore   **3.** however   **5.** including   **a)** pendant que   **c)** y compris   **e)** cependant
2. or else   **4.** while   **6.** since   **b)** ou bien   **d)** ainsi   **f)** puisque

---

Prepositions

Prepositions may not be much to look at, but size is no guarantee of power. These fellas are some of the most useful words in the French language — and, luckily, they're also some of the easiest to pronounce.

À — 'to', 'in' or 'at'

1) Prepositions are short words like 'to' and 'from'. They let you add extra information to sentences.

2) 'À' can mean 'to', 'in' or 'at'. It changes to 'au' and 'aux' when it's followed by 'le' and 'les' (see p.100).

> Je vais au magasin.
> *I'm going to the shop.*

> Je suis à la maison.
> *I'm at home.*

> J'habite aux États-Unis.
> *I live in the United States.*

You can't use 'à' for feminine countries, or countries beginning with a vowel. Look at the paragraph on 'en' below to find out more.

3) Some verbs are followed by 'à' when they go before a noun. Here are some examples:

(s')intéresser à	*to be interested in*	rendre visite à	*to visit (someone)*
jouer à	*to play (a game)*	penser à	*to think about*

'En' doesn't mean 'on'

See p.120 for the difference between 'en' and 'dans'.

1) 'En' can mean 'in' or 'to'. It's used instead of 'à' for feminine countries and countries starting with a vowel.

> Clare habite en France.   *Clare lives in France.*

> Je vais en Iran en mai.   *I'm going to Iran in May.*

For something happening in a specific season, month or year, you usually use 'en'.

2) You should use 'en' to say how long an action takes:

> Elle a lu l'article en cinq minutes.   *She read the article in five minutes.*

3) 'En' is also used to describe what something is made of.   une veste en cuir   *a leather jacket*

De — 'of' or 'from'

French doesn't have apostrophes to show belonging — it uses 'de' instead.

1) 'De' often means 'of'.

> une tasse de thé   *a cup of tea*

> Je porte la robe de ma mère.   *I'm wearing my mother's dress.*

2) 'De' can also mean 'from'. It changes to 'du', 'de la' or 'des' when it's next to a definite article (see p.100).

> Jean revient de la plage (f).   *Jean is coming back from the beach.*

3) Some verbs are followed by 'de' when they go before a noun. Learn these important examples:

Il s'agit de	*it's about*	avoir besoin de	*to need*	jouer de	*to play (an instrument)*
changer de	*to change*	avoir envie de	*to want*	partir de	*to leave*

Revise these prepositions carefully...

Translate these phrases into **French** using the correct prepositions.

1. I play football.
2. She visits Manu.
3. It's about a young boy.
4. a woollen jumper
5. I play the clarinet.
6. They live in France.
7. He's going to the bank.
8. You (sing, inf.) come from Wales.

Prepositions

Just for your enjoyment, here are some more handy prepositions...

Chez Natalie — At Natalie's

These prepositions are <u>really important</u> for your exams — try to learn them all.

avec	*with*	à cause de	*because of*	chez	*at the house of*
sans	*without*	au lieu de	*instead of*	grâce à	*thanks to*

Lots of prepositions relate to time

For more on telling the time, see p.2.

1) Prepositions of <u>time</u> tell you <u>when</u> something happened <u>in relation to</u> something else.

avant	*before*	depuis	*since / for*
après	*after*	jusqu'à	*until*
pour	*for*	pendant	*during / for*

> Florence a fini avant les autres.
> *Florence finished before the others.*

2) 'Pendant', 'depuis' and 'pour' are a little bit tricky because they can all be translated as 'for'.

3) Use '<u>pendant</u>' for actions that have <u>already happened</u>, or <u>will happen</u> in the future, but <u>aren't happening</u> now.

> J'ai travaillé dans un hôtel pendant deux ans.   *I worked in a hotel for two years.*

See p.124 and p.130 for more about 'depuis'.

4) Use '<u>depuis</u>' for actions that <u>began in the past</u>, but are <u>still continuing</u> today.

> J'habite dans le Cumbria depuis trois mois.   *I've lived in Cumbria for three months.*

5) '<u>Pour</u>' (*for*) is used very similarly to in English, but with time, it's <u>only used</u> in the <u>future tense</u>.

> Martine va aller en Suisse pour une semaine.   *Martine is going to go to Switzerland for a week.*

Use prepositions to describe position

1) Some prepositions describe the <u>location</u> of <u>something</u> or <u>someone</u>.

sur	*on*	dans	*in*	devant	*in front of*
sous	*under*	derrière	*behind*	à côté de	*next to*

2) '<u>Dans</u>' (*in*) is normally used to describe when something is <u>actually inside</u> something else.

'En' also means 'in', but it can't mean 'inside' — see p.119.

> Mon passeport est dans ma valise.   *My passport is in my suitcase.*

3) '<u>Dans</u>' is also used to say how much time will pass before an event. E.g. 'dans cinq minutes' (*in five minutes*).

Show off your knowledge of prepositions in the exams...

Choose the correct preposition to complete each of the sentences below.

1. Je suis (à / chez) Paul avec Dima.
2. Le magasin est (sous / dans) le pont.
3. Je vais aller en vacances (pendant / pour) deux semaines.
4. Je travaille à la pharmacie (depuis / pendant) six mois.

Quick Questions

Since we've got through another set of pages, it's time to test what you've learnt. If you can nail your prepositions, your examiner will be very impressed — and you'll be well on your way to good marks.

Quick Questions

1) Translate these conjunctions into English.
   a) mais
   b) ni...ni...
   c) lorsque
   d) comme
   e) ou
   f) quand
   g) depuis que
   h) pendant que
   i) parce que
   j) ou bien
   k) après que
   l) puis

2) These sentences contain the wrong conjunctions. Rewrite them using 'comme', 'puis', 'si', 'et' or 'mais.' You can only use each conjunction once.
   a) Je voudrais une pomme <u>car</u> une poire.
   b) C'est mon anniversaire <u>lorsque</u> je ne sors pas.
   c) <u>Ou</u> tu manges le champignon, je te tuerai.
   d) Je me douche, <u>quand</u> je m'habille.
   e) <u>Ou bien</u> j'étais en retard, j'ai manqué le bus.

3) Fill in the gaps in these sentences using 'à', 'aux', 'dans' or 'en'.
   a) J'habite .... Marseille.
   b) Je vais .... Pays-Bas.
   c) La voiture est .... le garage.
   d) Il va .... Paris ce week-end.
   e) Je voudrais aller .... Afrique.
   f) Mon gilet est .... cuir.
   g) Les chaussures sont .... la boîte.
   h) Il est .... États-Unis en ce moment.

4) Translate the underlined prepositions in the following sentences into French.
   a) The dog is <u>under</u> the table.
   b) Your bag is <u>on</u> the chair.
   c) I left the house <u>without</u> my coat.
   d) I'm going swimming <u>after</u> school.
   e) I had lunch <u>at</u> Juliette's.
   f) We will leave at <u>around</u> midday.
   g) I went to the cinema <u>with</u> my friends.
   h) I arrived <u>before</u> you.

5) Translate the following sentences into English.
   a) Mon père est très fatigué car il travaille tout le temps.
   b) Prends un chocolat si tu veux.
   c) Je suis fatiguée donc je vais me coucher.
   d) Qu'est-ce que tu vas faire pendant les vacances?
   e) Je joue au football avec mon frère.

6) Complete the following sentences using the correct form of 'à' or 'de.'
   a) Je viens .... France.
   b) Je vais donner des bonbons .... enfants.
   c) On peut changer de l'argent .... banque.
   d) Je m'intéresse .... tennis de table.
   e) Le train part .... quai numéro trois.
   f) C'est la voiture .... ma mère.
   g) Je l'ai vu .... télévision.
   h) Luc joue .... guitare.
   i) Pierre joue .... piano.
   j) Ce livre est .... Michel.

7) Translate these sentences into French using the prepositions in brackets.
   a) The school is opposite the swimming pool.   (en face de)
   b) I stayed at home because of the rain.   (à cause de)
   c) There is a supermarket next to the park.   (à côté de)
   d) Aix-en-Provence is near Marseilles.   (près de)

Verbs in the Present Tense

You need to know the present tense inside out and back to front — it crops up all over the place. It also provides the foundations for some trickier tenses later on, so learning it properly now is well worth it.

Verbs are action words

1) A <u>verb</u> is a word that describes an <u>action</u>. 'Eat', 'sing' and 'jump' are all <u>examples</u> of English <u>verbs</u>.

2) <u>Actions</u> can take place in different <u>times</u> — or <u>tenses</u> — the past, present or future.

3) To put a verb in a <u>tense</u>, you need to know its <u>infinitive</u>, e.g. 'être' (*to be*). They're in this <u>form</u> in the <u>dictionary</u>.

The present describes something happening now

1) Use the <u>present tense</u> to describe something <u>that's occurring now</u>.

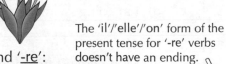
You can use the French present tense to say that something 'is happening' or that something 'happens'.

> Je mange une pomme.   *I am eating an apple. / I eat an apple.*

2) You should also use the <u>present tense</u> to describe something that <u>happens regularly</u>.

> Le lundi, je fais du jogging.   *I go jogging on Mondays.*

3) <u>Verbs</u> in the present tense have <u>different endings</u>, but you always start by finding the verb's <u>stem</u>.

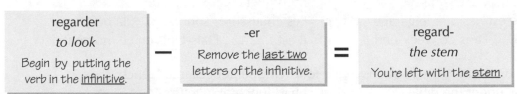

regarder				
to look		-er		regard-
				the stem
Begin by putting the verb in the <u>infinitive</u>.	**−**	Remove the <u>last two</u> letters of the infinitive.	**=**	You're left with the <u>stem</u>.

Infinitive	Stem
parler	parl-
finir	fin-
vendre	vend-

4) Then you add the correct <u>endings</u> to the <u>stem</u> (see below).

Add the right endings to the verb's stem

In French, there are <u>three groups</u> of verbs — verbs ending in '<u>-er</u>', '<u>-ir</u>' and '<u>-re</u>':

The 'il'/'elle'/'on' form of the present tense for '-re' verbs doesn't have an ending.

'-er' endings

I	je	-e
you (inf. sing)	tu	-es
he/she/it/one	il/elle/on	-e
we	nous	-ons
you (pl., formal)	vous	-ez
they (m/f)	ils/elles	-ent

'-ir' endings

I	je	-is
you (inf. sing)	tu	-is
he/she/it/one	il/elle/on	-it
we	nous	-issons
you (pl., formal)	vous	-issez
they (m/f)	ils/elles	-issent

'-re' endings

I	je	-s
you (inf. sing)	tu	-s
he/she/it/one	il/elle/on	—
we	nous	-ons
you (pl., formal)	vous	-ez
they (m/f)	ils/elles	-ent

E.g. 'regarder'   (*to watch*)
'regard-'   (the stem)
+ '-ons'   ('nous' ending)
nous regardons   (we watch)

E.g. 'finir'   (*to finish*)
'fin-'   (the stem)
+ '-issent'   ('elles' ending)
elles finissent   (they finish)

E.g. 'vendre'   (*to sell*)
'vend-'   (the stem)
+ nothing   ('elle' ending)
elle vend   (she sells)

You can't avoid the present tense, so make sure you learn it...

Have a go putting the verbs below into the present tense. The subject is given in brackets.

1. parler (je)
2. établir (il)
3. remplir (nous)
4. répondre (tu)
5. entendre (elles)
6. commencer (vous)
7. perdre (vous)
8. grossir (ils)
9. allumer (je)
10. vendre (on)

Irregular verbs don't follow a set pattern. This means that there aren't any concrete rules you can apply to them. The only way to revise them properly is to learn them off by heart.

Some of the most useful verbs are irregular

Lots of <u>important verbs</u> are <u>irregular</u> — this means that they <u>don't follow</u> the usual rules. Here are some of the <u>most common</u> ones that you <u>need to know</u> for your exams:

avoir — to have

I have	j'ai
you (inf. sing.) have	tu as
he/she/it/one has	il/elle/on a
we have	nous avons
you (pl., formal) have	vous avez
they have	ils/elles ont

Make sure you know the difference between 'a' from 'avoir' and the preposition 'à' (see p.119).

être — to be

I am	je suis
you (inf. sing.) are	tu es
he/she/it/one is	il/elle/on est
we are	nous sommes
you (pl., formal) are	vous êtes
they are	ils/elles sont

faire — to make / do

I make	je fais
you (inf. sing.) make	tu fais
he/she/it/one makes	il/elle/on fait
we make	nous faisons
you (pl., formal) make	vous faites
they make	ils/elles font

Remember, you don't usually pronounce the last letter of a word in French if it's a consonant. This means that some endings (e.g. 'fais' and 'fait') are spelt differently but sound exactly the same.

aller — to go

I go	je vais
you (inf. sing.) go	tu vas
he/she/it/one goes	il/elle/on va
we go	nous allons
you (pl., formal) go	vous allez
they go	ils/elles vont

devoir — must / to have to

I must	je dois
you (inf. sing.) must	tu dois
he/she/it/one must	il/elle/on doit
we must	nous devons
you (pl., formal) must	vous devez
they must	ils/elles doivent

'Devoir' is a verb, but 'les devoirs' is a noun meaning 'homework'.

vouloir — to want

I want	je veux
you (inf. sing.) want	tu veux
he/she/it/one wants	il/elle/on veut
we want	nous voulons
you (pl., formal) want	vous voulez
they want	ils/elles veulent

pouvoir — to be able to / can

I can	je peux
you (inf. sing.) can	tu peux
he/she/it/one can	il/elle/on peut
we can	nous pouvons
you (pl., formal) can	vous pouvez
they can	ils/elles peuvent

Don't mix up 'savoir' and 'connaître' — 'savoir' means to know something. To say that you know somebody, use 'connaître'.

savoir — to know

I know	je sais
you (inf. sing.) know	tu sais
he/she/it/one knows	il/elle/on sait
we know	nous savons
you (pl., formal) know	vous savez
they know	ils/elles savent

These verbs crop up everywhere, so you need to learn them...

Each verb below is spelt incorrectly — using the verb tables above, rewrite each of the phrases correctly.

1. nous doivons
2. je veut
3. vous êtez
4. tu doix
5. elle vat
6. ils faient
7. elles pouvent
8. on saix
9. ils avont
10. nous faions

More About the Present Tense

There's still more to learn about the present tense — round off your knowledge with these last few points.

Verbs sometimes stay in their infinitive

1) When one verb <u>follows</u> another in a sentence or phrase, the <u>first verb</u> needs to be in the right form, but the <u>second verb</u> is <u>always</u> in the <u>infinitive</u>.

> Je veux aider les autres.   *I want to help other people.*
>
> 'Je veux' is the <u>first verb</u> in the sentence — it's in the <u>first person singular</u> form of the present tense. Because '<u>aider</u>' comes <u>directly after</u> 'je veux', it's in the <u>infinitive</u> form.

2) Some <u>verbs</u> can be followed <u>directly</u> by an <u>infinitive</u>, but a few verbs need a <u>preposition</u> in between.

commencer à	*to begin*	essayer de	*to try*
réussir à	*to succeed*	décider de	*to decide*
apprendre à	*to learn*	(s')arrêter de	*to stop (oneself)*
arriver à	*to succeed in / to manage*	menacer de	*to threaten*

When 'venir de' is followed by an infinitive, its definition changes — it means 'to have just done something'.

'Arriver <u>à</u>' + an <u>infinitive</u> means 'to succeed' in doing something.

> J'essaie de faire plus de sport.   *I'm trying to do more sport.*

> J'apprends à conduire la voiture de mon père.   *I'm learning to drive my dad's car.*

'Depuis' can be used with the present tense

For when to use the imperfect with 'depuis', see p.130.

1) 'Depuis' means '<u>since</u>' or '<u>for</u>' (see p.120).

2) If the <u>action</u> you're talking about is <u>still going on</u> today, use the <u>present tense</u>.

> Il habite à Belfast depuis 1997.   *He's lived in Belfast since 1997.*

Even though the action began in the past, the person is still living in Belfast — so you need the present tense.

> Je travaille comme serveur depuis six mois.   *I've worked as a waiter for six months.*

Swap your subject and verb to form a question

Look at p.4-5 for more on how to ask questions.

1) To form a <u>question</u>, invert (or swap over) the <u>subject pronoun</u> and the <u>verb</u>.

2) When you do this, you <u>always</u> need to add a <u>hyphen</u> (-) between the <u>verb</u> and <u>subject pronoun</u>.

If the last letter of the verb and the first letter of the subject pronoun are both vowels, separate them by adding a 't'. This just makes it easier to pronounce — the 't' doesn't mean anything.

> Elle a mal au ventre. ⟹ A-t-elle mal au ventre?
>
> *She has a stomach ache.* ⟹ *Has she got a stomach ache?*

Remember that questions are important for your speaking exam...

Translate these sentences into **French**. Make sure you invert the subject and the verb for the questions.

1. I'm starting to understand. **3.** I've been studying French for 2 years. **5.** Do you like plums?

2. I want to eat some pizza. **4.** I've played football since 1999. **6.** Do you play the piano?

Quick Questions

It's essential you know how to use the present tense, so grab some paper and work through the questions below. Watch out for any irregular verbs — don't let them trip you up.

Quick Questions

1) How would you say the following in French?
   a) I speak   b) you listen   c) we play   d) they hate   e) he listens

2) Write out the correct form of each verb in the present tense. Make sure it matches the subject.
   a) agir — tu ....   f) punir — elles ....
   b) acheter — vous ....   g) battre — on ....
   c) finir — je ....   h) attendre — vous ....
   d) choisir — ils ....   i) mordre — elle ....
   e) partager — vous ....   j) vendre — je ....

3) Complete the following sentences by adding the correct verb endings in the present tense.
   a) Il rest...... à la maison. Il regard...... le match de rugby à la télé.
   b) Nous habit...... au troisième étage. Tu mont...... par l'escalier ou par l'ascenseur.
   c) Je mang...... des sandwichs tous les jours à midi. Mes amis mang...... à la cantine.
   d) Vous parl...... à votre amie au téléphone. Elle te donn...... de ses nouvelles.

4) Fill in the gaps in the following sentences with the correct form of the verb in brackets.
   a) Il .... du thé.   (boire)   d) Vous .... la porte.   (ouvrir)
   b) Ils .... toujours ça. (dire)   e) Elle .... la fenêtre.   (fermer)
   c) Je .... un journal.   (lire)   f) Nous .... sauter haut. (pouvoir)

5) Write in the present tense forms of the verbs below. Some are irregular.
   a) je .... **faire**   f) il / elle / on .... **faire**
   b) tu .... **aller**   g) nous .... **aller**
   c) il / elle / on .... **vouloir**   h) vous .... **vouloir**
   d) nous .... **devoir**   i) ils / elles .... **devoir**
   e) vous .... **faire**   j) je .... **aller**

6) Fill in the gaps in the following sentences with the correct present tense form of être.
   a) Nous .... heureux.   d) Vous .... anglais.
   b) Mon père .... ingénieur.   e) Je .... fatigué.
   c) Les devoirs .... ennuyeux.   f) Elle .... belle.

7) Translate these sentences into French using 'arriver à', 'commencer à' or 'apprendre à.'
   a) I'm learning to play the guitar.   c) It is starting to rain.
   b) I never manage to eat my breakfast.   d) I always manage to do my homework.

8) Write the correct form of the present tense of 'avoir' in the gaps.
   a) je ....   c) il / elle ....   e) vous ....
   b) tu ....   d) nous ....   f) ils / elles ....

9) Rearrange these statements to form questions.
   a) Elle mange de la viande.   d) Elle a un petit ami.
   b) Tu vas en ville ce matin.   e) Vous savez parler chinois.
   c) Il aime le chocolat.   f) Nous devons partir bientôt.

Talking About the Future

You need to be able to talk about things that'll happen in the future, too. Don't worry — there are no crystal balls involved, just some good old-fashioned verb conjugations. Everything you need to know is on this page.

Use 'I'm going' + infinitive

The immediate future is the easiest future tense — it uses the present tense form of 'aller' and an infinitive.

| je vais (*I am going*)
This is the present tense of 'aller'
(see p.123). You change this to
say 'you are going', 'he is going' etc. | **+** | danser (*to dance*)
The next verb goes in the
infinitive (see p.122). | **=** | Je vais danser.
(*I am going to dance.*)
A sentence about the future. |

| Il va déménager la semaine prochaine. | *He's going to move house next week.* |

| La forêt et ses animaux vont disparaître. | *The forest and its wildlife are going to disappear.* |

'I will' — the proper future tense

1) Using the proper future tense in French is the same as saying 'will' in English, e.g. 'I will bake'.

2) To form the future tense, you need find the verb's infinitive (see p.122) and add on the correct endings. The endings are the same for all verbs:

Future tense endings

I	je	-ai		we	nous	-ons
you (inf. sing.)	tu	-as		you (pl., formal)	vous	-ez
he/she/it/one	il/elle/on	-a		they (m/f)	ils/elles	-ont

These endings might look familiar because they're similar to the present tense of 'avoir'.

3) Verbs ending in '-re' are a bit different — you drop the final '-e' from the infinitive to get the stem.

Verb	Stem
regarder (*to look*)	regarder-
finir (*to finish*)	finir-
vendre (*to sell*)	vendr-

| je regarderai | *I will look* |

| il finira | *he will finish* |

| Ils vendront les fruits. | *They will sell the fruit.* |

Some important verbs have irregular stems

Some important verbs are irregular in the future tense — their stems aren't in the infinitive form:

Verb	Stem	Verb	Stem	Verb	Stem	Verb	Stem	Verb	Stem
aller	ir-	*avoir*	aur-	*venir*	viendr-	*voir*	verr-	*pouvoir*	pourr-
être	ser-	*faire*	fer-	*vouloir*	voudr-	*devoir*	devr-	*recevoir*	recev-

The stems are the only irregular part of these verbs — they all use the normal endings listed above.

You will need to use the future tense to access the highest marks...

Put each of these present tense phrases into the immediate and proper future tenses.

1. il va	**3.** nous finissons	**5.** elles disent	**7.** tu peux	**9.** ils sont
2. j'ai	**4.** tu regardes	**6.** vous faites	**8.** elle vient	**10.** on vend

Talking About the Past

Now you've got the hang of the present and future, it's time to look at the past — that's if you can remember what life was like before revision, of course. The perfect tense can be tricky, so read carefully.

Use the perfect tense for completed actions

1) Use the <u>perfect tense</u> to describe an action that <u>happened</u> and <u>finished</u> in the <u>past</u>.

2) In French, it has <u>three</u> parts — a <u>subject</u>, the <u>present tense</u> of '<u>avoir</u>' or '<u>être</u>' and a <u>past participle</u>.

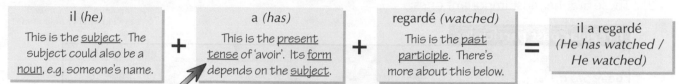

il *(he)*		a *(has)*		regardé *(watched)*		il a regardé
This is the <u>subject</u>. The subject could also be a <u>noun</u>, e.g. someone's name.	**+**	This is the <u>present tense</u> of 'avoir'. Its <u>form</u> depends on the <u>subject</u>.	**+**	This is the <u>past participle</u>. There's more about this below.	**=**	*(He has watched / He watched)*

3) You don't always need the 'have' part in English, but you <u>must</u> have it in French.

Most verbs use 'avoir' in the perfect tense

1) Use the <u>present tense</u> of '<u>avoir</u>' to make the '<u>have</u>' part of the perfect tense:

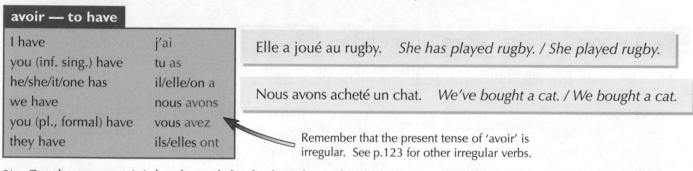

avoir — to have	
I have	j'ai
you (inf. sing.) have	tu as
he/she/it/one has	il/elle/on a
we have	nous avons
you (pl., formal) have	vous avez
they have	ils/elles ont

Elle a joué au rugby. *She has played rugby. / She played rugby.*

Nous avons acheté un chat. *We've bought a cat. / We bought a cat.*

Remember that the present tense of 'avoir' is irregular. See p.123 for other irregular verbs.

2) Get the <u>past participle</u> of a verb by finding the verb's <u>stem</u> (see p.122) and adding on the <u>correct ending</u>.

3) Verbs ending in '<u>-er</u>', '<u>-ir</u>' and '<u>-re</u>' each have a <u>different</u> ending:

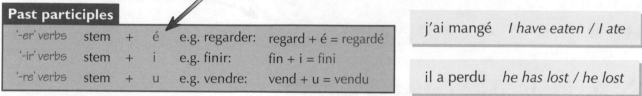

Past participles					
'-er' verbs	stem	+	é	e.g. regarder:	regard + é = regardé
'-ir' verbs	stem	+	i	e.g. finir:	fin + i = fini
'-re' verbs	stem	+	u	e.g. vendre:	vend + u = vendu

j'ai mangé *I have eaten / I ate*

il a perdu *he has lost / he lost*

Past participles agree with some direct objects

1) Past participles taking '<u>avoir</u>' only <u>change form</u> if there's a <u>direct object</u> or <u>direct object pronoun</u> (see p.114) <u>before</u> the verb.

2) When this happens, the <u>past participle</u> acts a bit like an adjective and <u>agrees</u> in <u>gender</u> and <u>number</u>.

Les voix (f) que j'ai entendues. *The voices that I heard.*

The object comes before the verb, so the verb needs to agree with it. 'Voix' is feminine and plural, so 'entendues' has an 'e' and an 's' on the end.

Don't move on until you're confident forming the perfect tense...

Change these phrases from the present to the perfect tense.

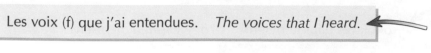

1. je parle   **3.** nous finissons   **5.** on grandit   **7.** je réponds

2. il élargit   **4.** tu vends   **6.** elles mangent   **8.** vous cherchez

Perfect Tense	# Talking About the Past

That's the easiest bit done and dusted. Now it's time to sit up straight, roll up your sleeves and discover why the perfect tense isn't so perfect after all. It's nothing you can't handle — just take it one step at a time.

'Vivre' becomes 'vécu'

1) Some really important verbs have <u>irregular past participles</u>. This means that they <u>don't use</u> the same endings as regular verbs (see p.127).

> Look out for the past participle of 'être' — it's spelt exactly the same way as the noun 'été' (*summer*).

2) These are the most important ones:

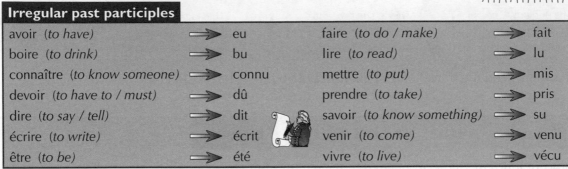

Irregular past participles

avoir (*to have*)	⟹ eu	faire (*to do / make*)	⟹ fait
boire (*to drink*)	⟹ bu	lire (*to read*)	⟹ lu
connaître (*to know someone*)	⟹ connu	mettre (*to put*)	⟹ mis
devoir (*to have to / must*)	⟹ dû	prendre (*to take*)	⟹ pris
dire (*to say / tell*)	⟹ dit	savoir (*to know something*)	⟹ su
écrire (*to write*)	⟹ écrit	venir (*to come*)	⟹ venu
être (*to be*)	⟹ été	vivre (*to live*)	⟹ vécu

Some verbs take 'être' instead of 'avoir'

> To see how the present tense of 'être' is formed, see p.123.

1) A few verbs use '<u>être</u>' instead of '<u>avoir</u>' to form the <u>perfect tense</u>.

aller	*to go*	partir	*to leave*	naître	*to be born*	tomber	*to fall*
venir	*to come*	sortir	*to go out*	mourir	*to die*	retourner	*to return*
revenir	*to come back*	descendre	*to go down*	devenir	*to become*	entrer	*to go in*
arriver	*to arrive*	monter	*to go up*	rester	*to stay*	rentrer	*to go back*

2) Just like '<u>avoir</u>' verbs, the correct <u>present tense form</u> of '<u>être</u>' is needed.

Luc est allé à l'épicerie.	*Luc went to the grocer's.*	Il s'est habillé.	*He got dressed.*

> All reflexive verbs (see p.133) take 'être' in the perfect tense.

Verbs that take 'être' have to agree

1) <u>All verbs</u> that take '<u>être</u>' in the perfect tense <u>have to agree</u> with their <u>subject</u>.

2) The <u>past participle</u> gains an '<u>s</u>' if the subject is <u>plural</u>, an '<u>e</u>' if it's <u>feminine</u> and '<u>es</u>' if it's <u>feminine and plural</u>.

> When a **reflexive verb** is in the **perfect tense**, the present tense of 'être' always goes between the reflexive pronoun and the past participle.

Les filles sont parties il y a une heure.	*The girls left an hour ago.*
Ils se sont lavés dans la rivière.	*They washed themselves in the river.*

It's vital you know which verbs take 'être' and which take 'avoir'...

Translate these phrases into **French**. Remember to check if they take 'être' or 'avoir'.

1. they (fem.) put
2. we've read
3. you (sing.) said
4. I went
5. she arrived
6. we had to
7. they (masc.) returned
8. I washed myself

Talking About the Past

Like English, French has more than one past tense — time is a complicated notion, after all. The imperfect tense is really useful though, and dead easy to form. Once you've got the hang of it, you won't look back.

Get the stem from the present tense 'nous' form

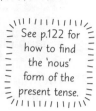

The only verb that's irregular in the imperfect tense is 'être' (see below).

1) To form the <u>imperfect tense</u>, you have to find <u>the stem</u> of the verb you want and <u>add on</u> the correct <u>ending</u>.

2) To get the <u>stem</u>, find the <u>present tense 'nous' form</u> of the verb and <u>take off</u> the '<u>-ons</u>'.

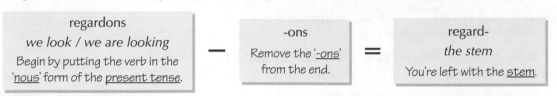

regardons		-ons		regard-
we look / we are looking				*the stem*
Begin by putting the verb in the 'nous' form of the present tense.	**−**	Remove the '-ons' from the end.	**=**	You're left with the stem.

See p.122 for how to find the 'nous' form of the present tense.

3) When you've got the stem, <u>add on</u> the <u>ending</u> you need. The endings are <u>the same</u> for <u>all</u> verbs:

Imperfect tense endings		
I	je	-ais
you (inf. sing.)	tu	-ais
he/she/it/one	il/elle/on	-ait
we	nous	-ions
you (pl., formal)	vous	-iez
they (m/f)	ils/elles	-aient

Verb	Stem	Imperfect form	
aller	all-	j'	allais
attendre	attend-	tu	attendais
venir	ven-	il/elle/on	venait
faire	fais-	nous	faisions
parler	parl-	vous	parliez
avoir	av-	ils/elles	avaient

'Être', 'avoir' and 'faire' crop up a lot

1) Some verbs crop up more than others, so it's a good idea to become <u>really familiar</u> with them.

2) '<u>Être</u>' is <u>irregular</u> in the <u>imperfect tense</u> — its stem is '<u>ét-</u>'. It uses the regular endings, though:

être (to be)		
I	j'	étais
you (inf. sing.)	tu	étais
he/she/it/one	il/elle/on	était
we	nous	étions
you (pl., formal)	vous	étiez
they (m/f)	ils/elles	étaient

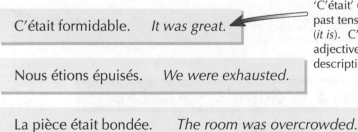

C'était formidable.   *It was great.*

'C'était' (*it was*) is the past tense of 'c'est' (*it is*). C'était + an adjective is useful for descriptions.

Nous étions épuisés.   *We were exhausted.*

La pièce était bondée.   *The room was overcrowded.*

3) All the other verbs are <u>regular</u> — they form the imperfect tense following the <u>normal rules</u>.

4) Make sure you learn '<u>avoir</u>' and '<u>faire</u>' inside out. They're used in lots of handy phrases.

Il y avait...   *There was... / There were...*

Il faisait froid.   *It was cold.*

You need to be able to form the imperfect tense...

These phrases are a mixture of the imperfect and present tense. List all of the phrases that are in the imperfect.

1. nous venions
2. j'attends
3. elle faisait
4. vous veniez
5. j'ai
6. nous remplissons
7. elles vendent
8. tu étais

Imperfect Tense

Talking About the Past

Now you know how to form the imperfect tense, it's a good idea to learn when to use it.

Use the imperfect for descriptions in the past

1) Use the imperfect tense to describe something or someone in the past.

| Il était une heure. | *It was one o'clock.* |

| Il faisait chaud. | It was hot. |

| Yann était heureux de la voir. | *Yann was happy to see her.* |

2) The imperfect tense also describes an action that 'was happening' in the past. It's different to the perfect tense (see p.127) because the action isn't complete.

| J'attendais le train. | *I was waiting for the train.* |

The person hadn't finished waiting for the train, so the action is incomplete.

| Il parlait à l'avocat. | *He was talking to the lawyer.* |

Imperfect	Perfect
I was going	I went
she was running	she ran
we were waiting	we waited

3) When one action interrupts another action in a past tense sentence, the first action is left unfinished. This means that it needs to be in the imperfect tense.

| Je lisais quand le téléphone a sonné. | *I was reading when the telephone rang.* |

The second action is in the perfect tense.

Use the imperfect for what used to happen

You can use the imperfect for something you used to do regularly, or something you used to do in general.

You also use the imperfect tense to talk about what you used to do.

| J'allais au cinéma tous les jeudis. | *I used to go to the cinema every Thursday.* |

This verb is describing someone.

| Quand j'avais dix ans, je jouais de la guitare. | *When I was ten, I used to play the guitar.* |

Imperfect + 'depuis' — had been

See p.124 for when to use 'depuis' with the present tense.

'Depuis' means 'for' or 'since' (see p.120). In French, when you want to say that something 'had been' happening 'for' or 'since' a certain time, use the imperfect tense with 'depuis'.

This could also mean 'It had been raining since two o'clock.'

| Il pleuvait depuis deux heures. | *It had been raining for two hours.* |

| Il attendait depuis six heures du matin. | *He had been waiting since six o'clock in the morning.* |

Learn the difference between the perfect and imperfect tenses...

Decide whether the verbs below should be in the perfect or the imperfect tense, then translate each sentence.

1. I ran.   **3.** You (sing.) were laughing.   **5.** It was terrifying.   **7.** I used to play basketball.
2. They have eaten.   **4.** He was annoying.   **6.** She cried.   **8.** I was tidying up when she arrived.

Quick Questions

Here's a double helping of questions about tenses. Remember — talking about what happened yesterday and what will happen tomorrow is just as important as talking about what's happening right now...

Quick Questions

1) Give the immediate future tense of these verbs, matching the person given.
   a) choisir — je   ....
   b) manger — tu   ....
   c) finir — ils   ....
   d) prendre — vous   ....

2) Give the future tense forms of these verbs.
   a) arriver — elles   ....
   b) danser — on   ....
   c) jouer — il   ....
   d) vendre — nous   ....

3) Fill the gaps with the future tense forms of the verbs in brackets.
   a) Vous .... s'il est permis d'amener les chiens.   (ask)
   b) Je te .... toutes les informations.   (give)
   c) Ils .... un article pour le magazine.   (write)
   d) Je .... par raconter une histoire amusante.   (finish)
   e) On .... un bruit très fort.   (hear)

4) What do these mean in English...?
   a) j'irai
   b) nous serons
   c) vous pourrez
   d) ils diront
   e) il devra
   f) elle voudra
   g) tu auras
   h) je ferai

5) Put these verbs into the perfect tense using the correct form of 'avoir' and the past participle.
   a) je (jouer)
   b) tu (vendre)
   c) vous (regarder)
   d) elles (dormir)
   e) il (écouter)
   f) je (manger)
   g) nous (finir)
   h) on (choisir)

6) Write down the past participle of each of these verbs.
   a) lire   ....
   b) avoir   ....
   c) être   ....
   d) mourir   ....
   e) craindre   ....
   f) devoir   ....
   g) conduire   ....
   h) mettre   ....
   i) prendre   ....
   j) vouloir   ....
   k) savoir   ....
   l) naître   ....

7) Put the verbs in brackets in these sentences into the past tense. Make sure you use the correct verb ('avoir' or 'être'), and make any necessary agreements.
   a) Hier soir mon frère (sortir) avec ses amis et il (rentrer) très tard.
   b) Je (vouloir) te téléphoner mais je (devoir) faire mes devoirs.
   c) Le film (finir) à huit heures, donc nous (pouvoir) en voir un autre.
   d) Quand vous (aller) à la discothèque, est-ce que vous (mettre) votre robe rouge?

8) Add the agreements to the past participles of the 'être' verbs below.
   a) Vous (masc. plural) êtes né...... pendant que votre père regardait le football.
   b) Elle est parti...... quand elle a entendu la voix de son copain.
   c) Elles sont entré...... dans une pièce qui était pleine de poissons morts.
   d) Il est venu...... me voir samedi après-midi.

132

Quick Questions

Quick Questions

9) Fill in the gaps in these sentences with the perfect tense of the irregular verb in brackets.
   a) Il .... le nouveau roman de son écrivain préféré.   (lire)
   b) Tu .... la tasse sur la table.   (mettre)
   c) Les parents .... une carte postale à leurs enfants.   (écrire)
   d) Vous .... en France.   (vivre)

10) Put these verbs into the perfect tense using the correct form of 'être' and the past participle.
   a) je (aller)   c) elle (sortir)   e) nous (monter)   g) tu (tomber)
   b) vous (devenir)   d) il (arriver)   f) ils (partir)   h) elle (entrer)

11) Turn these present tense sentences into the imperfect tense.
   a) Il y a un concert au théâtre.
   b) C'est trop facile.
   c) Dans ma chambre, il y a un lit et une armoire.

12) Write the correct form of 'faire', 'être' or 'avoir' in the imperfect tense.
   a) Les moutons .... du bruit au centre-ville.
   b) Nous .... bronzées après nos vacances.
   c) Tu .... la grippe.
   d) Tu .... très content de recevoir le paquet.
   e) Je .... la vaisselle avec mes doigts de pied.
   f) J' .... un melon et une courgette.

13) Put the verbs in brackets into the imperfect tense.
   a) je (dormir)   c) il (sembler)   e) vous (écouter)
   b) ils (finir)   d) tu (devoir)   f) nous (rester)

14) In each of these sentences there are two verbs. Put the one describing the key event into the perfect tense and the one describing the ongoing situation into the imperfect tense.
   a) Susie (téléphoner) pendant que tu (faire) tes devoirs.
   b) Je (manger) tout le gâteau pendant que ma mère (regarder) la télévision.
   c) Il (se casser) la jambe pendant que nous (jouer) au rugby.
   d) Pendant que vous (ranger) votre chambre, je (prendre) une douche.

15) Translate these sentences into English. Write them all as 'was / were ...ing'.
   a) Je regardais la télévision.   c) Nous attendions le facteur.
   b) Elle dansait dans la salle à manger.   d) Ils faisaient beaucoup de bruit.

16) Translate these sentences into English. Write them all as 'used to ...'.
   a) Je jouais du piano.   d) Tu croyais au père Noël.
   b) On allait au parc tous les jours.   e) Vous achetiez le journal.
   c) Nous regardions les actualités.   f) Il mangeait des haricots verts.

Reflexive Verbs and Pronouns

It's time to say goodbye to tenses and hello to reflexive verbs and pronouns. Lots of people get put off by the sight of these, but they're actually really simple — you just need to know a few rules.

Reflexive verbs have an extra part

Reflexive pronouns	
myself	me
yourself (inf. sing.)	te
himself/herself/itself/oneself	se
ourselves	nous
yourselves (pl., formal)	vous
themselves, each other (m/f)	se

1) <u>Reflexive verbs</u> describe <u>actions</u> that you do <u>to yourself</u>, like washing yourself or getting yourself up.

2) These verbs look different because they've got an <u>extra part</u> — a <u>pronoun</u> that means '<u>self</u>', e.g. 'se laver' (*to wash oneself*). The pronoun <u>changes</u> <u>form</u> depending on <u>who's doing</u> the action.

You can tell which verbs are reflexive by checking in the dictionary. If you look up 'to get up', it'll say 'se lever'.

Je me lave — I wash myself / have a wash

1) Reflexive verbs can end in '<u>-er</u>', '<u>-ir</u>' or '<u>-re</u>'. They form <u>tenses</u> in exactly the <u>same way</u> as other verbs:

For the present, imperfect and proper future tenses, the reflexive pronoun always goes between the subject and the verb.

se laver — to wash oneself			
I wash myself	je me lave	*one washes oneself*	on se lave
you (inf. sing.) wash yourself	tu te laves	*we wash ourselves*	nous nous lavons
he washes himself	il se lave	*you (pl., formal) wash yourselves*	vous vous lavez
she washes herself	elle se lave	*they wash themselves*	ils/elles se lavent

2) Reflexive verbs are really important — you'll need to use them to talk about your <u>hobbies</u> and your <u>daily routine</u>. Make sure you learn these useful examples:

se lever	*to get up*	se détendre	*to relax*	s'appeler	*to be called*
se coucher	*to go to bed*	se sentir	*to feel*	se plaindre	*to complain*
s'intéresser à	*to be interested in*	se disputer	*to argue*	s'amuser	*to enjoy oneself*

Reflexives keep their pronouns in all tenses

1) All reflexive verbs take '<u>être</u>' in the <u>perfect tense</u> — this means they <u>agree</u> with their <u>subject</u> (see p.128).

2) The <u>reflexive pronoun</u> (me, te, se, etc.) always goes between the <u>subject</u> and the <u>present tense</u> of '<u>être</u>'.

Je me suis levé(e) à sept heures ce matin.
I got up at seven o'clock this morning.

Elle s'est lavée.
She washed herself.

'Lavée' has an 'e' on the end here because its subject (elle) is feminine.

3) In the <u>immediate future tense</u> (see p.126), the reflexive <u>infinitive</u> needs the <u>pronoun</u> that <u>matches its subject</u>.

Je vais me coucher. *I'm going to go to bed.*

Ils vont se plaindre. *They're going to complain.*

Learn to express yourself with reflexive verbs...

Translate these phrases into **French**. Make sure you put the reflexive pronouns in the right places.

1. we're going to bed
2. you (pl.) argue
3. they (fem.) get up
4. he's interested in
5. you (sing.) enjoyed yourself
6. I'm going to relax
7. she felt
8. we're going to complain

Negative Forms

You've reached the page where you can grumble and moan. Take all your stress out on two of the most important French words ever — 'ne' and 'pas'. (Don't worry — they're only little but they can take it.)

'ne...pas' — not

1) In English, you change a sentence to mean the opposite by adding 'not'. In French, you add two words — 'ne' and 'pas'. They go either side of the verb.

> je suis d'accord ⟹ je ne suis pas d'accord
> I agree ⟹ I do not agree

'Suis' is the verb. The 'ne' goes before it, and the 'pas' goes after it.

2) For verbs in the perfect tense (see p.127-128), put the 'ne' and 'pas' around the bit of 'avoir' or 'être'.

> Je n'ai pas aimé l'école primaire.
> I did not like the primary school.

> Elle n'est pas encore arrivée.
> She hasn't arrived yet.

To say 'not yet', add the word 'encore' directly after the 'pas' in a normal negative sentence.

3) To make an infinitive negative, put the 'ne' and the 'pas' in front of it.

> Elle préfère ne pas parler de son talent.   She prefers not to talk about her talent.

'ne...jamais' — never

There are other negatives that work in the same way as 'ne...pas'. Here are some of the most common ones:

ne...jamais	never	ne...personne	nobody / anyone
ne...rien	nothing	ne...ni...ni	neither...nor
ne...plus	no more / no longer	ne...que	only / nothing but

These negatives position themselves around the verb in the same way as 'ne...pas'.

> Je ne vais plus à York.
> I don't go to York any more.

> Je ne vais jamais à York.
> I never go to York.

> Je ne vais ni à York ni à Belfast.
> I neither go to York nor Belfast.

> Il n'y a rien ici.
> There's nothing here.

> Je n'en ai plus.
> I don't have any more of them.

'Y' and 'en' always go between the 'ne' and the verb.

Articles change to 'de' after a negative

After a negative, indefinite articles ('un / une') and partitives ('du', 'de la', 'des' — see p.100) usually become 'de'.

> Elle n'a plus de pain.   She doesn't have any more bread.

'Ne...que' doesn't follow this rule — it keeps its articles. E.g. 'Je n'ai que du café.' (I only have coffee.)

The 'de' is only shortened if the next word begins with a vowel or an 'h' which takes 'l'. E.g. 'd'animaux', 'd'hôpital'.

> Je ne veux pas d'argent.   I don't want any money.

This page should help you feel more positive about being negative...

Translate these sentences into **French** using the negative phrases you've learnt on this page.

1. I never eat meat.
2. He doesn't have a dog.
3. You (sing.) only drink water.
4. They (masc.) don't like anyone.
5. We don't live together any more.
6. You (pl.) never go there.

Would, Could and Should

The conditional is a bit of a mish-mash of different tenses. On the plus side, you already know half of it...

The conditional = future stem + imperfect endings

1) The <u>conditional</u> is where you'd say '<u>would</u>', '<u>could</u>' or '<u>should</u>' in English.

2) Forming the conditional is pretty straightforward — you take the verb's <u>stem</u> from the <u>future tense</u> and add on the <u>endings</u> you learnt for the <u>imperfect tense</u>.

> Be careful — the imperfect 'je' ending ('-ais') sounds just like the future 'je' ending ('-ai'). This can make the future and conditional tenses tricky to tell apart.

je regarderai
(I will look)
This is the first person singular <u>future tense</u> of 'regarder' (see p.126). The verb is <u>regular</u>, so its stem is its <u>infinitive</u> — '<u>regarder</u>'.

+

je regardais
(I was looking)
This is the first person singular <u>imperfect tense</u> of 'regarder' (see p.129). Its ending is '<u>-ais</u>'.

=

je regarderais
(I would look)
This is the first person singular <u>conditional</u> of 'regarder'.

> Remember that '-re' verbs drop the '-e' off their infinitive to get their future / conditional stem.

Verb	Future stem	Imperfect ending	Conditional
manger (to eat)	je mangerai	je mangeais	je mangerais *(I would eat)*
finir (to finish)	je finirai	je finissais	je finirais *(I would finish)*
vendre (to sell)	je vendrai	je vendais	je vendrais *(I would sell)*
être (to be)	je serai	j'étais	je serais *(I would be)*

Some verbs, like 'être', have irregular stems (see p.126).

3) '<u>Si</u>' + <u>the imperfect tense</u> is always followed by a verb in the <u>conditional</u>.

> Si j'étais riche, je voyagerais autour du monde.   *If I was rich, I'd travel around the world.*

4) To say '<u>could</u>' in French, use the conditional form of '<u>pouvoir</u>' (*to be able to*) followed by <u>an infinitive</u>. To say '<u>should</u>', use the conditional form of '<u>devoir</u>' (*to have to*) followed by <u>an infinitive</u>.

> Elle pourrait aller en France.   *She could go to France.*

> Tu devrais te plaindre.   *You should complain.*

'Je voudrais' and 'j'aimerais' — I would like

These two verbs are really useful in the <u>conditional</u> — you can use them lots in your <u>speaking assessment</u>:

vouloir (to want)	
I would like	je voudrais
you (inf. sing.) would like	tu voudrais
he/she/it/one would like	il/elle/on voudrait
we would like	nous voudrions
you (pl., formal) would like	vous voudriez
they (m/f) would like	ils/elles voudraient

> Both of these verbs are often followed by an infinitive. Look at p.124 for more on infinitives.

aimer (to like)	
I would like	j'aimerais
you (inf. sing.) would like	tu aimerais
he/she/it/one would like	il/elle/on aimerait
we would like	nous aimerions
you (pl., formal) would like	vous aimeriez
they (m/f) would like	ils/elles aimeraient

> Je voudrais aller à l'hôpital.   *I'd like to go to the hospital.*

> J'aimerais du lait.   *I would like some milk.*

The examiner would like to see that you can use the conditional...

Put these verbs into the conditional. The subject has been given to you in brackets.

1. améliorer (tu)
2. élargir (il)
3. rendre (nous)
4. faire (je)
5. aller (elles)
6. venir (vous)
7. être (on)
8. avoir (elle)
9. se laver (ils)
10. chercher (vous)

| Imperative | **Giving Orders** |

Learning to order other people about is a pretty important life skill, whatever language you're speaking in. Putting verbs in their imperative lets you do just that — it's really useful and very easy to form.

Imperatives use the present tense

1) <u>Imperatives</u> are words that give an <u>order</u>. They tell someone <u>to do something</u>, or <u>suggest</u> doing something together, e.g. 'sit down' or 'let's eat'.

For when to choose 'tu' or 'vous', see p.112

2) In French, imperatives are formed using the <u>present tense</u> of the '<u>tu</u>', '<u>nous</u>' and <u>vous</u>' parts of a verb:

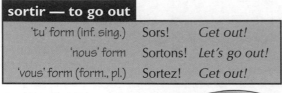

sortir — to go out		
'tu' form (inf. sing.)	Sors!	*Get out!*
'nous' form	Sortons!	*Let's go out!*
'vous' form (form., pl.)	Sortez!	*Get out!*

'Tu', 'nous' and 'vous' never appear with an imperative verb — otherwise they would be in the present tense.

Vendons la voiture! | *Let's sell the car!*

The 'nous' form always means 'let's'. The action has to involve you and someone else.

Écoutez ceci! | *Listen to this!*

Take off the '-s' from the 'tu' form of '-er' verbs

Regular '-er' verbs in the 'tu' form of the present tense normally end in '-es', e.g. 'tu parles'.

1) Watch out for '<u>tu</u>' forms that <u>end</u> in '<u>-es</u>' — you have to <u>lose</u> the <u>final '-s</u>' from the <u>present tense</u>. This means you have to be careful with <u>regular '-er'</u> verbs.

Arrête de me parler! | *Stop talking to me!*

Regarde Jean-Paul! | *Look at Jean-Paul!*

2) Some verbs have <u>irregular</u> imperatives. They're nothing like the present tense, so you have to <u>learn</u> them.

Imperative form	être — to be	avoir — to have	savoir — to know	aller — to go
tu (*you inf. sing.*)	sois	aie	sache	va
nous (*we*)	soyons	ayons	sachons	allons
vous (*form., pl.*)	soyez	ayez	sachez	allez

Only the 'tu' form of 'aller' has an irregular imperative.

Negative imperatives use 'ne...pas' normally

1) To make an imperative verb <u>negative</u>, put '<u>ne</u>' <u>before</u> the verb and '<u>pas</u>' <u>after</u> it (see p.134).

Ne vendez pas la voiture! | *Don't sell the car!*

N'écoute pas! | *Don't listen!*

2) Imperative <u>reflexive verbs</u> (see p.133) have an <u>emphatic pronoun</u> (see p.114) that goes <u>after</u> the verb.

Tu te lèves. ⟹ Lève-toi!
You get up. ⟹ *Get up!*

The emphatic pronoun is always joined to the verb by a dash (-).

Tu ne te lèves pas. ⟹ Ne te lève pas!
You don't get up. ⟹ *Don't get up!*

3) When <u>reflexive verbs</u> are <u>imperative</u> and <u>negative</u>, they use their <u>normal pronouns</u> (me, te, etc.). The '<u>ne</u>' goes <u>before</u> the pronoun, and the '<u>pas</u>' goes <u>after</u> the verb.

It's imperative that you learn this page...

Translate these phrases into **French**.

1. Finish your homework! (pl.)
2. Let's organise a party!
3. Listen! (sing.)
4. Let's eat!
5. Don't go! (sing.)
6. Don't run! (pl.)
7. Go to bed! (sing.)
8. Don't argue! (pl.)

Quick Questions

This page covers lots of important grammar points, so don't move on until you can answer each question. After all, knowing how to use negatives and give commands could come in handy...

Quick Questions

1) Fill in the gaps using the correct form of the verb in brackets.
   a) Je .... — j'ai cassé votre vase.   (s'excuser)
   b) Nous .... toujours avec du savon particulier.   (se laver)
   c) Vous .... quand vous jouez au football?   (s'amuser)
   d) Les appartements .... de l'autre côté du supermarché.   (se trouver)
   e) J'ai laissé ma sœur à la maison, parce qu'elle .... mal.   (se sentir)
   f) Mes deux petits frères ne .... jamais de bonne heure.   (se coucher)

2) Add any missing agreements to these reflexive verbs in the perfect tense.
   a) Ce matin, elle s'est levé...... à huit heures.
   b) Les élèves (masc.) se sont excusé...... après le cours.
   c) Il s'est lavé...... trois fois avant son rendez-vous avec la princesse.
   d) Elles se sont amusé...... au marché de Noël.

3) Rewrite these sentences to make them negative.
   a) Je mange de la viande.   c) Tu as beaucoup d'argent.
   b) Elle aime faire les courses.   d) Nous allons au cinéma ce soir.

4) Translate these sentences into French.
   a) I eat neither peas nor carrots.   c) We've never been to Russia.
   b) She only wears blue socks.   d) They (fem.) don't speak to anyone.

5) Put the verbs in brackets into the correct conditional form.
   a) Je .... rester à la maison.   (préférer)
   b) Nous .... voir un match de football.   (détester)
   c) Je .... au hockey, si je n'avais pas mal à la jambe.   (jouer)
   d) Ils ont dit qu'ils .... le train cet après-midi.   (prendre)

6) Translate these sentences into French.
   a) I'd go to the cinema, but I don't have enough money.
   b) We would like to help.
   c) You (informal singular) should arrive at 11 o'clock.

7) Put the missing verb into the French sentences. They all need to be in the imperative form.
   a) .... tes légumes ! (manger)   c) .... à la patinoire !   (aller — nous)
   b) .... gentils ! (être — vous) d) .... tes devoirs !   (finir)

8) Change these French sentences into commands.
   a) Tu me prêtes ton stylo.   c) Vous vous taisez.   e) Vous vous asseyez.
   b) Tu te couches.   d) Tu t'assieds.   f) Nous nous levons.

9) Make these commands negative.
   a) Sors !   b) Allons à la piscine !   c) Couche-toi !   d) Lève-toi !

Pluperfect, Present Participle, Perfect Infinitive	'Had done' and '-ing'

It may sound like a made-up tense, but the pluperfect tense is real and you need to know how to use it. It's fairly straightforward, though — plus, you can learn about the present participle once you're done...

J'avais fait — I had done

1) The <u>pluperfect</u> tense is for saying what you <u>had done</u>. It's like the <u>perfect tense</u> — which describes what you <u>have done</u> — but it deals with actions <u>further in the past</u>.

For more about the perfect tense, see p.127-128. For the imperfect tense, look at p.129-130.

2) The pluperfect is made up of the <u>imperfect</u> version of '<u>avoir</u>' or '<u>être</u>' + a <u>past participle</u>.

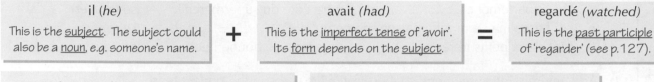

il *(he)*		avait *(had)*		regardé *(watched)*
This is the <u>subject</u>. The subject could also be a <u>noun</u>, e.g. someone's name.	**+**	This is the <u>imperfect tense</u> of 'avoir'. Its <u>form</u> depends on the <u>subject</u>.	**=**	This is the <u>past participle</u> of 'regarder' (see p.127).

J'avais écrit une lettre. *I had written a letter.*	Elles s'étaient disputées. *They had argued.*

Verbs taking 'avoir' don't agree with their subject, but verbs taking 'être' always do.

With reflexive verbs, the word order is exactly the same as it would be for the perfect tense — the reflexive pronoun goes before the bit of 'avoir' or 'être'.

'Doing', 'saying' and 'thinking' are present participles

1) To form the <u>present participle</u>, get the <u>imperfect stem</u> of the verb (see p.129) and add '<u>-ant</u>':

Verb	Imperfect stem	Present participle
regarder	regard-	regardant *(watching)*
finir	finiss-	finissant *(finishing)*
vendre	vend-	vendant *(selling)*
faire	fais-	faisant *(doing / making)*

Careful — to say you're 'doing something', e.g. 'I am laughing', you should use the present tense (see p.122-124). If you use two verbs together, e.g. 'I like writing', you use the present tense with an infinitive (see p.124).

Renonçant à l'idée, Clare est retournée chez elle. Giving up on the idea, Clare returned home.

2) '<u>En</u>' + the <u>present participle</u> usually means '<u>while doing something</u>' or '<u>by doing something</u>'.

Il lit le journal en déjeunant. *He reads the paper whilst having lunch.*

3) Some verbs have <u>irregular stems</u> in the present participle.

Il a réussi en sachant les faits. *He succeeded by knowing the facts.*

Verb	Irregular stem
avoir *(to have)*	ay-
être *(to be)*	ét-
savoir *(to know)*	sach-

Après avoir mangé — After having eaten

'<u>Avoir</u>' / '<u>être</u>' + '<u>past participle</u>' means '<u>having done something</u>'. This is called the <u>perfect infinitive</u>.

Il regrette d'avoir joué au foot. *He regretted having played football.*	Après être arrivées, elles... *After having arrived, they...*

Because 'arriver' takes 'être', it needs to agree with its subject.

After having learnt the page, the student attempted the questions...

Translate the following phrases into **French**.

1. I had played
2. we had argued
3. you (pl.) had arrived
4. they (fem.) had been
5. whilst helping
6. by staying
7. after having left
8. after having destroyed

The Passive

Passive sentences in French are structured just like passive sentences in English, so they're dead easy to recognise. But for that theory to work, you need to know what all this passive stuff is in the first place...

La tasse est cassée — The cup is broken

1) In most sentences, there's a person or thing <u>doing</u> the verb, e.g. '<u>The fly bit</u> the man'. These are <u>active sentences</u>. In a <u>passive</u> sentence, the person or thing has <u>something done to it</u>, e.g. '<u>The man was bitten</u> by the fly'.

2) The <u>present passive</u> is made up of a <u>person</u> or <u>thing</u> followed by the <u>present tense</u> of '<u>être</u>' + a <u>past participle</u>.

> Il est aidé par ses parents.   *He is helped by his parents.*

See p.127-128 for more on past participles.

3) The <u>past participle</u> has to <u>agree</u> with the <u>person</u> or <u>thing</u> that is having the <u>action done to it</u>.

> La télé réalité est regardée par beaucoup de gens.
> *Reality TV is watched by lots of people.*

This is passive — 'reality TV' is having something done to it. 'Regardée' has an 'e' so it agrees with 'la télé'.

In the past and the future, only the 'être' bit changes

1) The passive voice can also be <u>in the past</u> or <u>future</u> tenses. It's formed in <u>the same way</u> as it is in <u>the present</u> — the only thing that changes is <u>the tense</u> of '<u>être</u>'.

2) The <u>perfect passive</u> tells you about a passive event that happened in the <u>past</u>. It's formed using the <u>perfect tense</u> of '<u>être</u>' (see p.128) and a <u>past participle</u>.

> La photo a été prise.   *The photo was taken.*

You don't need to be able to form the passive — you just have to know how to recognise it.

3) The <u>imperfect passive</u> describes a passive action that '<u>was happening</u>'. It's formed using the <u>imperfect tense</u> of 'être' (see p.129) and a <u>past participle</u>.

> Le livre était écrit pendant la guerre.   *The book was being written during the war.*

4) The <u>future passive</u> is made up of the <u>future tense</u> of '<u>être</u>' and a <u>past participle</u>.

> Tu seras puni(e).   *You will be punished.*

> Les déchets seront jetés.   *The rubbish will be thrown away.*

French often uses 'on' instead of the passive

The passive isn't used very much in French. French speakers often use '<u>on</u>' (*one*) with an <u>active sentence</u> instead.

'One didn't see' sounds quite formal in English, so you'd normally use the passive voice instead.

> On n'a pas vu l'homme.   *One didn't see the man. / The man wasn't seen.*

Don't forget — you only need to be able to recognise the passive...

Identify all of the passive sentences in the list below.

1. L'homme est heurté par la voiture.   3. Le match est intéressant.   5. On regarde la télé.
2. La fille perd le ballon.   4. La pomme sera mangée par mon oncle.   6. La tasse a été cassée.

Impersonal Verbs and the Subjunctive

Right, you're almost there now — just one last page until you're granted grammar freedom. The subjunctive is the crème de la crème of French grammar, but luckily you only have to recognise it in the exam.

Impersonal verbs only work with 'il'

1) <u>Impersonal verbs</u> always have '<u>il</u>' as their subject. Here are some common examples:

il faut	*you must / it is necessary to*	il est nécessaire de	*it's necessary to*
il s'agit de	*it's about*	il pleut / neige	*it's raining / snowing*
il semble	*it seems*	il fait chaud / froid	*it's hot / cold*

Il s'agit d'une mère et ses enfants.   *It's about a mother and her children.*

Il semble injuste d'ignorer la décision.   *It seems unfair to ignore the decision.*

You often use impersonal verbs to talk about the weather. For more about the weather, see p.56.

2) '<u>Il faut</u>' and '<u>il est nécessaire de</u>' are always followed by an <u>infinitive</u>:

See p.124 to learn more about infinitives.

Il faut aller au lycée tous les jours.
You must go to school every day.

Il est nécessaire de lutter contre le réchauffement de la Terre.
It's necessary to fight against global warming.

You may see the subjunctive instead of the infinitive

1) The subjunctive <u>doesn't have</u> an <u>equivalent</u> in English. You don't have to use it in your exams, but you do have to be able to <u>recognise common verbs</u> in the subjunctive:

avoir	être	faire	aller	pouvoir
j'aie	je sois	je fasse	j'aille	je puisse
tu aies	tu sois	tu fasses	tu ailles	tu puisses
il/elle/on ait	il/elle/on soit	il/elle/on fasse	il/elle/on aille	il/elle/on puisse
nous ayons	nous soyons	nous fassions	nous allions	nous puissions
vous ayez	vous soyez	vous fassiez	vous alliez	vous puissiez
ils/elles aient	ils/elles soient	ils/elles fassent	ils/elles aillent	ils/elles puissent

The 'tu' and 'vous' forms of 'avoir' in the subjunctive are the same as its imperatives (see p.136). This is true for 'être', as well.

2) Certain expressions need to be followed by the <u>subjunctive</u> rather than the <u>infinitive</u>, e.g. '<u>il faut que</u>'.

Il faut que tu fasses la vaisselle.
You must do the washing up.

Il est nécessaire que vous soyez sages.
It is necessary that you're well behaved.

The subjunctive is often used after 'que'.

3) The subjunctive is also used with certain <u>constructions</u>. '<u>Bien que</u>' (*although*), '<u>avant que</u>' (*before*) and '<u>pour que</u>' (*so that*) are all followed by the subjunctive too.

Bien qu'elle ait deux enfants...
Although she has two children...

Avant que vous partiez...
Before you leave...

Pour qu'il fasse ses devoirs...
So that he does his homework...

If I were you, I'd learn this page...

List all phrases below that contain a verb in the subjunctive.

1. Il faut commencer.   **3.** avant que vous alliez   **5.** Il me semble ridicule.   **7.** le stylo que j'ai

2. Le livre que tu veux.   **4.** bien qu'elles soient   **6.** pour que nous puissions   **8.** bien qu'il puisse

Quick Questions

Congrats on reaching the last page of quick questions. Don't speed through it just because it's at the end — give it the time and attention it deserves. You'll kick yourself if you don't revise properly...

1) Write out the pluperfect forms of the infinitives below, matching the person given.
   a) décrire — il
   b) faire — vous
   c) partir — elles
   d) vivre — il
   e) dire — ils
   f) manquer — tu
   g) aller — nous
   h) manger — je

2) Translate these sentences into English.
   a) J'avais fini.
   b) Mark avait oublié de fermer la fenêtre.
   c) Michelle et Sharon étaient arrivées.
   d) Elle s'était levée à trois heures.
   e) Nous avions perdu la vache.
   f) J'étais parti en voiture.

3) Turn the infinitives below into present participles.
   a) vouloir
   b) donner
   c) acheter
   d) finir
   e) rendre
   f) choisir
   g) perdre
   h) faire
   i) dire
   j) aller
   k) savoir
   l) boire

4) Translate these sentences into English.
   a) Nous nous amusons en lisant des bandes dessinées.
   b) Il reste en forme en jouant au tennis.
   c) Je fais mes devoirs en regardant la télévision.

5) Translate these sentences into French, using the perfect infinitive.
   a) After having made the cake, I ate it.
   b) After having left, he came back.

6) The following sentences are in the passive. Translate them into English.
   a) Elle est renversée par l'escargot.
   b) Je suis regardé par tout le monde au théâtre.
   c) Louis et Carlo étaient punis par leur prof.
   d) Vous avez été trouvés par les pompiers.

7) What do the following phrases mean...?
   a) il faut
   b) il est nécessaire de
   c) il semble
   d) il s'agit de
   e) il neige
   f) il fait chaud

8) Match up the French sentences with the English translations.
   a) Il est étrange de voir ces choses.
   b) Il neige aujourd'hui.
   c) Il est important de porter de vêtements.
   d) Il s'agit d'un homme et d'un chat.
   i) It's snowing today.
   ii) It is important to wear clothes.
   iii) It's about a man and a cat.
   iv) It is strange to see these things.

9) For each of the sentences below, underline the verb in the subjunctive and translate the whole sentence into English.
   a) Il faut que tu viennes — tout le monde sera là !
   b) Il semble qu'ils aient une maladie grave.
   c) Je veux qu'il me dise toute l'histoire.
   d) Il est possible que nous y allions ce soir.

Revision Summary for Section Nine

This section has a lot of information to take in, so practice is the only way to see if you know your stuff. After doing all those quick questions, there shouldn't be anything on this page that can trip you up.

Nouns and Articles (p.99-100) ☑

1) Underline all of the nouns in the following sentences.
   a) Elle aime manger des carottes.
   b) On parle français au Canada.
   c) J'ai reçu un cadeau de Marcel.
   d) Les cochons nagent.
   e) La poste est fermée.
   f) Samantha habite près de mon frère.

2) Write down the definite ('the'), indefinite ('a') and partitive ('some') articles for the following words.
   a) maison
   b) jeux
   c) chien
   d) journal
   e) chaussure
   f) soleil
   g) travail
   h) jeu

Adjectives and Adverbs (p.101-109) ☑

3) Using the word 'vert' with the correct endings, translate these phrases into French.
   a) the green mountain
   b) the green coat
   c) the green eyes
   d) the green apples
   e) the green man
   f) the green grass

4) Translate these sentences into French, using the adverb formed from the adjective in brackets:
   a) He swims well. (bon)
   b) Eleanor sings badly. (mauvais)

Pronouns (p.112-116) ☑

5) Write the correct subject pronouns in the gaps:
   a) Ma souris est malade. .... ne mange rien.
   b) Leur père est infirmier. .... travaille dans un hôpital.
   c) Ses parents sont en vacances. .... rentrent à la maison la semaine prochaine.

Joining Words (p.118) ☑

6) Fill in the gaps with the correct conjunction from the options in brackets:
   a) Je veux me promener, ... il pleut.   (ou, puis, mais)
   b) Il est resté à la maison .... il faisait mauvais.   (ou bien, et, pendant que)
   c) Je bois du chocolat chaud .... il fait froid.   (quand, puis, ou)
   d) J'aime mon cousin .... il est très sympa.   (mais, parce que, ou bien)
   e) Nous allons à l'école .... nous nous amusons.   (puis, si, lorsque)

Different Tenses and the Imperative (p.122-136) ☑

7) What do each of these sentences mean in English? Name the tense used in each one:
   a) Je mange un gâteau.
   b) J'ai mangé un gâteau.
   c) Je mangeais un gâteau.
   d) Je mangerai un gâteau.
   e) J'avais mangé un gâteau.
   f) Je mangerais un gâteau.

8) Change these sentences from the present tense into the imperative.
   a) Tu arrêtes de faire ça.
   b) Nous ne regardons pas le film.
   c) Vous êtes tranquille.
   d) Tu te lèves.
   e) Nous allons au Portugal.

The Passive and the Subjunctive (p.139-140) ☑

9) You hear this headline on the radio: "Un homme a été écrasé par deux chiens géants."
   Rewrite it so it's an active sentence, making sure you don't change the meaning.

10) Final question. What does the following sentence mean?
   "Il faut que tu apprennes toutes les choses dans ce livre avant de le jeter."

The Listening Exam

These pages are crammed full of advice to help you tackle your exams head on, so listen up.

There are four exams for GCSE French

1) Your Edexcel French GCSE is assessed by four separate exams — Listening, Speaking, Reading and Writing.

2) Each exam is worth 25% of your final mark. You'll get a grade between 1 and 9 (with 9 being the highest).

3) You won't sit all of the papers at the same time — you'll probably have your speaking exam a couple of weeks before the rest of your exams.

The Listening Exam has two sections

If you're sitting foundation tier papers, the format of your exams will be slightly different, but this advice will still be useful.

1) For the listening paper, you'll listen to various recordings of people speaking in French and answer questions on what you've heard.

2) The paper is 45 minutes long (including 5 minutes reading time) and is split into Section A and Section B.

3) Section A is the shorter section — the questions will be multiple choice, with the instructions in French. Section B is longer, but the questions are in English and your answers will be, too.

Read through the paper carefully at the start of the test

1) Before the recordings begin, you'll be given five minutes to read through the paper.

2) Use this time to read each question carefully. Some are multiple choice, and others require you to write some short answers — make sure you know what each one is asking you to do.

3) In particular, look at the questions in Section A, which are written in French. Try to work out what the questions mean. There's a list of exam-style French question words and phrases on the inside front cover of this book to help you prepare for this.

4) Reading the question titles, and the questions themselves, will give you a good idea of the topics you'll be asked about. This should help you predict what to listen out for.

5) You can write on the exam paper, so scribble down anything that might be useful.

Make notes while listening to the recordings

1) You'll hear each audio track twice, and then there'll be a pause for you to write down your answer.

2) While you're listening, it's a good idea to jot down a few details — e.g. dates, times, names or key words. But make sure you keep listening while you're writing down any notes.

Listen to the speaker's tone, too — this will hint at their mood, e.g. angry or excited.

3) Listen right to the end, even if you think you've got the answer — sometimes the person will change their mind or add an important detail at the end.

4) Don't worry if you can't understand every word that's being said — just listen carefully both times and try to pick out the vocabulary you need to answer the question.

Don't worry if you don't quite catch the answer...

If you've heard a track twice, and you're still not sure of the answer, scribble one down anyway — you never know, it might be the right one. You may as well write something sensible just in case — it's worth a shot.

The Speaking Exam

The Speaking Exam can seem daunting, but remember — no one is trying to catch you out, so try to stay calm.

There are three parts to the Speaking Exam

During your preparation time, you can make notes to take in with you for the first two tasks. You can't keep the notes for the conversation.

1) Your speaking exam will be conducted and recorded by your teacher.

2) The exam is in three parts. Before you start, you'll get 12 minutes to prepare for the first two sections:

① Role play (~2 min.)	② Picture-based task (~3 min.)	③ Conversation (~6 min.)
You'll get a card with a scenario on it. It'll have five bullet points — two will be notes on what to say, in French. The '!' means you'll be asked an unknown question, and '?' shows you have to ask a question about the words next to it. See p.5 for an example.	Before the exam, you'll receive a photo and five bullet points relating to it (there's an example on p.22 for you to have a look at). Your teacher will ask you questions based on the prompts on the picture card, as well as one question you haven't seen.	You and your teacher will have a conversation. The conversation will have two parts. In the first part, you'll talk about the theme that you've chosen. Then, you'll discuss another theme that hasn't been covered in the second task.

3) The role play card will tell you if you should use 'tu', but otherwise, use 'vous' to talk to your teacher.

Try to be imaginative with your answers

You need to find ways to show off the full extent of your French knowledge. You should try to:

1) Use a range of tenses — e.g. for a question on daily routine, think of when something different happens.

Mais demain ce sera différent car je jouerai au snooker après les cours.	*But tomorrow it will be different because I will play snooker after lessons.*

2) Talk about other people, not just yourself — it's fine to make people up if that helps.

J'aime le foot, mais ma mère le déteste.	*I like football, but my mum hates it.*

If you can't remember a word, just say something suitable that you do know instead, e.g. swap 'snooker' for 'hockey', or 'mum' for 'sister'.

3) Give loads of opinions and reasons for your opinions.

À mon avis, il faut faire plus de recyclage parce qu'on produit trop de déchets.	*In my opinion, we must do more recycling because we produce too much rubbish.*

If you're really struggling, ask for help in French

1) If you get really stuck trying to think of a word or phrase, you can ask for help — as long as it's in French.

2) For example, if you can't remember how to say 'homework' in French, ask your teacher. You won't get any marks for vocabulary your teacher's given you though.

Comment dit-on 'homework' en français?	*How do you say 'homework' in French?*

3) If you don't hear something clearly, just ask:

Pouvez-vous répéter, s'il vous plaît?	*Could you repeat that, please?*

You could also ask this if you're desperately in need of time to think of an answer.

Making mistakes isn't the end of the world...

Don't panic if you make a mistake in the speaking exam — what's important is how you deal with it. You won't lose marks for correcting yourself, so show the examiner that you know where you went wrong.

The Reading Exam

The Reading Exam is split into three parts, so make sure you know what to do for each one.

Read the questions and texts carefully

1) The <u>higher tier</u> reading paper is <u>1 hour long</u>, and has <u>three sections</u>.

2) In Sections A and B, you'll be given a <u>variety of French texts</u> and then asked questions about them. The texts could include blog posts, emails, newspaper reports, adverts and literary texts. <u>Section A</u> has questions and answers <u>in English</u>, and <u>Section B</u> has questions and answers <u>in French</u>.

3) <u>Section C</u> is a <u>translation</u> question — you'll have to translate a short passage of text from French <u>into English</u>. See p.147 for more tips on tackling translation questions.

4) In Sections A and B, <u>scan through the text</u> first to <u>get an idea</u> of what it's about. Then read the <u>questions</u> that go with it carefully, making sure you understand <u>what information</u> you should be looking out for.

5) Next, <u>go back through the text</u>. You're not expected to understand every word, so don't get distracted by trying to work out what everything means — <u>focus</u> on finding the <u>information you need</u>.

The inside front cover of this book has a list of common French question words, phrases and instructions.

Don't give up if you don't understand something

1) Use the <u>context</u> of the text to help you understand what it might be saying. You might be able to find some clues in the <u>title of the text</u> or the <u>type of text</u>.

2) Knowing how to spot <u>different word types</u> (e.g. nouns, verbs) can help you work out what's happening in a sentence. See the <u>grammar section</u> (p.99-142) for more.

3) You can <u>guess</u> some French words that look or sound the <u>same as English</u> words, e.g. le problème — *problem*, la musique — *music*, dangereux — *dangerous*.

Look for words that look like ones you know, e.g. 'le sac de couchage'. 'Le sac' means 'bag', and 'se coucher' means 'to sleep', so you can guess it means 'sleeping bag'.

4) Be careful though — you might come across some '<u>false friends</u>'. These are French words that look like an English word, but have a <u>completely different meaning</u>:

sensible	*sensitive*	mince	*slim*	la journée	*day*	le car	*coach*	les affaires (f)	*things*
grand(e)	*big*	joli(e)	*pretty*	la cave	*cellar*	le médecin	*doctor*	les baskets (f)	*trainers*
large	*wide*	le genre	*type / kind*	la veste	*jacket*	le crayon	*pencil*	attendre	*to wait*

Keep an eye on the time

1) There are quite a few questions to get through in the reading exam, so you need to work at a <u>good speed</u>.

2) If you're having trouble with a particular question, you might want to <u>move on</u> and <u>come back to it later</u>.

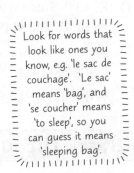

3) Don't forget that the <u>last question</u> in the paper (Section C) is a <u>translation</u> — this is worth <u>more marks</u> than any other question, so you should leave <u>plenty of time</u> to tackle it.

4) Make sure you put an answer down for <u>every question</u> — lots of the questions are multiple choice, so even if you can't work out the answer, it's always worth putting down one of the options.

Familiarise yourself with the structure of the exam...

Don't forget, the questions in Section B will be in French. Don't panic if you don't understand them — search for any familiar vocabulary and use any answer lines or boxes to help you guess what you have to do.

The Writing Exam

The Writing Exam is a great way of showing off what you can do — try to use varied vocabulary, include a range of tenses, and pack in any clever expressions that you've learnt over the years.

There'll be three tasks in the Writing Exam

1) The <u>higher tier</u> writing paper is <u>1 hour and 20 minutes long</u> and has <u>three tasks</u>.

2) Each task is worth a <u>different number of marks</u>, so you should spend more time on the higher-mark tasks.

① Informal writing (20 marks)	② Formal writing (28 marks)	③ Translation (12 marks)
There will be <u>two tasks</u> to choose from. You'll be asked to write <u>about 80-90 words</u> in French, based on <u>four bullet points</u>. You'll need to write about each bullet point and give <u>opinions</u>. The scenario for the task will be <u>informal</u>, so use the '<u>tu</u>' form.	There will also be <u>two tasks</u> to choose from. You'll need to write <u>about 130-150 words</u> in French, based on <u>four bullet points</u>. Make sure you include some <u>opinions</u> and justify your <u>reasons</u>. You'll need to be more formal in this task, so use the '<u>vous</u>' form.	You'll be given an <u>English passage</u> to translate <u>into French</u>. The passage could be on <u>any topic</u> you've studied. Make sure you leave plenty of <u>time</u> for this task. There's more advice for doing translations on p.147.

Read the instructions carefully, and spend some time planning

1) Read the instructions for questions 1 and 2 carefully — you'll need to make sure you cover <u>all of the bullet points</u>. You can often use <u>words from the question</u> in your answer too.

2) Spend a few minutes for each question <u>planning out</u> your answer. Decide <u>how</u> you're going to cover everything that's required and <u>in what order</u> you're going to write things.

> Try to use varied vocab and a range of tenses.

3) Write the <u>best answer</u> you can, using the French <u>that you know</u> — it doesn't matter if it's not true.

Check through your work thoroughly

Checking your work is <u>really important</u> — even small mistakes can cost marks. Take a look at this checklist:

- Are all the <u>verbs</u> in the <u>right tense</u>?
  Demain, je travaillais dans le jardin. ✗   Demain, je travaill**erai** dans le jardin. ✓

- Are the <u>verb endings</u> correct?
  Tu n'aime pas les framboises? ✗   Tu n'aime**s** pas les framboises? ✓

- Do your <u>adjectives agree</u> with their nouns?
  La cuisine est grand. ✗   La cuisine est grand**e**. ✓

  > All of the points on this checklist are covered in the grammar section — see p.99-142.

- Are your <u>adjectives</u> in the <u>right place</u>?
  Il porte une rose chemise. ✗   Il porte une chemise rose. ✓

- Do your <u>past participles</u> agree?
  Ils sont parti. ✗   Ils sont parti**s**. ✓

- Have you <u>spelt</u> everything correctly, including using the right <u>accents</u>?
  Ele ecoute de la music avec ma mere. ✗   E**ll**e **é**coute de la musi**que** avec ma m**è**re. ✓

Make sure you cover every aspect of the tasks...

When you're nervous and stressed, it's dead easy to miss out something the question has asked you to do. For tasks one and two, try to write about the bullet points in order, and tick them off as you go along.

The Translation Tasks

When you're studying French, you do little bits of translation in your head all the time. For the translation questions, you just need to apply those skills — one sentence at a time — to a couple of short passages.

In the Reading Exam, you'll translate from French to English

1) The final question of the reading paper will ask you to translate a <u>short French passage</u> (about 50 words) <u>into English</u>. The passage will be on a <u>topic you've studied</u>, so most of the vocabulary should be familiar.

2) Here are some <u>top tips</u> for doing your translation:

- Read the whole text <u>before you start</u>. Make some <u>notes in English</u> to remind you of the main ideas.

- Translate the text <u>one sentence at a time</u>, rather than word by word — this will avoid any of the French word order being carried into the English.

Elle achète la pomme rouge.	*She buys the apple red.* ✖	*She buys the red apple.* ✔
Thomas l'a mangée.	*Thomas it ate.* ✖	*Thomas ate it.* ✔

- Keep an eye out for <u>different tenses</u> — there will definitely be a variety in the passage.

- <u>Read through</u> your translation to make sure it sounds <u>natural</u>. Some words and phrases don't translate literally, so you'll need to make sure that your sentences sound like <u>normal English</u>:

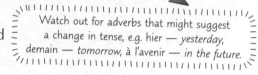
Watch out for adverbs that might suggest a change in tense, e.g. hier — *yesterday*, demain — *tomorrow*, à l'avenir — *in the future*.

La semaine dernière, elle a fait du camping.	*The week last, she did some camping.* ✖	*Last week, she went camping.* ✔

3) Make sure you've translated <u>everything</u> from the original text — you'll lose marks if you miss something.

In the Writing Exam, you'll translate from English to French

1) In the writing paper, you will have to translate <u>a short English passage</u> (about 50 words) <u>into French</u>.

2) Here are <u>some ideas</u> for how you could approach the translation:

- <u>Read</u> through the <u>whole text</u> before you get started so you know exactly what the text is about.

- Tackle the passage <u>one sentence at a time</u> — work slowly and carefully through each one.

- <u>Don't</u> translate things <u>literally</u> — think about what each English sentence means and try to write it in the <u>most French way</u> you know. Don't worry — the translation is likely to include similar sentences to the ones you've learnt.

- Work on the <u>word order</u> — remember that most French adjectives follow the noun. If the sentence is <u>negative</u>, check you've got 'ne' in the <u>right place</u> (see p.134).

Don't try to write a perfect translation first time — do it roughly first, and then write it up properly, crossing out any old drafts. Remember to keep an eye on the time.

3) Once you've got something that you're happy with, go back through and <u>check that you've covered everything</u> that was in the English.

4) Now <u>check</u> your French text thoroughly using the <u>list from p.146</u>.

Thankfully, none of that got lost in translation...

There's no set way of translating a text, but following these ideas is a good place to start. Now you've taken all this advice on board, it's time to test it out — have a go at tacking the practice exam.

Practice Exam

Once you've been through all the questions in this book, you should be starting to feel prepared for the final exams. As a last piece of preparation, here's a practice exam for you to have a go at. It's been designed to give you the best exam practice possible for the Edexcel Higher Tier papers. Good luck!

General Certificate of Secondary Education

GCSE French
Higher Tier

Listening Paper

Centre name					
Centre number					
Candidate number					

Surname
Other names
Candidate signature

CGP

Practice Exam Paper
GCSE French

Time Allowed: 40 minutes approximately
+ 5 minutes reading before the test.

Instructions
*   Write in black ink.
*   You have 5 minutes at the start of the test during which you may read through the questions and make notes. Then start the recording.
*   Answer **all** questions in the spaces provided.
*   The questions in Section A are in **French**.
*   The questions in Section B are in **English**.
*   Give all the information you are asked for, and **write neatly**.

Advice
*   Before each new question, read through all the question parts and instructions carefully.
*   Listen carefully to the recording. There will be a pause to allow you to reread the question, make notes or write down your answers.
*   Listen to the recording again. There will be a pause to allow you to complete or check your answers.
*   You may write at any point during the exam.
*   Each item on the CD is repeated once.
*   You are **not** allowed to ask questions or interrupt during the exam.

Information
*   The maximum mark for this paper is **50**.
*   The number of marks for each question is shown in brackets.
*   You are **not** allowed to use a dictionary.

Section A

Un mode de vie sain

1   Un médecin parle de l'exercice.

Choisis la bonne réponse et mets une croix dans la case.

Exemple: Aujourd'hui, de plus en plus de gens...

☐	**A** font beaucoup d'exercice.
☒	**B** ne font pas d'exercice.
☐	**C** font assez d'exercice.

a)   Selon ce médecin, pour rester en bonne forme...

☐	**A** il faut faire de l'exercice.
☐	**B** il faut manger moins de viande.
☐	**C** il faut boire de l'eau.

[1 mark]

b)   Le médecin dit que les gens ne font pas d'exercice parce qu'...

☐	**A** ils trouvent cela ennuyeux.
☐	**B** ils sont trop occupés.
☐	**C** ils doivent se reposer.

[1 mark]

c)   Le médecin recommande...

☐	**A** de l'exercice quotidien.
☐	**B** de s'inscrire à un gymnase.
☐	**C** de réfléchir à sa routine quotidienne.

[1 mark]

d)   Au lieu de conduire au travail, le médecin suggère...

☐	**A** aller à pied ou à vélo.
☐	**B** faire du jogging.
☐	**C** trouver un nouvel itinéraire.

[1 mark]

e)   Les gens qui prennent l'autobus pourraient...

☐	**A** aller à pied.
☐	**B** descendre un arrêt plus tôt.
☐	**C** quitter la maison plus tôt.

[1 mark]

Turn over

Les matières scolaires

2 Yannick parle des matières qu'il étudie au collège.

Complète les phrases en choisissant un mot dans la case. Il y a des mots que tu n'utiliseras pas.

EPS	ennuyeuse	~~compliqué~~	intéressante
chimie	aviron	utile	anglais
informatique	fantastique	histoire	biologie

Exemple: Selon lui, l'allemand est ....*compliqué*.............. .

a) La géographie est la matière la plus .... *[1 mark]*

b) Il trouve que l'..................................... est intéressante. *[1 mark]*

c) Il est mauvais en .... *[1 mark]*

d) À son avis, l'..................................... est utile pour rester actif. *[1 mark]*

e) L'..................................... est pratique pour la carrière qu'il a choisie. *[1 mark]*

Section B

Christmas

3   You've asked your French classmate, Amélie, about her plans for Christmas.

Complete the sentences by putting a cross in the correct box for each question.

Example: Amélie likes the end of the year because...

☐	**A** that's when she goes on holiday.
☒	**B** it's when her favourite festivals are celebrated.
☐	**C** there are lots of celebrations.
☐	**D** her birthday is in December.

a)   Next week, Amélie is going to...

☐	**A** go into town to see the Christmas lights.
☐	**B** stay with her aunt for a few days.
☐	**C** decorate her aunt's house.
☐	**D** decorate the Christmas tree.

[1 mark]

b)   This year, her family are spending Christmas...

☐	**A** outside France.
☐	**B** in the north of France.
☐	**C** in the south of France.
☐	**D** in a city.

[1 mark]

c)   It's usually difficult for her family to meet up because...

☐	**A** everyone is disorganised.
☐	**B** there are a lot of family members.
☐	**C** there isn't enough time during school holidays.
☐	**D** her relatives live far away from each other.

[1 mark]

d)   The present that Amélie hasn't bought yet is...

☐	**A** a train set for her little brother.
☐	**B** a horse figurine for her stepmother.
☐	**C** a necklace for her grandmother.
☐	**D** a computer game for her cousin.

[1 mark]

Turn over

Weather Forecasts

4   Listen to the weather forecast for these Belgian cities.

What does the presenter talk about? Put a cross in each one of the **three** correct boxes.

Example	cloudy weather in Liège	X
A	the forecast for the north of the country	☐
B	sunshine in Bruges	☐
C	a weather warning for Brussels	☐
D	high temperatures in Brussels	☐
E	the forecast for the east of the country	☐
F	heavy rain in the south	☐
G	poor visibility due to mist	☐

[3 marks]

School Life

5   During a video call with your penfriend, Chantal, you ask about her life at school.

Answer the questions in **English**.

Example: What is the problem with Chantal's lessons?

Some students like to disrupt them.

a)   What does Chantal say her school could improve?

....   [1 mark]

b)   Who would this change benefit?

....   [1 mark]

c)   Write down **one** alternative interest that Chantal mentions.

....   [1 mark]

Music

6   Two members of a well-known Swiss band have agreed to take part in an international radio debate to discuss their views on online music streaming.

Put a cross in the **two** correct boxes for each question.

a)   What **two** advantages are mentioned by Alain and Michelle?

A	Online music streaming is great for established artists.	☐
B	It's easy to find the music you want.	☐
C	You can listen to music straight away.	☐
D	It can be accessed by everyone.	☐
E	The sound quality is better than a CD.	☐

[2 marks]

b)   What **two** disadvantages are mentioned by Alain and Michelle?

A	It isn't good for new bands who need to make money.	☐
B	You can only use it at certain times.	☐
C	Online streaming isn't available without a subscription.	☐
D	The sound quality isn't as good as a CD.	☐
E	It makes it easier for people to pirate music.	☐

[2 marks]

Social Media

7 Your cousin sends you a podcast in French about how people use social media.

Answer the questions in **English**.

Example: According to Paul, why is social media so popular?

It's the easiest way to contact people and it's free.

a) How do Paul's friends use social media?

Give **two** examples.

1. ....

2. .... *[2 marks]*

b) Why does Paul use his phone to send messages on social media?

Give **two** reasons.

1. ....

2. .... *[2 marks]*

c) Why is social media important for Paul's mother?

.... *[1 mark]*

d) What does Paul's brother think about social media?

.... *[1 mark]*

Voluntary Work

8   You hear this interview with students who have done voluntary work.

Answer the following questions **in English**.

(i) a) What do you learn about the charity that Florian worked for? Give **two** details.

....

....   *[2 marks]*

b) Why would Florian recommend this kind of voluntary work?

....   *[1 mark]*

c) What did Sandrine spend nine months doing?

....   *[1 mark]*

(ii) a) What was the aim of Zayna's expedition?

....   *[1 mark]*

b) Why did Kassim choose his voluntary placement?

....   *[1 mark]*

c) What did Kassim do to help out? Give **two** details.

....

....   *[2 marks]*

Future Plans

9   Two exchange students have recorded an interview about their future plans.

Put a cross in each one of the **two** correct boxes for each question.

(i) a) What does Jamil say about his future plans?

☐	**A** He hopes to be on television.
☐	**B** He is getting relevant experience now.
☐	**C** He is going to do work experience in the summer.
☐	**D** He has chosen this career so that he can travel.
☐	**E** He wants to work in an office.

[2 marks]

(ii) a) What does Marie say about her plans when she was younger?

☐	**A** She wanted to do a creative job.
☐	**B** Her parents encouraged her to follow her dream.
☐	**C** Her parents did not approve of her choice.
☐	**D** She wanted to be a doctor.
☐	**E** She considered being a lawyer like her father.

[2 marks]

b) What does Marie say about her current plans for the future?

☐	**A** She wants to teach languages in a primary school.
☐	**B** She has changed her mind.
☐	**C** She would like to travel.
☐	**D** She wants to become a travel agent.
☐	**E** She wants to volunteer at an animal sanctuary.

[2 marks]

Brittany

10   Listen to this advertisement from a tourist office in Brittany.

Answer the questions in **English**.

(i) a)   Who in particular would enjoy a visit to Brittany?

.... *[1 mark]*

b)   What can you do on the Sept-Îles?

.... *[1 mark]*

(ii) a)   What historical attractions are mentioned in the advertisement?

....

.... *[2 marks]*

b)   Give **one** traditional savoury dish you can try in Brittany.

.... *[1 mark]*

c)   What is a kouign-amann?

.... *[1 mark]*

END OF QUESTIONS

General Certificate of Secondary Education

GCSE French
Higher Tier

Centre name					
Centre number					
Candidate number					

CGP

Practice Exam Paper
GCSE French

Surname	
Other names	
Candidate signature	

Speaking Paper

Time Allowed: 10-12 minutes
+ 12 minutes of supervised preparation time.

Instructions to candidates
- Find a friend or parent to read the teacher's part for you.
- You will have **12 minutes** to prepare the role play and picture-based task.
- You may make notes on one side of A4 paper during the preparation time.
- You must not use any notes during the conversation.
- The conversation in this paper will be based on the following themes:
  School; International and global dimension.

Instructions to teachers
- It is essential that you give the student every opportunity to use the material they have prepared.
- You may repeat questions and use the set prompts to allow the student to give a detailed response.
  You must remember **not** to provide students with any key vocabulary.

Information
- The test consists of **3** tasks.
- You may only prepare the role play and the picture-based task during the preparation time.
- The role play will last approximately 2 minutes.
- The picture-based task will last approximately 3 minutes.
- The conversation will last between 5 and 6 minutes.
- You are **not** allowed to use a dictionary at any time during the preparation time or the test.

> In the actual exam, you will nominate one theme to talk about in the conversation. This will determine your picture-based task theme and the remaining theme for the conversation. For this practice paper, you don't need to nominate a theme as there's only one picture-based task, so the conversation will use two themes not covered by the picture-based task.

ROLE PLAY
CANDIDATE'S MATERIAL

Instructions to candidate

You are staying with the family of a French friend, talking to your friend about where you live.

- Your teacher will play the role of your French friend. They will speak first.

- You must use *tu* to address your friend.

- ! – means you will have to respond to something you have not prepared.

- ? – means you will have to ask your friend a question.

> Tu parles d'où tu habites avec ton ami(e) français(e).
>
> - Ta maison — description
>
> - Ta ville — opinion
>
> - !
>
> - ? Sa ville — activités pour les jeunes
>
> - ? Changer quelque chose dans sa ville — quoi

PICTURE-BASED TASK
CANDIDATE'S MATERIAL

Instructions to candidate

- You should look carefully at the photo during the preparation time.

- You can make notes on a separate piece of paper.

© iStock.com/Chad McDermott

Regarde la photo et prépare des réponses sur les points suivants :

- la description de la photo

- si tu aimes le sport

- comment tu passerais un week-end de rêve

- si tu as assez de temps libre

- !

ROLE PLAY
TEACHER'S MATERIAL

Instructions to teacher

- You begin the role play.

- You should address the candidate as *tu*.

- Do not supply the candidate with key vocabulary.

- You must ask the questions below exactly as they are written.

Begin the role play by using the introductory text below.

Introductory text: *Tu parles d'où tu habites avec ton ami(e) français(e). Moi, je suis ton ami(e).*

1   *Comment est ta maison ?*

        Allow the candidate to talk about what his / her house is like.

2   *Qu'est-ce que tu penses de ta ville ? ... Pourquoi ?*

        Allow the candidate to say what s/he thinks about their town and why.

3   !   *Où habitais-tu quand tu étais plus jeune?*

        Allow the candidate to talk about where s/he lived when s/he was younger.

        C'est très bien.

4   ?   Allow the candidate to ask you about activities for young people in your town

        Give an appropriate brief response.

5   ?   Allow the candidate to ask you if there's something in your town that you want to change.

        Give an appropriate brief response.

Turn over

PICTURE-BASED TASK & CONVERSATION
TEACHER'S MATERIAL

Picture-based task

Theme: Identity and culture   **Topic**: Cultural life

This part of the test should last for a maximum of **three and a half minutes**. It may be less than that for some candidates. Candidates can use any notes they made during the preparation time.

Begin the conversation by asking the candidate the first question from the list below. Then ask the remaining four questions in order. You may not re-phrase the questions. You can repeat any questions that the candidate does not understand, but no more than twice. Allow the candidate to develop his / her answers as much as possible.

- Décris-moi la photo.

- Est-ce que tu aimes le sport ? ... Pourquoi / pourquoi pas ?

- Quel serait ton week-end de rêve ?

- Est-ce que tu penses que tu as assez de temps libre ? ... Pourquoi ?

- Qu'est-ce que tu as fait hier soir ?

Conversation

The conversation follows the picture-based task. It should last between **five** to **six minutes**, and a similar amount of time should be spent on each theme. You should allow the candidate to start with his / her chosen topic, and talk for approximately one minute uninterrupted. Sample questions for a range of topics within each theme have been provided below, but these lists are not exhaustive.

Themes and sample questions for the conversation:

International and global dimension

1) Quel type de travail bénévole voudrais-tu faire ? Pourquoi ?

2) À ton avis, pourquoi le travail des associations charitables est-t-il important ?

3) Parle-moi d'un événement charitable auquel tu as participé.

4) Qu'est-ce qu'on pourrait faire pour aider les sans-abri ?

5) Qu'est-ce qui se passera si on ne peut pas empêcher le réchauffement de la Terre ?

6) Que fais-tu pour être vert(e) ?

School

1) Qu'est-ce que tu penses des pressions scolaires ?

2) Comment est ton collège ?

3) Qu'est-ce que tu fais pendant une journée typique au collège ?

4) Quelle est ta matière préférée ? Pourquoi ?

5) Que penses-tu des échanges scolaires ?

6) Où aimerais-tu aller en excursion scolaire ? Pourquoi ?

General Certificate of Secondary Education

GCSE French
Higher Tier

Reading Paper

Centre name						CGP
Centre number						Practice Exam Paper GCSE French
Candidate number						
Surname						
Other names						
Candidate signature						

Time Allowed: 1 hour

Instructions
- Write in black ink.
- Answer **all** questions in the spaces provided.
- Answer the questions in Section A in **English**.
- Answer the questions in Section B in **French**.
- In Section C, translate the passage into **English**.
- Give all the information you are asked for, and **write neatly**.
- Cross out any rough work that you do not want to be marked.

Advice
- Read the question carefully before starting your answer.
- If you have time at the end, check through your work.

Information
- The maximum mark for this paper is **50**.
- The number of marks for each question is shown in brackets.
  Use this to work out how long to spend on each question.
- You are **not** allowed to use a dictionary.

Section A

1   **TV**

Read the comments about a new Belgian TV programme in which people are sent on blind dates.

Étienne

J'ai regardé cette émission hier soir, et elle m'a beaucoup plu — tu dois la regarder ! Ce n'était pas une émission sérieuse, et pour moi les rendez-vous avec les femmes différentes étaient drôles. Malheureusement, aucune d'entre elles n'a choisi l'homme comme petit ami — c'était très triste pour lui.

Susi

Je pense que cette émission est complètement stupide. Il s'agit d'un homme qui dîne avec trois femmes pendant une semaine, mais elles sont présentées de manière très négative. Je n'ai aucune intention de la regarder à nouveau. Cependant, je suis désolée pour l'homme principal — je crois qu'il ne trouvera jamais de petite amie !

Who says what about the Belgian TV programme?
Enter either **Étienne** or **Susi** in the gaps below.

a)   .... says that the programme is sexist.   *[1 mark]*

b)   .... says that the man will stay single forever.   *[1 mark]*

c)   .... says that the programme is worth watching.   *[1 mark]*

d)   .... says that the man has meals with different women.   *[1 mark]*

2 **Poverty and homelessness**

Read the article.

> La pauvreté en France a fortement augmenté à partir de 2008, et on estime que le pays compte environ 4,9 millions de pauvres. On est décrit comme 'pauvre' quand on gagne moins de 50% du revenu moyen national.
>
> Le nombre de sans-abri à Paris est estimé à 28.000, et la plupart sont des hommes. L'approche de l'hiver est un souci majeur et le conseil municipal a permis aux deux associations caritatives d'ouvrir 20 centres de refuge — un dans chaque arrondissement — pour éviter le pire. Cependant, il reste beaucoup à faire pour trouver la meilleure solution à long terme.

© iStock.com/ruchos

Answer the questions **in English**.

a) What has happened to the number of poor people since 2008?

.... *[1 mark]*

b) What does the article say about the majority of homeless people in Paris?

.... *[1 mark]*

c) What is being done to help them?

.... *[1 mark]*

d) What still needs to be done?

.... *[1 mark]*

3 **Education post-16**

Read the email.

From: claude305@internetz.fr
Subject: Après les examens

Salut !

Il ne me reste que 2 semaines avant de passer mes examens. J'ai étudié très dur et j'ai fait beaucoup de révisions, donc j'espère obtenir de bonnes notes, mais je m'inquiète quand même. Après les examens, j'irai en vacances pour me détendre. Pourtant, je ne sais pas quoi faire après les vacances. Je pourrais aller à l'université si mes notes sont bonnes mais j'en ai assez d'étudier. Mon père pense que je devrais faire un apprentissage mais pour ça j'aurais besoin de choisir une carrière et je n'ai aucune idée de l'emploi qui me convient. Je pense que j'essayerai de trouver un travail bénévole et puis je pourrai prendre une décision plus tard.

Qu'en penses-tu ?

Claude

Put a cross in the correct box.

a) How does Claude say he feels about his exams?

☐	**A** confident
☐	**B** worried
☐	**C** relaxed
☐	**D** angry

[1 mark]

b) Why doesn't Claude want to go to university?

☐	**A** He doesn't want to leave home.
☐	**B** He doesn't know which subject to study.
☐	**C** His marks won't be good enough.
☐	**D** He is fed up of studying.

[1 mark]

c)   Why is Claude reluctant to do an apprenticeship?

☐	**A** He has no idea which career would suit him.
☐	**B** He wants to go back to school after summer.
☐	**C** It's what his father wants.
☐	**D** He doesn't want to have a career.

[1 mark]

d)   What does Claude say he thinks he will do?

☐	**A** Find a part-time job.
☐	**B** Go to college later.
☐	**C** Find some voluntary work.
☐	**D** Find some well-paid work.

[1 mark]

Turn over

4 **Relationships**

Read this letter.

> Mon copain et moi sommes ensemble depuis six mois. Nous nous sommes rencontrés à la fête d'une de mes amies. On s'entend bien et je suis tombée vraiment amoureuse de lui. Pourtant, je crois qu'il a perdu tout intérêt pour moi. D'habitude on se voit tous les deux jours, et les jours où on ne se voit pas, on parle sur les réseaux sociaux ou il m'envoie un texto. Récemment, chaque fois que j'ai proposé un rendez-vous il a dit qu'il était fatigué ou qu'il avait trop à faire. Il ne m'a pas contactée depuis cinq jours. Je m'inquiète parce qu'il a peut-être trouvé une autre copine.
>
> Aidez-moi !
>
> Francine

Put a cross in the correct box.

a) Francine and her boyfriend...

☐	**A** met at a music festival
☐	**B** have been together for over a year
☐	**C** usually exchange messages when they don't see each other
☐	**D** chat on social media once a week

[1 mark]

b) Francine's boyfriend...

☐	**A** says he's too busy to meet up
☐	**B** hasn't spoken to her for a week
☐	**C** told her that he is tired of her
☐	**D** has been spending lots of time with his friends

[1 mark]

5   **A wedding**

Read this extract from 'Un Mariage' by Ernest Laut. The narrator is talking about a wedding procession.

Tout de suite, j'ai supposé qu'on allait célébrer le mariage du chef de quelque grosse industrie, et j'ai pensé que tous les ouvriers de l'usine s'étaient rassemblés là pour faire honneur au patron.

Mais j'étais surpris lorsque, au lieu des brillants équipages que j'attendais, j'ai vu apparaître, au bout de la rue de la Mairie, le cortège* nuptial, cortège pédestre et simple s'il en a été : en tête les deux époux, derrière les quatre témoins — c'était tout !

L'enthousiasme des spectateurs n'en a été pas moins bouillant, je dois le dire.

Ils se sont rangés de chaque côté de la rue, et quand les époux ont passé entre ces deux haies** humaines, une immense clameur s'est élevée :

— Vive la mariée !

*cortège — procession
**haies — hedges

Answer the questions **in English**.

a)   Whose marriage did the narrator originally assume was taking place?

.... *[1 mark]*

b)   How many people were in the wedding procession?

.... *[1 mark]*

c)   Where were the spectators standing?

.... *[1 mark]*

Turn over

6   Film reviews

Read Yasin's film reviews.

La femme en blanc	J'ai beaucoup aimé ce film. C'est un film d'horreur qui raconte l'histoire d'une femme qui est morte le jour de son mariage. La tension était incroyable et je l'ai trouvé très effrayant.
Julian et Fabien	Le film explore le voyage de deux vrais jumeaux qui sont séparés à la naissance. Après leur première rencontre, ils s'embarquent dans beaucoup d'aventures ensemble. Le film est inspiré de faits réels mais c'était difficile de suivre l'histoire.
Bataille extra-terrestre	Il s'agit d'une armée de soldats extra-terrestres super-méchants qui essaye d'envahir la Terre, et d'un homme et sa famille qui dirigent la résistance. En général, je ne regarde pas les films de science fiction, mais ce film est spectaculaire avec beaucoup d'effets spéciaux.
Le crépuscule	Ce film décrit l'histoire d'une femme qui cherche l'homme qu'elle avait aimé quand elle était très jeune — son premier amour. Malheureusement, l'actrice principale m'a énervé parce qu'elle était trop sentimentale. Je ne le recommande pas.

a)   What do the reviews tell us?
Put a cross next to each one of the **three** correct boxes.

Example	Yasin really liked 'La femme en blanc'.	☒
A	'La femme en blanc' is about a woman who died the day after her wedding.	☐
B	Yasin found 'La femme en blanc' too frightening.	☐
C	Julian and Fabien are twin brothers who were separated at birth.	☐
D	In 'Bataille extra-terrestre', aliens are defeated by one man and his family.	☐
E	'Bataille extra-terrestre' is not the sort of film that Yasin would usually watch.	☐
F	'Le crépuscule' is a romantic film.	☐
G	Yasin thought that the main actress in 'Le crépuscule' was not emotional enough.	☐

[3 marks]

Answer the questions **in English**.

b) What problem did Yasin encounter when watching 'Julian et Fabien'?

.... *[1 mark]*

c) What did Yasin find positive about 'Bataille extra-terrestre'?

.... *[1 mark]*

d) What does the main character in 'Le crépuscule' want to do?

.... *[1 mark]*

172

7   Smartphones

Read this blog post.

Merci aux progrès technologiques, presque tout le monde possède un téléphone intelligent : un smartphone. Un smartphone n'est pas seulement un téléphone : on peut l'utiliser pour accéder à Internet, écouter de la musique, regarder les films, prendre des photos et même pour trouver son chemin — la liste est infinie. Pourtant, nous commençons à nous attacher trop à nos portables. Tout le monde connaît au moins une personne dans son entourage qui est 'accro' à son portable — une personne qui ne peut pas s'empêcher d'envoyer des textos pendant un repas et qui doit afficher chaque détail de leur vie sur les réseaux sociaux.

Les scientifiques disent que les conséquences de cette addiction sont inquiétantes. Certaines personnes se sentent anxieuses si elles sont séparées de leur smartphone, et si on passe trop de temps à regarder les portables, la lumière de l'écran peut perturber le sommeil. La recommandation : nous devrions essayer de séparer la vie virtuelle et la vie réelle.

Answer the questions **in English**.

a)   According to the blog post, what can a smartphone be used for besides communicating? Give **two** details.

1. ....

2. .... *[2 marks]*

b)   What actions does the blog post suggest are typical of smartphone addicts? Give **two** details.

1. ....

2. .... *[2 marks]*

c)   What do scientists say about smartphone screens?

.... *[1 mark]*

Section B

8   **Un email**

Lis cet email.

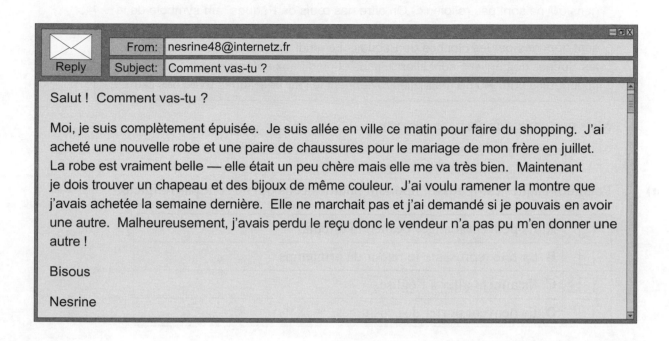

From: nesrine48@internetz.fr
Subject: Comment vas-tu ?

Salut ! Comment vas-tu ?

Moi, je suis complètement épuisée. Je suis allée en ville ce matin pour faire du shopping. J'ai acheté une nouvelle robe et une paire de chaussures pour le mariage de mon frère en juillet. La robe est vraiment belle — elle était un peu chère mais elle me va très bien. Maintenant je dois trouver un chapeau et des bijoux de même couleur. J'ai voulu ramener la montre que j'avais achetée la semaine dernière. Elle ne marchait pas et j'ai demandé si je pouvais en avoir une autre. Malheureusement, j'avais perdu le reçu donc le vendeur n'a pas pu m'en donner une autre !

Bisous

Nesrine

Réponds aux questions **en français**. Il n'est pas nécessaire d'écrire des phrases complètes.

Exemple   À quel événement familial ira-t-elle en juillet ?

.... *Le mariage de son frère.* ....

a)   Qu'est-ce que Nesrine a acheté ?
      Donne **deux** détails.

      1. ....

      2. .... *[2 marks]*

b)   Quel était le problème avec la montre ?

      .... *[1 mark]*

c)   Pourquoi n'a-t-elle pas pu avoir une autre montre ?

      .... *[1 mark]*

Turn over

9 **Pâques**

Lis cet article.

> Pâques est une fête très importante en France. C'est la fête religieuse la plus importante de l'Église catholique mais de nombreuses coutumes destinées à célébrer le retour du printemps s'y attachent, donc c'est important même pour les gens qui ne sont pas religieux. On offre des œufs de Pâques : un symbole de la naissance et du retour du printemps. Mais en France la légende dit que les œufs sont apportés par les cloches de Pâques. Le jeudi avant le dimanche de Pâques, les cloches des églises sont silencieuses et on dit aux enfants que les cloches sont parties pour Rome mais elles reviennent le jour de Pâques avec des œufs.

Mets une croix dans la case correcte.

a) Pourquoi Pâques est-il aussi important pour les gens qui ne sont pas religieux ?

☐	**A** Ils peuvent manger beaucoup d'œufs.
☐	**B** La fête représente le retour du printemps.
☐	**C** Ils aiment aller à l'église.
☐	**D** Ils peuvent porter des costumes.

[1 mark]

b) Selon la légende, d'où viennent les œufs de Pâques en France ?

☐	**A** Rome
☐	**B** Le lapin de Pâques
☐	**C** L'église
☐	**D** Les cloches

[1 mark]

c) Qu'est-ce qui se passe dans les églises avant le dimanche de Pâques ?

☐	**A** Les cloches sont nettoyées.
☐	**B** Les cloches sont rendues silencieuses.
☐	**C** On sonne les cloches.
☐	**D** On offre des œufs aux enfants.

[1 mark]

10   Demande d'emploi

Lis ces demandes d'emploi.

Réponds aux questions **en français**. Il n'est pas nécessaire d'écrire des phrases complètes.

> J'aimerais poser ma candidature pour le poste de promeneur de chiens. Je voudrais ce poste car j'aime travailler avec les animaux. Je pense que je serais idéal pour ce poste parce que je comprends les chiens et l'année dernière j'ai travaillé pendant deux mois dans un refuge pour animaux.

a)   Le candidat dit qu'il veut le poste pour quelle raison ?

    .... *[1 mark]*

b)   Quel type d'expérience a-t-il ?

    .... *[1 mark]*

> J'ai lu votre annonce et je voudrais poser ma candidature pour le poste de vendeuse dans le nouveau magasin de vêtements. Je m'intéresse beaucoup à la mode et je pense que je serais parfaite pour ce poste. Je suis travailleuse et j'ai déjà deux ans d'expérience comme vendeuse dans un petit magasin à Nantes.

c)   Pourquoi veut-elle ce poste ?

    .... *[1 mark]*

d)   Quelle qualité possède-t-elle qui l'aiderait dans ce poste ?

    .... *[1 mark]*

Turn over

11 Les trois mousquetaires

Lis cet extrait du livre '*Les trois mousquetaires*' d'Alexandre Dumas.
Un gentilhomme est en train de donner des conseils à son fils.

> Mon fils, avait dit le gentilhomme gascon, mon fils, ce cheval est né dans la maison de votre père, il y a treize ans, et y est resté depuis ce temps-là, ce qui doit vous porter à l'aimer. Ne le vendez jamais, laissez-le mourir tranquillement et honorablement de vieillesse.
>
> À la cour, a continué M. d'Artagnan père, si toutefois vous avez l'honneur d'y aller, soutenez dignement votre nom de gentilhomme, qui a été porté dignement par vos ancêtres depuis plus de cinq cents ans. C'est par son courage qu'un gentilhomme fait son chemin aujourd'hui. Quiconque tremble une seconde laisse peut-être échapper la chance que la fortune lui tendait. Vous êtes jeune, vous devez être brave pour deux raisons : la première, c'est que vous êtes Gascon, et la seconde, c'est que vous êtes mon fils. Ne craignez pas les occasions et cherchez les aventures.

Mets une croix dans la case correcte.

a) Le garçon ne doit pas...

☐	**A** aimer son cheval
☐	**B** garder son cheval
☐	**C** vendre son cheval
☐	**D** monter à son cheval

[1 mark]

b) La famille de M. d'Artagnan est très...

☐	**A** célèbre
☐	**B** vieille
☐	**C** faible
☐	**D** généreuse

[1 mark]

c) Selon M. d'Artagnan père, un gentilhomme doit toujours...

☐	**A** être courageux
☐	**B** réfléchir avant d'agir
☐	**C** avoir de la chance
☐	**D** augmenter sa fortune

[1 mark]

d) Le fils doit être brave...

☐	**A** parce qu'il est jeune
☐	**B** parce qu'il est un garçon
☐	**C** pour devenir riche
☐	**D** pour honorer son père

[1 mark]

Section C

Translation

12   Translate this passage **into English**.

> Quelles terribles vacances ! Je viens de revenir de mon voyage en Allemagne
> et c'était vraiment affreux. Je suis allé à Berlin avec mes cousins. La ville était
> incroyable, mais l'hôtel où nous sommes restés était désagréable. Il n'y avait pas
> d'eau chaude ! Si je retournais un jour à Berlin, je trouverais un autre logement.

[7 marks]

....

....

....

....

....

....

....

....

....

....

END OF QUESTIONS

General Certificate of Secondary Education

GCSE French
Higher Tier

Centre name				
Centre number				
Candidate number				

CGP
**Practice Exam Paper
GCSE French**

Surname
Other names
Candidate signature

Writing Paper

Time Allowed: 1 hour 20 minutes

Instructions
- Write in black ink.
- Give all the information you are asked for, and **write neatly**.
- You must answer **three** questions.
- Answer **either** Question 1 a) **or** Question 1 b). Do **not** answer both questions.
- Answer **either** Question 2 a) **or** Question 2 b). Do **not** answer both questions.
- You **must** answer Question 3.
- All questions must be answered in **French**.
- In the actual exam, you must write your answers in the spaces provided. Do **not** write on blank pages.
- You may plan your answers in the exam booklet. Make sure you cross through any work you do
  not want to be marked.

Information
- This paper contains **3** writing tasks.
- The maximum mark for this paper is **60**.
- The number of marks for each question is shown in brackets.
  Use this to work out how long to spend on each question.
- You should spend around 15 minutes on the translation question.
- You are **not** allowed to use a dictionary.

Answer **either** Question 1 a) **or** Question 1 b)

Le travail

1 a) Michèle, ta correspondante française, t'a envoyé un email au sujet du travail.

Écris une réponse à Michèle. Tu **dois** faire référence aux points suivants :

- un stage que tu as déjà fait

- ton opinion sur les stages en général

- ton travail idéal

- les avantages et les désavantages de ce travail

Écris 80-90 mots environ **en français**.   *[20 marks]*

Les problèmes environnementaux

1 b) Un magazine français pour les jeunes cherche des articles sur les problèmes environnementaux.

Écris un article pour ce magazine. Tu **dois** faire référence aux points suivants :

- les problèmes environnementaux causés par les voitures

- les avantages des transports en commun

- une activité récente que tu as faite pour sauvegarder l'environnement

- tes idées pour sauvegarder l'environnement à l'avenir.

Écris 80-90 mots environ **en français**.   *[20 marks]*

180

Answer **either** Question 2 a) **or** Question 2 b)

Les campagnes charitables

2 a)   Une organisation bénévole française cherche des articles sur les campagnes charitables pour son nouvel site Internet.

Écrivez un article dans lequel vous donnez vos opinions sur les campagnes charitables.

Vous **devez** faire référence aux points suivants :

- ce que vous pensez généralement des campagnes charitables

- une campagne qui a eu lieu dans votre ville

- votre opinion de cette campagne

- un événement mondial auquel vous aimeriez participer à l'avenir.

Justifiez vos idées et vos opinions.

Écrivez 130-150 mots environ **en français**.   *[28 marks]*

Les réseaux sociaux

2 b)   Vous voulez participer à une compétition dans un journal français pour gagner un nouveau smartphone. Les participants doivent discuter des réseaux sociaux.

Écrivez une lettre pour participer à la compétition.

Vous **devez** faire référence aux points suivants :

- comment vous utilisez les réseaux sociaux

- les avantages et les désavantages des réseaux sociaux

- une expérience récente qui vous est arrivée sur les réseaux sociaux

- ce qu'on pourrait faire pour réduire les risques en ligne.

Justifiez vos idées et vos opinions.

Écrivez 130-150 mots environ **en français**.   *[28 marks]*

You **must** answer Question 3

Le shopping

3   Traduis le passage suivant **en français**.

> Sometimes Damien likes to do online shopping because it is faster. However, last week he went to the supermarket to do the shopping. He bought fruit, vegetables and some bread. Now, he wants some new shoes and he will have to go to the shops to buy them because he will need to try them on.

[12 marks]

Vocabulary

Section One — General Stuff

Conjunctions (p.118)

à cause de	because of
à part	apart from
ainsi	therefore / so
alors	so / therefore / then
aussi	also
car	because
cependant	however
c'est-à-dire	that is to say
comme	as / like
d'un côté / de l'autre côté	on the one hand / on the other hand
donc	therefore / so
enfin / finalement	finally
ensuite	then / next
et	and
évidemment	obviously
lorsque	when / as soon as
mais	but
même si	even if
ni...ni	neither...nor
ou	or
ou bien	or else
par contre	on the other hand
parce que	because
par exemple	for example
pendant que	while
pourtant	however
puis	then
puisque	seeing that / since
quand	when
sans doute	undoubtedly / without doubt
si	if
tout d'abord	first of all
y compris	including

Comparisons (p.104 & 109)

aussi...que	as...as
plus / moins	more / less
plus que / moins que	more than / less than
bon(ne) / meilleur(e) / le/la meilleur(e)	good / better / the best
mauvais(e) / pire / le/la pire	bad / worse / the worst
bien / mieux / le/la mieux	well / better / the best
mal / plus mal / le/la plus mal	badly / worse / the worst
beaucoup / plus / le/la plus	lots / more / the most
peu / moins / le/la moins	few / less / the least

Prepositions (p.119-120)

à	to / in / at
à côté de	next to
à travers	across / through
après	after
au bord de	at the side / edge of
au bout de	at the end of (length, rather than time)
au-dessous de	beneath / below
au-dessus de	above / over
au fond de	at the back of / at the bottom of
au lieu de	instead of
au milieu de	in the middle of
autour de	around
avant	before
avec	with
chez	at the house of
contre	against
dans	in
de	of / from
depuis	since / for
derrière	behind
devant	in front of
en	in / to
en dehors de	outside (of)
en face de	opposite
entre	between
jusqu'à	up to / until
loin de	far from
malgré	despite / in spite of
parmi	amongst
pendant	during
pour	for / in order to
près de	near
sans	without
selon	according to
sous	under
sur	on
vers	towards

Negatives (p.134)

ne...aucun(e)	not any / not a single
ne...jamais	never
ne...ni...ni	neither...nor
ne...pas	not
ne...personne	nobody / no one
ne...plus	no more / no longer
ne...que	only / nothing but
ne...rien	nothing
pas encore	not yet

Numbers (p.1)

zéro	zero
un	one
deux	two
trois	three
quatre	four
cinq	five
six	six

sept	seven
huit	eight
neuf	nine
dix	ten
onze	eleven
douze	twelve
treize	thirteen
quatorze	fourteen
quinze	fifteen
seize	sixteen
dix-sept	seventeen
dix-huit	eighteen
dix-neuf	nineteen
vingt	twenty
vingt et un	twenty-one
vingt-deux	twenty-two
trente	thirty
quarante	forty
cinquante	fifty
soixante	sixty
soixante-dix	seventy
soixante et onze	seventy-one
soixante-douze	seventy-two
quatre-vingts	eighty
quatre-vingt-un	eighty-one
quatre-vingt-dix	ninety
quatre-vingt-onze	ninety-one
quatre-vingt-dix-huit	ninety-eight
cent	one hundred
mille	one thousand
dix mille	ten thousand
cent mille	one hundred thousand
un million	one million
premier / première	first
deuxième	second
troisième	third
quatrième	fourth
cinquième	fifth
sixième	sixth
septième	seventh
huitième	eighth
neuvième	ninth
dixième	tenth
quatre-vingt-dix-neuvième	ninenty-ninth
une dizaine	about ten
des dizaines	lots / dozens
une douzaine	a dozen
une vingtaine	about twenty
un nombre de	a number of

Times and Dates (p.2-3)

lundi	Monday
mardi	Tuesday
mercredi	Wednesday
jeudi	Thursday

vendredi	Friday	et demie	half past	**Weights and Measures**	
samedi	Saturday	la fin	end	assez	enough / quite
dimanche	Sunday	hier	yesterday	bas(se)	low
janvier	January	il y a	ago	la boîte	box / tin / can
février	February	le jour	day	la bouteille	bottle
mars	March	la journée	day	court(e)	short
avril	April	le lendemain	the next day	le demi	half
mai	May	longtemps	for a long time	un demi-litre	half a litre
juin	June	maintenant	now	encore de	more
juillet	July	le matin	morning	étroit(e)	narrow
août	August	moins le quart	quarter to	un gramme	a gram
septembre	September	le mois	month	gros	fat
octobre	October	normalement	normally	haut(e)	high
novembre	November	la nuit	night	un kilogramme	a kilogram
décembre	December	parfois	sometimes	large	wide
l'hiver (m)	winter	le passé	past	un litre	a litre
le printemps	spring	pendant	during	maigre	skinny / thin
l'été (m)	summer	plus tard	later	mince	slim / thin
l'automne (m)	autumn	presque	almost / nearly	la moitié	half
à la fois	at the same time	prochain(e)	next	le morceau	piece
à l'avenir	in the future	la quinzaine / les quinze jours (m)	fortnight	moyen / moyenne	medium / average
à l'heure	on time			le nombre	number
à temps partiel	part-time	quelquefois	sometimes	le paquet	packet
à temps plein	full-time	rarement	rarely	pas mal de	quite a few
l'an (m)	year	récemment	recently	peser	to weigh
l'année (f)	year	la semaine	week	plein de	full of / lots of
après	after	seulement	only	la pointure	size (for shoes)
après-demain	the day after tomorrow	le siècle	century	la portion	portion
		le soir	evening	le quart	quarter
l'après-midi (m / f)	afternoon	soudain	suddenly	suffisamment	sufficiently
l'aube (f)	dawn	souvent	often	la taille	size (for clothes)
au début	at the start	suivant(e)	following	tout(e)	all
aujourd'hui	today	(être) sur le point de	(to be) about to	la tranche	slice
auparavant	formerly / in the past			tranché(e)	sliced
avant	before	tard	late	les trois-quarts (m)	three quarters
avant-hier	the day before yesterday	tôt	early	trop	too much
		toujours	always / still		
bientôt	soon	tous les jours	every day	**Materials**	
le coucher du soleil	sunset	tout à coup	suddenly / all of a sudden	l'argent (m)	silver
d'abord	at first / firstly			le béton	concrete
d'habitude	usually	tout de suite	immediately	le bois	wood
de bonne heure	early	vite	quickly	le cuir	leather
de l'après-midi	in the afternoon	le week-end	weekend	le fer	iron
de nouveau	again			la laine	wool
de temps en temps	from time to time	**Colours and Shapes**		l'or (m)	gold
le début	start	blanc / blanche	white	la soie	silk
déjà	already	bleu(e)	blue	le verre	glass
dès que	as soon as	châtain	light brown		
demain	tomorrow	clair(e)	light	**Access**	
dernier / dernière	last	foncé(e)	dark	complet / complète	full
du matin	in the morning	gris(e)	grey	l'entrée (f)	entry / entrance
du soir	in the evening	jaune	yellow	fermé(e)	closed
en attendant	whilst waiting (for)	marron	brown	fermer	to close
en avance	in advance	noir(e)	black	interdit(e)	forbidden
en ce moment	at the moment	noisette	hazel	libre	free / vacant / unoccupied
en retard	late	orange	orange	occupé(e)	taken / occupied / engaged
en train de (faire...)	in the process of (doing)	pourpre	purple		
		rose	pink	ouvert(e)	open
en même temps	at the same time	rouge	red	ouvrir	to open
encore une fois	once more	vert(e)	green	la sortie	exit
enfin	at last / finally	carré(e)	square		
environ	about	rond(e)	round		
et quart	quarter past				

Vocabulary

Questions (p.4-5)

Combien ?	How much / How many?
Comment ?	How?
Est-ce que ?	expression put before a verb that makes a sentence into a question
lequel / laquelle	Which one?
Où ?	Where?
Pourquoi ?	Why?
Quand ?	When?
Que ?	What?
Quel / Quelle ?	Which?
Qu'est-ce que ?	What?
Qu'est-ce qui ?	What?
Qu'est-ce que c'est ?	What is it?
Qui ?	Who?
Quoi ?	What?
À quelle heure ?	At what time?
Que veut dire... ?	What does... mean?
Quelle heure est-il ?	What time is it?

Being Polite (p.6-7)

à bientôt	see you soon
à demain	see you tomorrow
à tout à l'heure	see you soon / later
allô	hello (on phone)
amitiés	best wishes
au revoir	goodbye
Au secours !	Help!
bienvenue	welcome
bonjour	hello
Bonne chance !	Good luck!
bonne idée	good idea
bonne nuit	good night
bonnes vacances	have a good holiday
bonsoir	good evening
ça va bien, merci	(I am) fine, thanks
ça ne va pas bien	(I am) not well
comme ci, comme ça	so-so / OK
Comment ça va ?	How are you? (informal)
Comment allez-vous ?	How are you? (formal)
d'accord	OK / fine
de rien	you're welcome
désolé(e)	sorry
enchanté(e)	pleased to meet you
Et toi ?	And you? (informal)
Et vous ?	And you? (formal)
excusez-moi	excuse me (formal)
Félicitations !	Congratulations!
j'aimerais...	I would like...
je me sens...	I feel...
je ne sais pas	I don't know
je voudrais...	I would like...
merci (beaucoup)	thank you (very much)
pardon	excuse me (informal)
pas mal	not bad
Puis-je... ?	May I.... ?
Puis-je te présenter... ?	May I introduce... ? (informal)
Puis-je vous présenter... ?	May I introduce...? (formal)
quel dommage	what a shame
salut	hi
Santé !	Cheers!
s'il te plaît	please (informal)
s'il vous plaît	please (formal)
Super !	Great!
voici...	this is... / here is...

Opinions (p.8-10)

à mon avis	in my opinion
absolument	absolutely
adorer	to love
agaçant(e)	annoying
aimer	to like / to love
aimer bien	to like
affreux / affreuse	awful
agréable	pleasant
amical(e)	friendly
amusant(e)	funny
l'avantage (m)	advantage
barbant(e)	boring
bien entendu	of course
bien sûr	of course, certainly
bon(ne)	good
ça dépend	it depends
ça m'énerve	it gets on my nerves
ça me fait rire	it makes me laugh
ça me fait pleurer	it makes me cry
ça me plaît	I like it
ça m'est égal	I don't care
ça ne me dit rien	it means nothing to me / I don't fancy that / I don't feel like it
ça suffit	that's enough
car	because
casse-pieds	annoying
certainement	certainly
cher / chère	expensive
chouette	great
compliqué(e)	complicated
content(e)	happy
croire	to believe
désagréable	unpleasant
désirer	to want
détester	to hate
dire	to say / to tell
doué(e)	gifted / talented
drôle	funny
embêtant(e)	annoying
en général	in general
enchanté(e)	delighted
ennuyeux / ennuyeuse	boring
espérer	to hope
Es-tu d'accord ?	Do you agree?
étonné(e)	astonished / amazed
facile	easy
faible	weak

fantastique	fantastic
formidable	great
franchement	frankly
généralement	generally
génial(e)	brilliant
grâce à	thanks to
grave	serious
habile	clever
l'inconvénient (m)	disadvantage
intéressant(e)	interesting
s'intéresser à	to be interested in
inutile	useless
incroyable	incredible
inquiet / inquiète	worried
marrant(e)	funny
en avoir marre (de)	to be fed up (with)
mauvais(e)	bad
merveilleux / merveilleuse	marvellous
mignon / mignonne	cute
moche	ugly
(moi) non plus	(me) neither
nouveau / nouvelle	new
nul / nulle	rubbish
par contre	on the other hand
parfait(e)	perfect
passionnant(e)	exciting
la peine	the bother
penser	to think
personnellement	personally
peut-être	perhaps
pourtant	however
pratique	practical
préférer	to prefer
promettre	to promise
Quel est ton avis sur... ?	What is your opinion of...?
ridicule	ridiculous
rigolo / rigolote	funny
sage	well-behaved
selon moi...	in my opinion...
sembler	to seem
sensass	sensational
super	great
supporter	to put up with
sympa / sympathique	nice (person)
utile	useful
vouloir	to wish / to want
vraiment	really / truly

Correctness

avoir raison	to be right
avoir tort	to be wrong
corriger	to correct
l'erreur (f)	error / mistake
la faute	fault / mistake
il (me) faut	you (I) must
juste	correct
obligatoire	compulsory
sûr(e)	certain / sure
se tromper	to make a mistake

Abbreviations

le CES (collège d'enseignement secondaire)	secondary school
l'HLM (habitation à loyer modéré) (f)	council / social housing
le SDF (sans domicile fixe)	homeless person
le TGV (train à grande vitesse)	high-speed train
le VTT (vélo tout terrain)	mountain bike

Dialogues and Messages

à l'appareil	speaking / on the line
à l'attention de	for the attention of
appelle-moi / appelez-moi	call me (formal / informal)
le bip sonore	tone
le combiné	receiver (telephone)
composer le numéro	dial the number
envoi de	sent by
le faux numéro	wrong number
l'indicatif (m)	area code
un instant	one moment
je reviens tout de suite	I'll be right back
je vous écoute	I'm listening
je vous le / la passe	I will put you through
le mail / le courriel	email
la messagerie vocale	voicemail
ne quittez pas	stay on the line
patientez	wait
suite à	further to / following

Section Two — About Me

You and Your Family (p.16-17)

adopté(e)	adopted
aîné(e)	elder
l'anniversaire (m)	birthday
s'appeler	to be called
avoir...ans	to be...years old
le beau-frère	brother-in-law
le beau-père	step-father
le bébé	baby
la belle-mère	step-mother
la belle-sœur	sister-in-law
le cousin / la cousine	cousin
le demi-frère	half-brother / step-brother
la demi-sœur	half-sister / step-sister
divorcé(e)	divorced
d'origine...	of... origin
la famille proche	close relatives
la famille élargie	extended family
la fille	daughter / girl
le fils	son
le fils / la fille unique	only child
le frère	brother
la grand-mère	grandmother
le grand-père	grandfather
les grands-parents (m)	grandparents
le jumeau / la jumelle	twin
la maison de retraite	old people's home
la maman	mum
la mamie / mémé	grandma / granny
la mère	mother
mort(e)	dead
mourir	to die
la naissance	birth
naître	to be born
né(e) le...	born on the...
le neveu	nephew
la nièce	niece
le nom	surname
nous sommes...	there are... of us
l'oncle (m)	uncle
le papa	dad
le papy / pépé	grandad
le parent / la parente	relative
le / la partenaire	partner
le père	father
le / la petit(e) ami(e)	boyfriend / girlfriend
la petite-fille	granddaughter
le petit-fils	grandson
plus âgé(e)	older
plus jeune	younger
le prénom	first name
la sœur	sister
la tante	aunt

Describing People (p.18-19)

aimable	kind
l'apparence (f)	appearance
autoritaire	bossy
avoir l'air	to look (e.g. angry)
la barbe	beard
bavard(e)	chatty / talkative
beau / bel / belle	handsome / beautiful
bête	stupid / silly
les bijoux (m)	jewellery
blond(e)	blonde
bouclé(e)	curly
le bouton	spot / pimple
brun(e)	brown
le caractère	personality
les cheveux (m)	hair
la cicatrice	scar
clair(e)	light
compréhensif / compréhensive	understanding
court(e)	short (hair)
de mauvaise humeur	bad-tempered
de taille moyenne	of medium height
égoïste	selfish
équilibré(e)	well-balanced
l'esprit (m)	mind
étonnant(e)	amazing
étrange	strange
fâché(e)	angry
fiable	reliable
fier / fière	proud
foncé(e)	dark
fou / fol / folle	mad, crazy
frisé(e)	curly
gêner	to annoy
généreux / généreuse	generous
gentil / gentille	kind, nice
le grain de beauté	mole (on skin)
grand(e)	tall
gros / grosse	fat
heureux / heureuse	happy
honnête	honest
insupportable	unbearable
jaloux / jalouse	jealous
jeune	young
la jeunesse	youth
joli(e)	pretty
laid(e)	ugly
long / longue	long
les lunettes (f)	glasses
méchant(e)	naughty
mi-long / mi-longue	medium length
mince	slim
ondulé(e)	wavy
paresseux / paresseuse	lazy
pénible	annoying
la personnalité	personality
petit(e)	short
raide	straight
roux / rousse	ginger
le sens de l'humour	sense of humour
sensible	sensitive
sportif / sportive	sporty
sûr(e) de soi	self-confident
sympa	kind / nice
têtu(e)	stubborn
timide	shy
tranquille	quiet / calm
travailleur / travailleuse	hard-working
triste	sad
vaniteux / vaniteuse	conceited
vieux / vieil / vieille	old
vif / vive	lively
les vrais jumeaux (m) / les vraies jumelles (f)	identical twins
les yeux (m)	eyes

Pets (p.20)

affectueux / affectueuse	affectionate
allergique à	allergic to
le chat	cat
le cheval	horse
le chien	dog
le cochon d'Inde	guinea pig
effronté(e)	cheeky
fidèle	loyal / faithful
le hamster	hamster
le lapin	rabbit
mignon(ne)	cute
l'oiseau (m)	bird
le poil	animal hair
le poisson rouge	goldfish
le poisson tropical	tropical fish
le serpent	snake
la tortue	tortoise

Style and Fashion (p.21)

la bague	ring
les boucles d'oreille (f)	earrings
la casquette	cap
le collier	necklace
le collant	tights
la confiance en soi	self-confidence
le costume	suit
en coton	made of cotton
en cuir	made of leather
d'occasion	second-hand

se faire coiffer	to have one's hair done
se faire couper les cheveux	to have one's hair cut
habillé / vêtu de	dressed in
en laine	made of wool
large	loose
le maquillage	make-up
se maquiller	to put on make-up
la mode	fashion
le parfum	perfume
à points	spotted
porter	to wear
rayé(e)	striped
le rouge à lèvres	lipstick
serré(e)	tight
le tatouage	tattoo
teint	dyed (hair)
en velours	made of velvet

Relationships (p.22-24)

l'amitié (f)	friendship
l'amour (m)	love
casse-pieds	a pain in the neck
célibataire	single
la confiance	trust
connaître	to know (a person)
le copain / la copine	friend / mate
se disputer	to argue
ensemble	together
s'entendre (avec)	to get on (with)
épouser	to marry
être fâché(e)	to be angry

se faire des amis	to make friends
la femme	wife / woman
la fête familiale	family celebration
les fiançailles (f)	engagement
gâter	to spoil
gâté(e)	spoilt
injuste	unfair
joyeux / joyeuse	happy
le mari	husband
le mariage	marriage
se marier	to get married / to marry
le / la meilleur(e) ami(e)	best friend
mépriser	to despise
se mettre en colère	to get angry
le modèle	role model
les noces (f)	wedding
partager	to share
le / la partenaire	partner
participer à	to take part in
passer du temps avec	to spend time with
le petit ami	boyfriend
la petite amie	girlfriend
les rapports (m)	relationships
le sentiment	feeling
séparé(e)	separated
se rendre compte	to realise
sortir	to go out
soutenir	to support
le surnom	nickname
traîner avec	to hang out with

Section Three — Daily Life

Everyday Life (p.30)

aider	to help
l'argent (m) de poche	pocket money
le bricolage	DIY (do it yourself)
se brosser les dents	to brush your teeth
se coucher	to go to bed
les courses (f)	shopping
cuisiner	to cook
devoir	to have to
se doucher	to shower
faire le lit	to make the bed
la fleur	flower
garder	to look after
s'habiller	to get dressed
le jardinage	gardening
laver	to wash
se laver	to wash (yourself)
la lessive	laundry
se lever	to get up
mettre la table	to lay the table
nettoyer	to clean
passer l'aspirateur	to vacuum

la pelouse	lawn
prendre le petit-déjeuner	to eat breakfast
propre	clean, tidy
ranger	to tidy
la tâche	task
la vaisselle	washing-up

Food (p.31)

avoir faim	to be hungry
avoir soif	to be thirsty
l'agneau (m)	lamb
l'ail (m)	garlic
allergique à	allergic to
amer / amère	bitter
l'ananas (m)	pineapple
l'artichaut (m)	artichoke
l'assiette (f)	plate / dish
le beurre	butter
le bifteck	steak
le bœuf	beef
les bonbons (m)	sweets
la boulette	meatball
la brochette	kebab
le canard	duck

la cerise	cherry
le champignon	mushroom
les chips (m)	crisps
le chou	cabbage
le chou-fleur	cauliflower
les choux de Bruxelles	brussels sprouts
le citron	lemon
la confiture	jam
la côtelette (de porc / d'agneau)	(pork / lamb) chop
la crêpe	pancake
le croque-monsieur	toasted ham and cheese sandwich
cuisiner	to cook
le déjeuner	lunch
la dinde	turkey
le dîner	evening meal
épicé(e)	spicy
les épinards (m)	spinach
l'espèce (f)	type / kind
essayer	to try
fait(e) maison	homemade
la fraise	strawberry
la framboise	raspberry

Vocabulary

le fromage	cheese
le fromage de chèvre	goat's cheese
les frites (f)	chips
les fruits (m)	fruit
les fruits (m) de mer	seafood
fumé	smoked
le gâteau	cake
la glace	ice cream
le goût	taste
goûter	to taste
les haricots (m) verts	green beans
le jambon	ham
le lait	milk
les légumes (m)	vegetables
manger	to eat
les nouilles (f)	noodles
la noix	nut
nourrissant(e)	nourishing
la nourriture	food
l'œuf (m)	egg
l'oignon (m)	onion
le pain	bread
le pamplemousse	grapefruit
les pâtes (f)	pasta
la pêche	fishing / peach
le petit-déjeuner	breakfast
les petits pois (m)	peas
piquant(e)	spicy
le plat cuisiné	ready meal
la poire	pear
les poireaux (m)	leeks
le poisson	fish
le poivre	pepper
le poivron	pepper (vegetable)
la pomme	apple
la pomme de terre	potato
le potage	soup
le poulet	chicken
la prune	plum
les raisins (m)	grapes
le repas	meal
le riz	rice
rôti(e)	roast
salé(e)	salty
la sauce vinaigrette	salad dressing
la saucisse	sausage
le saucisson	cold sliced meat
le saumon	salmon
le sel	salt
le steak haché	burger
le sucre	sugar
sucré(e)	sweet
le thon	tuna
végétalien(ne)	vegan
végétarien(ne)	vegetarian
la viande	meat
la viande hachée	mince
le yaourt	yoghurt

Shopping (p.32-33)

abîmé(e)	damaged
les baskets (f)	trainers
besoin (m) (avoir... de)	need (to need)
la boîte	box / tin / can
le blouson	coat / jacket
bon marché	cheap
les bottes (f)	boots
Ça me va.	It suits me.
la caisse	till
la carte bancaire	bank card
la ceinture	belt
le centre commercial	shopping centre
C'est combien, s'il vous plaît ?	How much is it, please?
le caleçon	leggings
le chapeau	hat
les chaussettes (f)	socks
les chaussures (f)	shoes
la chemise	shirt
cher / chère	expensive
le choix	choice
la chose	thing
les courses (f)	shopping
la cravate	tie
défectueux / défectueuse	faulty
dépenser	to spend (money)
l'écharpe (f)	scarf
endommagé(e)	damaged
en espèces	with cash
en ligne	online
essayer	to try on
l'étiquette (f)	label
faire la queue	to queue
se faire rembourser	to get a refund
le foulard	scarf
les gants (m)	gloves
le gilet	waistcoat
le grand magasin	department store
la grande surface	superstore
gratuit(e)	free (of charge)
l'imperméable (m)	raincoat
le jean	jeans
la jupe	skirt
un kilogramme	a kilogram
le lèche-vitrine (faire du)	window shopping (to go window shopping)
un litre	litre
livrer	to deliver
le magasin	shop
le maillot (de sport)	sports shirt
le manteau	coat
la marque	make / label / brand
la mode	fashion
la moitié	half
le morceau	piece
le pantalon	trousers

un paquet	packet
perdre	to lose
peser	to weigh
le polo	polo shirt
le portefeuille	wallet
le porte-monnaie	purse
la portion	portion
pouvoir	to be able
pratique	convenient
le prix	price
les provisions (f)	food shopping
le pull	jumper
le pull à capuche	hoodie
le pyjama	pyjamas
le quart	quarter
le rayon	department
réduire	to reduce
réduit(e)	reduced
je regarde	I'm browsing
rembourser	to refund
la robe	dress
le sac à main	handbag
les soldes (m)	sale
le survêtement / le jogging	tracksuit
le sweat	sweatshirt
la taille	size
le ticket de caisse	receipt
la tranche	slice
tranché(e)	sliced
le tricot	sweater / jumper
le vendeur / la vendeuse	shop assistant
vendre	to sell
la veste	jacket
les vêtements (m)	clothes
la vitrine	shop window

Technology (p.34-35)

à cause de	because of
l'abonné (m) / l'abonnée (f)	subscriber
acheter	to buy
afficher	to post
au lieu de	instead of
l'avantage (m)	advantage
le bloggeur	blogger
chercher	to look for
le clavier	keyboard
cliquer	to click
le compte	account
la console de jeux	games console
le courrier électronique	email
la cyber-intimidation	cyberbullying
dangereux / dangereuse	dangerous
le désavantage	disadvantage
les détails (m) personnels	personal details
l'écran (m) tactile	touch screen
l'écrivain (m)	author

effacer	*to delete*	le lecteur MP3	*MP3 player*	recevoir	*to receive*
en ligne	*online*	le logiciel	*software*	remplir	*to fill (in)*
enregistrer	*to record*	le mail / le courrier électronique	*e-mail*	le réseau social	*social network*
envoyer	*to send*			rester en contact	*to stay in contact*
être accro à	*to be addicted to*	mettre	*to put*	le risque	*risk*
faire attention	*to be careful*	mettre en ligne	*to upload*	sauvegarder	*to save*
faire des recherches	*to do research*	le moniteur	*monitor*	le site internet / web	*website*
le fichier	*file*	le mot de passe	*password*	les sites sociaux	*social media sites*
le forum	*chat room*	naviguer (sur)	*to browse*	la souris	*mouse*
la fraude	*fraud*	numérique	*digital*	surfer sur Internet	*to surf the internet*
le genre	*type / kind*	l'ordinateur (m)	*computer*	la tablette	*tablet*
grâce à	*thanks to*	l'ordinateur (m) portable	*laptop*	taper	*to type*
l'imprimante (f)	*printer*			tchatter	*to talk online*
imprimer	*to print*	la page d'accueil	*welcome page*	télécharger	*to download*
l'inconvénient (m)	*disadvantage / drawback*	la page internet	*internet page*	le texto	*text message*
		partager	*to share*	la toile / le web	*web*
l'internaute (m)	*internet user*	passer du temps	*to spend time*	la touche	*key*
Internet (m)	*Internet*	la pile	*battery*	le traitement de texte	*word processing*
le jeu	*game*	le portable	*mobile (phone)*		
le lecteur DVD	*DVD player*	pratique	*practical*	la vie privée	*private life*

Section Four — Free-Time Activities

Books and Reading (p.43)

la bande dessinée (BD)	*comic book*
collectionner	*to collect*
les connaissances (f)	*knowledge*
le journal	*newspaper*
la lecture	*reading*
la liseuse électronique	*e-reader*
le livre	*book*
le livre électronique	*e-book*
le magazine	*magazine*
le plaisir	*pleasure / amusement*
la revue	*magazine*
le roman	*novel*
le roman policier	*detective story*
romantique	*romantic*

Celebrations and Festivals (p.44-45)

l'Aïd (f) al-Fitr	*Eid al-Fitr*
athée	*atheist*
Bonne année !	*Happy New Year!*
Bon anniversaire !	*Happy birthday!*
Bonne chance !	*Good luck!*
la bougie	*candle*
la bûche de Noël	*yule log*
le cadeau	*present*
le Carême	*Lent*
célébrer	*to celebrate*
chanter	*to sing*
chrétien(ne)	*Christian*
commercial(e)	*commercial*
la couronne	*crown*
la danse	*dance*
le défilé	*procession*
la dinde	*turkey*

l'église (f)	*church*
l'événement (m)	*event*
Félicitations !	*Congratulations!*
la fête	*festival / celebration / party*
la fête des mères / pères	*Mother's / Father's Day*
la fête des rois	*Epiphany / Twelfth Night*
la fête du travail	*May Day*
la fête nationale	*Bastille Day*
fêter	*to celebrate*
les feux (m) d'artifice	*fireworks*
la fève	*charm*
la foi	*faith*
la galette des rois	*cake for Epiphany*
le gâteau des rois	*cake for Epiphany*
la Hanoukka	*Hanukkah*
historique	*historical*
impressionnant(e)	*impressive*
jouer un tour	*to play a trick*
le Jour de l'An	*New Year's Day*
le jour férié	*bank holiday*
Joyeux Noël !	*Merry Christmas!*
juif / juive	*Jewish*
le lundi de Pâques	*Easter Monday*
la messe	*mass*
la mosquée	*mosque*
musulman(e)	*Muslim*
l'oie (f)	*goose*
le pain calendal	*Christmas loaf*
Pâques	*Easter*
la Pentecôte	*Whitsuntide*
la plaisanterie	*joke*
le poisson d'avril	*April Fools' Day*
Poisson d'avril !	*April Fool!*
prier	*to pray*
le ramadan	*Ramadan*

la reine	*queen*
religieux / religieuse	*religious*
la réunion	*meeting*
le réveillon	*meal eaten after midnight in France*
le roi	*king*
la Saint Valentin	*Valentine's Day*
la Saint-Sylvestre	*New Year's Eve*
le sapin de Noël	*Christmas tree*
sentimental(e)	*sentimental*
la synagogue	*synagogue*
la Toussaint	*All Saints Day*
les vacances	*holidays*
la veille de Noël	*Christmas Eve*
le vendredi saint	*Good Friday*

Music, Film and TV (p.46-47)

s'abonner	*to subscribe*
l'acteur (m) / l'actrice (f)	*actor / actress*
les actualités (f)	*news*
l'ado (m / f)	*adolescent*
apprendre à	*to learn to*
l'argent (m)	*money*
la bande-annonce	*trailer*
la batterie	*drums*
le billet	*ticket*
célèbre	*famous*
la chaîne de télé	*TV channel*
la chanson	*song*
chanter	*to sing*
le chanteur / la chanteuse	*singer*
la chorale	*choir*
les clips (m)	*music videos*
la comédie musicale	*musical comedy (a musical)*
commencer	*to start*

le concert	concert	regarder	to watch	faire de la gymnastique	to do gymnastics
la dance	dance music	relaxant(e)	relaxing	faire du vélo	to cycle
débuter	to begin	rencontrer	to meet	faire une randonnée	to go on a walk / hike
le dessin animé	cartoon	répéter	to rehearse / practise	gagner	to win
diffuser	to broadcast			fana de	a fan of
divertissant(e)	entertaining	se reposer	to rest	le foot / football	football
le documentaire	documentary	la séance	performance	le hockey	hockey
écouter de la musique	to listen to music	la série	series	le jeu de société	board game
		la série historique	period drama	le lieu (avoir lieu)	place (to take place)
les effets (m) spéciaux	special effects	les sous-titres (m)	subtitles	marquer un but / un essai	to score a goal / a try
l'émission (f)	programme	le spectacle	show (e.g. theatre)	se motiver	to motivate oneself
entraînant(e)	catchy	le tarif réduit	reduced price	la musculation	body building
faire partie de	to take part in	la télé réalité	reality TV	nager	to swim
le feuilleton	soap opera	la télévision satellite	satellite TV	la natation	swimming
le film d'action / d'aventure	action film	le temps libre	free time	le netball	netball
		la vedette	film star	le parapente	paragliding
le film d'amour / romantique	romantic film	le violon	violin	participer (à)	to take part (in)
		voir	see	le patin à glace	ice skating
le film d'animation	animated film			la patinoire	ice rink
le film comique	comedy film	**Sport (p.48)**		la pêche	fishing
le film de guerre	war film	à l'intérieur	inside	perdre	to lose
le film d'horreur / d'épouvante	horror film	à l'extérieur	outside	la piscine	swimming pool
		les arts martiaux (m)	martial arts	la planche à voile	wind-surfing
le film policier	detective film	l'athlétisme (m)	athletics	la plongée sous-marine	scuba diving
le film de science-fiction	science fiction film	l'aviron (m)	rowing		
		le badminton	badminton	pratiquer un sport	to do a sport
le film / l'histoire (f) de suspense	thriller (film / book)	le basket	basketball	la promenade	walk
		la boxe	boxing	régulièrement	regularly
la flûte	flute	le canoë-kayak	canoeing	le rugby	rugby
le genre	genre / type / kind	captivant(e)	engaging	le skate	skateboarding
le groupe	band	le centre sportif	sports centre	le ski (nautique)	(water) skiing
la guitare	guitar	le cheval	horse	sportif / sportive	sporty
l'histoire (f)	storyline	le club des jeunes	youth club	les sports (m) d'hiver	winter sports
les informations (f)	news	compétitif / compétitive	competitive	les sports (m) extrêmes	extreme sports
s'intéresser à	to be interested in				
l'intrigue (f)	plot	courir	to run	le stade	stadium
le jeu télévisé	game show	la course	race	le surf	surfing
jouer (d'un instrument)	to play (an instrument)	les échecs (m)	chess	le tennis	tennis
		l'entraînement (m)	sports practice	le terrain de sport	sports field
le musicien / la musicienne	musician	s'entraîner	to train	le tir à l'arc	archery
		l'équipe (f)	team	la tournée	tour
la musique folk	folk music	l'équitation (f)	horse riding	le tournoi	tournament
la musique pop	pop music	l'escalade (f)	rock climbing	tricher	to cheat
la musique rock	rock music	l'escrime (f)	fencing	la voile	sailing
l'orchestre (m)	orchestra	l'événement (m)	event	le volley	volleyball
le personnage	character				
la publicité	advert(s)				

Section Five — Where You Live

Where You Live (p.54-55)

à la campagne	in the countryside	la banque	bank	le canapé	sofa
à la montagne	in the mountains	le bâtiment	building	la cave	cellar
au bord de la mer	by the sea	la bibliothèque	library	célèbre	famous
au premier / deuxième étage (m)	on the first / second floor	la bijouterie	jeweller's shop	le centre commercial	shopping centre
		la boucherie	butcher's		
animé	lively	la boulangerie	bakery	le centre-ville	town centre
l'appartement (m)	flat	le bowling	bowling alley	la chaise	chair
l'arbre (m)	tree	le bruit	noise	la chambre	bedroom
l'armoire (f)	wardrobe	bruyant	noisy	le champ	field
la banlieue	suburb	le bureau	office / study / desk	la charcuterie	delicatessen
		calme	quiet	le cinéma	cinema

la circulation	traffic	le musée	museum	le brouillard	fog
la colline	hill	tout(e) neuf / neuve	brand new	la brume	mist
les commerces (m)	shops	le parc	park	la chaleur	heat
le commissariat	police station	la pâtisserie	cake shop	chaud(e)	hot
la cuisine	kitchen / cooking	pauvre	poor	le ciel	sky
déménager	to move house	la pièce	room	clair(e)	bright
démodé	old-fashioned	la piste cyclable	cycle path	le climat	climate
les distractions (f)	things to do	pittoresque	picturesque	couvert(e)	overcast
l'embouteillage (m)	traffic jam	le placard	cupboard	doux / douce	mild
emménager	to move in	la place	square	l'éclair (m)	lightning
l'endroit (m)	place	le pont	bridge	l'éclaircie (f)	bright spell
l'escalier (m)	staircase	la poste	post office	ensoleillé(e)	sunny
l'espace (m) vert	park / green space	le quartier	area	faire beau	to be fine (weather)
l'étage (m)	floor / storey	la quincaillerie	ironmonger's /	faire mauvais	to be bad (weather)
la fenêtre	window		hardware shop	froid(e)	cold
la ferme	farm	quitter	to leave	geler	to freeze
la fermeture	closure	le rez-de-chaussée	ground floor	grêler	to hail
le four	oven	le risque	risk	la glace	ice
le foyer	home	sale	dirty	humide	humid / wet
la gare	railway station	la salle à manger	dining room	la météo	weather report
la gare routière	bus station	la salle de bains	bathroom	mouillé(e)	wet
les gens (m)	people	le salon	living room / lounge	neiger	to snow
la grande ville	city	la sécurité	safety	le nuage	cloud
le grenier	loft	le sous-sol	basement	nuageux / nuageuse	cloudy
l'habitant (m)	inhabitant	la station-service	service station	l'ombre (m)	shade, shadow
l'HLM (f)	council housing	le supermarché	supermarket	l'orage (m)	storm
l'hôpital (m)	hospital	surchargé	overcrowded	orageux / orageuse	stormy
l'hôtel (m) de ville	town hall	le tabac	newsagent's	pleuvoir	to rain
l'immeuble (m)	block of flats	le théâtre	theatre	la pluie	rain
le lac	lake	les transports (m)	public transport	les prévisions	weather forecast
la librairie	bookshop	en commun		météo (f)	
le lit	bed	travailler	to work	sec / sèche	dry
le loyer	rent	se trouver	to be situated	le soleil	sun
la lumière	light	l'usine (f)	factory	la température	low temperature
la mairie	town hall	la vie	life	basse	
la maison	house	le village	village	la température	high temperature
(individuelle /	(detached /	la ville	town	élevée	
jumelée /	semi-detached /	vivre	to live	la température	average
mitoyenne)	terraced)	le voisin / la voisine	neighbour	moyenne	temperature
le marché	market	la zone piétonne	pedestrian zone	la tempête	storm
le métro	underground railway			le temps	weather
les meubles (m)	furniture	**Weather (p.56)**		le tonnerre	thunder
la moquette	carpet	agité(e)	turbulent	tremper	to soak
multiculturel/le	multicultural	l'averse (f)	shower	variable	changeable
le mur	wall	briller	to shine	le vent	wind

Section Six — Travel and Tourism

Where to Go (p.62)

à la montagne	in the mountains	l'Asie (f)	Asia	la Corse	Corsica
à l'étranger	abroad	asiatique	Asian	la côte	coast
l'Afrique (f)	Africa	l'Autriche (f)	Austria	le Danemark	Denmark
africain(e)	African	autrichien(ne)	Austrian	danois(e)	Danish
l'Algérie (f)	Algeria	la Belgique	Belgium	le département	administrative area
algérien(ne)	Algerian	belge	Belgian		of France
l'Allemagne (f)	Germany	la Bourgogne	Burgundy	Douvres	Dover
allemand(e)	German	le Brésil	Brazil	l'Écosse (f)	Scotland
les Alpes (f)	the Alps	brésilien(ne)	Brazilian	écossais(e)	Scottish
l'Amérique (f) du Sud	South America	la Bretagne	Brittany	l'Espagne (f)	Spain
américain(e)	American	le Canada	Canada	espagnol(e)	Spanish
l'Angleterre (f)	England	canadien(n)	Canadian	les États-Unis (m)	United States
anglais(e)	English	la Chine	China	l'Europe (f)	Europe
		chinois(e)	Chinese	européen(ne)	European

la France	France
français(e)	French
la frontière	border / frontier
la Grande-Bretagne	Great Britain
britannique	British
la Grèce	Greece
grec(que)	Greek
la Guyane	French Guiana
l'île (f)	island
l'Inde (f)	India
indien(ne)	Indian
l'Irlande (f)	Ireland
irlandais(e)	Irish
l'Italie (f)	Italy
italien(ne)	Italian
le Japon	Japan
japonais(e)	Japanese
Londres	London
la Manche	English Channel
le Maroc	Morocco
marocain(e)	Moroccan
la Méditerranée	Mediterranean
la mer	sea
le monde	world
la Normandie	Normandy
Paris	Paris
les Pays-Bas (m)	Netherlands
néerlandais	Dutch
le pays de Galles	Wales
gallois(e)	Welsh
la Picardie	Picardy
la plage	beach
le Royaume-Uni	United Kingdom
la Réunion	Reunion
la Russie	Russia
russe	Russian
le Sénégal	Senegal
la Suisse	Switzerland
suisse	Swiss
la Tunisie	Tunisia
tunisien(ne)	Tunisian
la Turquie	Turkey
turc / turque	Turkish

Preparation (p.63-64)

l'accueil (m)	welcome / reception
l'agence (f) de voyages	travel agency
l'aire (f) de jeux	play area
l'ascenseur (m)	lift
l'auberge (f) de jeunesse	youth hostel
les bagages (m)	luggage
le camping	campsite
le camping-car	campervan
la caravane	caravan
casser	to break
la chambre	room
la chambre d'hôte	bed and breakfast
la chambre de famille	family room

la chambre pour deux personnes	double room
chercher	to look for
la clé	key
la climatisation	air conditioning
la colonie de vacances	holiday / summer camp
la demie-pension	half board
déranger	to disturb
descendre	to go down
donner sur	to overlook
le dortoir	dormitory
dresser	to put up (tent)
durer	to last
l'échange (m)	exchange
l'emplacement (m)	pitch
en plein air	in the open air
expliquer	to explain
héberger	to lodge / accommodate
l'hôtel (m) (de luxe)	(luxury) hotel
inconnu(e)	unknown
jumelé(e)	twinned
le lavabo	wash basin
lever	to lift
le lit	bed
le lit à deux places	double bed
les lits (m) jumeaux	twin beds
les lits (m) superposés	bunk beds
le logement	accommodation
loger	to stay / to lodge
le passeport	passport
la pension complète	full board
la pièce d'identité	ID
les préparatifs (m)	preparations
prêt(e)	ready
le projet	plan
le / la propriétaire	owner
remercier	to thank
réserver	to book / to reserve
rester	to stay
le sac de couchage	sleeping bag
la salle de séjour	lounge
le séjour	stay / visit
la station balnéaire	seaside resort
la tente	tent
les vacances (f)	holidays
la valise	suitcase
la vue de mer	sea view

Getting There (p.65)

l'aéroport (m)	airport
aller-retour (m)	return ticket
aller-simple (m)	single ticket
l'arrivée (f)	arrival
s'asseoir	to sit down
attendre	to wait (for)
atterrir	to land
l'auto (f)	car
l'autobus (m)	bus
l'autoroute (f)	motorway

l'avion (m)	plane
le bateau	boat
le car	coach
la carte	map
le chemin	way / path
le chemin de fer	railway
conduire	to drive
la correspondance	connection
décoller	to take off
le départ	departure
en provenance de	coming from
en retard	late
s'enregistrer	to check in
l'essence (f)	petrol
le gasoil	diesel
l'horaire (m)	timetable
lentement	slowly
la location de voitures	car rental
louer	to rent / to hire
manquer	to miss
se mettre en route	to set off
la moto	motorbike
partir	to leave
le permis de conduire	driving licence
ralentir	to slow down
le retour	return
retourner	to return
revenir	to come back
la route	way / road
le train	train
le trajet	journey
la traversée	crossing
la voiture	car
le vol	flight
voler	to fly
le voyage	journey / trip
voyager	to travel

What To Do (p.66)

l'aventure (f)	adventure
l'avis (m)	opinion
se baigner	to bathe, swim
le bord de la mer	seaside
la carte postale	postcard
la cathédrale	cathedral
le château	castle
le concours	competition
la crème solaire	sun cream
la culture	culture
se débrouiller	to get by
les distractions (f)	entertainment / things to do
l'événement (m)	event
l'étranger (m) / l'étrangère (f)	stranger / foreigner
explorer	to explore
l'exposition	exhibition
se faire bronzer	to sunbathe
faire du camping	to go camping
faire la connaissance	to get to know

faire la grasse matinée	to lie in / sleep in
la foire	fair
se garer	to park
s'habituer à	to get used to
l'herbe (f)	grass
le lac	lake
laver	to wash
le loisir	free time (activity)
louer	to hire
les lunettes (f) de soleil	sunglasses
le maillot de bain	swimming costume
marcher	to walk
la montagne	mountain
monter	to go up / ascend
le musée	museum
nager	to swim
la nature	nature
l'office (m) de tourisme	tourist office
paraître	to seem
le parc d'attractions	theme park
la plage	beach
plaire	to please
le plan de ville	town plan
se présenter	to introduce oneself
se promener	to go for a walk
la randonnée	walk / hike
remarquer	to notice
le rendez-vous	meeting
les renseignements (m)	information
se réveiller	to wake up
la rivière	river
le sable	sand
la salle de jeux	games room
le site touristique	tourist attraction
le sommet	summit
le spectacle	show
le tour	tour
le tour en bateau	boat tour
le tourisme	tourism
tourner	to turn
traduire	to translate
la visite guidée	guided tour
le zoo	zoo

Eating Out (p.67)

l'addition (f)	the bill
l'auberge (f)	inn (traditional)
bien cuit(e)	well cooked
la bière	beer
boire	to drink
la boisson	drink

le café	coffee
la carte	menu
le chocolat chaud	hot chocolate
choisir	to choose
commander	to order
coûter	to cost
le couvert	place setting
les cuisses (f) de grenouille	frogs' legs
le dessert	dessert
l'eau (f) minérale	mineral water
l'eau (f) plate / gazeuse	still / fizzy water
emporter	to take away
l'escargot (m)	snail
fermé(e)	closed
le hors d'œuvre	starter
le menu à prix fixe	fixed price menu
payer	to pay (for)
prendre	to take
se plaindre	to complain
le plat principal	main meal / dish
le pourboire	tip
la pression	beer (from the pump)
le restaurant	restaurant
le serveur / la serveuse	waiter / waitress
la tasse	cup
le thé	tea
un verre de...	a glass of
le vin	wine

Practical Stuff (p.68)

le bureau des objets trouvés	lost property office
cassé(e)	broken
le commissariat	police station
composter	to validate (ticket)
le contrôleur / la contrôleuse	ticket inspector
défense de / interdit de	(it is) forbidden to...
l'endommagement (m)	damage
la facture	bill (invoice)
les freins (m)	brakes
garantir	to guarantee
laisser	to leave (behind)
la livraison	delivery
le mode d'emploi	instructions for use
la perte	loss
se plaindre	to complain
la plainte	complaint
le pneu crevé	flat tyre
le portefeuille	wallet

le porte-monnaie	purse
le quai	platform
remplacer	to replace
réparer	to repair
le retard	delay
le service client	customer services
tomber en panne	to break down
le vol	robbery / theft
voler	to steal

Directions (p.69)

à droite	on / to the right
à gauche	on / to the left
le carrefour	crossroads
C'est loin d'ici ?	Is it far from here?
de chaque côté	on each side
de l'autre côté	on the other side
en bas	down(stairs)
en face de	opposite
en haut	up(stairs)
environ	about
l'est (m)	east
les feux (m) (de signalisation)	(traffic) lights
la grande rue	high street / main street
ici	here
juste à côté de	right next to
jusqu'à	until / as far as
là	there
là-bas	over there
loin de	far from
le nord	north
nulle part	nowhere
Où est...?	Where is...?
l'ouest (m)	west
le panneau	sign
par	by
partout	everywhere
le péage	toll
la place	square
le pont	bridge
pour aller à... ?	how do I get to...?
près de	near to
quelque part	somewhere
le rond-point	roundabout
la rue	street
situé(e)	situated
le sud	south
tout droit	straight ahead
tout près	very near
toutes directions	all directions
traverser	to cross
le trottoir	pavement
se trouver	to be situated

Section Seven — Current and Future Study and Employment

School Subjects (p.75)

| l'allemand (m) | German |
| apprendre | to learn |

| l'art (m) dramatique | drama |
| les arts (m) ménagers | food technology |

la chimie	chemistry
la couture	sewing
le dessin	art

Vocabulary

l'espagnol (m)	Spanish
l'EPS (éducation physique et sportive) (f)	PE (physical education)
l'étude (f) des médias	media studies
le français	French
l'histoire-géo (f)	humanities
il ne sert à rien	it's useless
l'informatique (f)	ICT
l'instruction (f) civique	personal and social education (PSE)
s'intéresser à	to be interested in
la langue	language
les langues vivantes (f)	modern languages
le latin	Latin
la littérature anglaise	English literature
la matière (obligatoire)	(compulsory) subject
la physique	physics
préféré(e)	favourite
la religion	religious studies
les sciences (f) naturelles	biology
la technologie	DT (design technology)

School Life (p.76-78)

aller à pied	to go on foot
l'ambiance (f)	atmosphere
bien équipé(e)	well equipped
le bulletin scolaire	school report
la calculette	calculator
la cantine	canteen
le car de ramassage	school bus
la chorale	choir
le collège	secondary school
comprendre	to understand
le contrôle	class test / assessment
le couloir	corridor
le cours	lesson
de bonne heure	early
demander	to ask
les devoirs (m)	homework
la difficulté	difficulty
le diplôme	qualification
le directeur	headmaster
la directrice	headmistress
distribuer	to give out
doué(e)	gifted / talented
le droit	right
échouer	to do badly / fail
l'école (f) confessionnelle	religious school
l'école maternelle	nursery school
l'école (f) primaire	primary school
l'école (f) privée	private school
l'école (f) publique	state school

l'école (f) secondaire	secondary school
l'élève (m / f)	pupil
l'emploi (m) du temps	timetable
en retard	late
en seconde	in year 11
enseigner	to teach
les études (f)	study
l'étudiant (m)	student
l'examen (m)	examination
l'expérience (f)	experiment
faire attention	to pay attention
fatigant(e)	tiring
les grandes vacances (f)	summer holidays
le groupe théâtral	drama group
le gymnase	sports hall
l'heure du déjeuner	lunch break
les incivilités (f)	rudeness
l'injure (f)	insult
l'instituteur (m) / l'institutrice (f)	primary school teacher
interdit(e)	forbidden
l'internat / le pensionnat (m)	boarding school
une journée typique	a typical day
le laboratoire	laboratory
le laboratoire de langues	language lab
la leçon	lesson
la lecture	reading
lire	to read
le lycée	sixth form college
mal équipé(e)	badly equipped
le maquillage	make up
la maternelle	nursery school
le niveau	achievement, performance
la note	mark / grade
oublier	to forget
passer (en classe supérieure)	to move up (to the next form / year)
passer un examen	to sit an exam
la pause	break / pause
penser	to think
permettre	to allow / permit
la piscine	swimming pool
porter	to wear / carry
la pression	pressure
le / la professeur	teacher
le progrès	progress
le proviseur	head teacher
la récré(ation)	break
la rédaction	essay
redoubler	to repeat a year
la règle	rule
le règlement	school rules
la rentrée	return to school (after the holidays)
répéter	to repeat
la réponse	reply
le résultat	result

la retenue	detention
réussir un examen	to pass an exam
la salle de classe	classroom
savoir	to know
scolaire	school (adj)
sécher les cours	to skip lessons
la semaine	week
le succès / la réussite	success
le tableau	board
le terrain de sport	sports ground
le trimestre	term
l'uniforme (m) scolaire	school uniform
les vestiaires (m)	changing rooms

School Events (p.79)

à l'étranger	abroad
un(e) correspondante	penfriend / pen pal
l'échange (m) (scolaire)	(school) exchange
l'excursion (f) scolaire	school trip
le groupe scolaire	school group / party
participer à	to take part
la remise des prix	prize giving
la rencontre parents-professeurs	parents' evening
la réunion	meeting

Education Post-16 (p.80)

l'année (f) sabbatique	gap year
l'apprenti(e) (m / f)	apprentice
l'apprentissage (m)	apprenticeship
l'avenir (m)	future
avoir envie de	to want to
avoir l'intention de	to intend to
le bac(calauréat)	A-levels
le but	aim / goal
le conseiller / la conseillère d'orientation	careers adviser
le diplôme	qualification
le droit	law (study of)
en première	in year 12
en terminale	in year 13
l'enseignement (m) postscolaire	further education
l'épreuve (f)	test
l'établissement (m)	establishment
étudier	to study
la faculté	university / faculty
former	to train
laisser tomber	to drop
la liberté	freedom
la licence	degree
le lycée	sixth form college / grammar school
le lycée professionnel	technical college
la médecine	medicine (study of)

les projets pour l'avenir	future plans	le fermier / la fermière	farmer
le travail bénévole	voluntary work	le / la fonctionnaire	civil servant
l'université (f)	university	gagner	to earn / win

varié(e) — varied
le vendeur / la vendeuse — shop assistant
venir de — to have just
le / la vétérinaire — vet

Career Choices (p.81)

à peine	scarcely
à temps partiel	part-time
à temps plein	full-time
l'agent de police (m)	police officer
l'architecte (m / f)	architect
l'artiste (m / f)	artist
assis(e)	sitting
l'avenir (m)	future
l'avocat(e) (m / f)	lawyer
le babysitting	babysitting
bien payé	well paid
le boulot	job (informal)
le candidat	candidate
le coiffeur / la coiffeuse	hairdresser
le commerce	business
le / la comptable	accountant
compter (sur)	to count (on)
le cuisinier / la cuisinière	cook
le débouché	job opportunity / prospect
debout	standing
le / la dentiste	dentist
le dessinateur / la dessinatrice de mode	fashion designer
disponible	available
élargir	to widen
l'électricien(ne) (m / f)	electrician
l'emploi (m)	job (formal)
l'employé(e) (m / f)	employee
l'employeur (m) / l'employeuse (f)	employer
enrichissant(e)	enriching / rewarding
l'entreprise (f)	firm / enterprise
l'entretien (m)	interview
espérer	to hope
le facteur / la factrice	postman / postwoman

l'hôtesse (f) de l'air	air hostess
l'idée (f)	idea
l'infirmier (m) / l'infirmière (f)	nurse
l'informaticien(ne) (m / f)	computer scientist
l'ingénieur (m / f)	engineer
l'instituteur (m) / l'institutrice (f)	primary school teacher
l'interprète (m / f)	interpreter
le journal	newspaper
le / la journaliste	journalist
la livre (sterling)	pound (sterling)
le maçon	builder
mal payé	badly paid
le mécanicien / la mécanicienne	mechanic
le médecin	doctor
mettre de l'argent de côté	to save money
le monde du travail	the world of work
le musicien / la musicienne	musician
l'outil (m)	tool
le patron / la patronne	boss
le petit job	part-time job
le pharmacien / la pharmacienne	pharmacist
le plombier	plumber
le policier / la policière	police officer
le / la professeur	teacher
le programmeur	programmer
la retraite	retirement
le rêve	dream
rêver	to dream
le salaire	salary
le steward de l'air	air steward
le traducteur / la traductrice	translator
le travailleur social / la travailleuse sociale	social worker

Languages for the Future (p.82)

l'assistant(e) (m / f) de langue	language assistant
communiquer	to communicate
discuter	to talk / to discuss
s'exprimer	to express oneself
les langues (f) étrangères	foreign languages
obtenir un métier	to get a job
parcourir le monde	to travel the world
parler couramment	to speak fluently
les possibilités (f) d'avancement	promotion prospects
rencontrer quelqu'un	to meet someone
la société multiculturelle	multicultural society

Applying for Jobs (p.83)

l'annonce (f) de recrutement	job advertisement
bénévolement	voluntarily / without pay
les compétences (f)	skills
les conditions (f) d'emploi	terms of employment
les diplômes requis	the required qualifications
faire un stage	to do work experience
joindre	to attach / enclose
le jour de congé	(a) day's leave
la lettre de motivation	application letter
l'offre (f) d'emploi	job offer
poser sa candidature	to apply for a job
le poste	position
postuler	to apply
les possibilités (f) d'avancement	promotion prospects
qualifié	qualified
remplir un formulaire	to fill in a form

Section Eight — Global Issues

Problems in Society (p.89)

affamé(e)	starving
agresser	to attack
améliorer	to improve
l'attaque (f)	attack
avoir besoin de	to need
la bande	gang
battu(e)	hit
les biens	possessions
blessé(e)	injured

la bonne action	good deed
le chômage	unemployment
combattre	to combat
coupable	guilty
un défi	a challenge
déprimé(e)	depressed
la dette	debt
la discrimination	discrimination
les droits (m) de l'homme	human rights

égal(e)	equal
l'égalité (f)	equality
l'émeute (f)	riot
l'enquête (f)	enquiry
entouré(e)	surrounded
éradiquer	to eradicate
l'espionnage (m)	spying
la faim	hunger
gratifiant(e)	rewarding
la guerre	war

194

le harcèlement	bullying / harassment
Il vaut la peine.	It's worthwhile.
l'immigration (f)	immigration
l'immigré (m)	immigrant
l'inégalité (f) sociale	social inequality
lourd(e)	heavy / serious
lutter	to struggle
malheureux / malheureuse	unfortunate / needy
mal nourri(e)	malnourished
la manifestation	demonstration
mener une campagne	to lead a campaign
mentir	to lie
se moquer de	to make fun of
les morts (f)	deaths / fatalities
mourir	to die
la paix	peace
les pauvres	the poor
la pauvreté	poverty
les personnes (f) défavorisées	disadvantaged people
se plaindre	to complain
le / la politicien(ne)	politician
prioritiser	to prioritise
produire	to provide / to produce
le racisme	racism
reconnaissant(e)	grateful
le réfugié	refugee
le / la sans-abri	homeless person
les SDF	homeless people
la sécurité	security
socialement exclu(e)	socially excluded
supporter	to tolerate / put up with
supprimer	to suppress / eliminate
le témoin	witness
le travail bénévole / volontaire	voluntary work
le troisième âge	old age
tuer	to kill
la victime	victim
vivre	to live
voler	to steal
le voyou	yob / hooligan
vulnérable	vulnerable

The Environment (p.90-92)

allumer	to switch on
améliorer	to improve
les animaux (m)	animals
augmenter	to increase
le bain	bath
la boîte (en carton)	(cardboard) box
le boîte (en aluminium)	(aluminium) can
la campagne	campaign
la catastrophe naturelle	natural disaster

le centre de recyclage	recycling centre
le charbon	coal
le chauffage central	central heating
climatique	climate (adjective)
le commerce équitable	fair trade
contaminer	to contaminate
la couche d'ozone	ozone layer
cultiver	to grow
le déboisement	deforestation
les déchets (m)	rubbish
décomposer	to decompose
le désastre	disaster
détruire	to destroy
disparaître	to disappear
la douche	shower
l'eau (f) douce	fresh water
l'eau (f) potable	drinking water
économiser	to save
écologique	environmentally friendly
l'effet (m) de serre	greenhouse effect
effrayant(e)	frightening
l'électricité (f)	electricity
l'emballage (m)	packaging
empêcher	to prevent
en danger	in danger
endommager	to damage
l'énergie (f) éolienne	wind power
les énergies (f) fossiles	fossil fuels
l'énergie (f) renouvelable	renewable energy
l'énergie (f) solaire	solar power
l'ennui (m)	problem, worry
l'environnement (m)	environment
l'éolienne (f)	wind turbine
l'espace (m) vert	green area
l'espèce (f)	species
l'état (m)	state
être vert(e)	to be green
faire du compost	to make compost
faire du recyclage	to recycle
la famine	famine
gaspiller	to waste
le gaz carbonique	carbon dioxide
le gaz d'échappement	exhaust fumes
les habitats (m)	habitats
l'incendie (m)	fire
l'inondation (f)	flood
inonder	to flood
s'inquiéter	to worry
instantané(e)	instant
jeter	to throw (away)
s'inquiéter	to worry
le manque (de)	lack (of)
la marée	tide
les matières (f) premières	raw materials
menacé(e)	threatened

menacer	to threaten
mener à	to lead to
le monde	world
mondial(e)	worldwide
le niveau	level
les ordures (f)	rubbish
l'organisation (f) charitable	charity
l'ouragan (m)	hurricane
le papier	paper
le paysage	countryside / landscape
le pétrole	oil
la planète	planet
pollué(e)	polluted
polluer	to pollute
la pollution	pollution
potable	drinkable
la poubelle	dustbin
les produits (m) bio	green products
protéger	to protect
ramasser	to pick up
le réchauffement de la Terre	global warming
recyclable	recyclable
le recyclage	recycling
les ressources (f) naturelles	natural resources
le risque sanitaire	health hazard
le robinet	tap
le sac en plastique	plastic bag
sauver	to save
sauvegarder	to keep safe
la sécheresse	drought
le souci	worry / concern
survivre	to survive
la terre	earth
le tremblement de terre	earthquake
trier	to sort
le trou	hole
utiliser	to use
la vague	wave
le verre	glass
le volcan	volcano

Global Events (p.93)

l'aide (f) financière	funding
assister à	to attend
bénéficier	to benefit
la bonne cause	good cause
collecter des fonds	to raise money
la coupe du monde	world cup
l'événement (m)	event
le festival (de musique)	(music) festival
les Jeux (m) olympiques	Olympic Games
la rencontre sportive	sports event
rester en contact	to stay in touch

VocabularyVocabulary

Answers

The answers to the translation questions are sample answers only, just to give you an idea of one way to translate them. There may be different ways to translate these passages that are also correct.

Section One — General Stuff

Page 1: Numbers

1) Il a trois sœurs. (Il n'a pas de frère.)
2) la première maison de la rue Phillipe
3) C'est la troisième rue après le parc.
4) une vingtaine

Page 3: Times and Dates

1) a) 6.45 am   c) Tuesdays and Thursdays
   b) 8.30 am   d) 1996

Page 9: Opinions

1) Maurice le Pain is not very funny.   4)   Because he is handsome.
2) He is really talented.   5)   He is great.
3) They are always great.

Page 10: Putting it All Together

1) (i) a) son équipe   c) regarder des films
      b) sport

   (ii) a) ennuyeux   c) agaçantes
       b) lire

Page 11: Listening Questions

1) a) about 10   b) €256   c) about 20
2) (i) A and D   (ii) C and D

Page 13: Reading Questions

1) a) 73   b) 20   c) 17   d) 14   e) 47   f) 16
2) a) le mardi soir, à sept heures
   b) un concours
   c) le lundi soir et le samedi matin
   d) la semaine prochaine

Page 14: Writing Questions

1) Le lundi, je vois mes ami(e)s. La semaine dernière, nous avons regardé un film d'action. Ce week-end, je vais faire les magasins avec mes cousin(e)s.

2) Mon sport préféré, c'est le rugby parce que c'est très passionnant. Je joue au rugby depuis sept ans. Le week-end, j'aime regarder le sport à la télévision avec mes amis, mais je ne m'intéresse pas au football. Je pense que les joueurs sont arrogants. Dans le futur / À l'avenir, je voudrais être prof.

Section Two — About Me

Page 17: Your Family

In my family, there are three people — my mother, my father and me. Unfortunately, I don't have any brothers or sisters, so I'm an only child. On the other hand, I have lots of cousins and I see them often. Last weekend, for example, we went to the cinema together and we really enjoyed ourselves.

Page 18: Describing People

1) (i) A and D   (ii) C and D

Page 20: Pets

1) a) He walks his dog for him every week.
   b) Duc is a very young dog.
   c) They are cute. **or** They are affectionate.
   d) cats and dogs

Page 21: Style and Fashion

1) Sylvie   2) Jérôme   3) Jérôme   4) Pauline

Page 24: Partnership

1)   C   2)   B

Page 25: Listening Questions

1) a) les magazines   c) passionnants
   b) blouson   d) coiffer
2) a) B   b) A   c) B

Page 27: Reading Questions

1) a) One from: Elle est assez grande. / Elle a les cheveux blonds et courts. / Elle a les yeux verts. / Elle est sportive.
   b) Il est (déjà) plus grand que leur père.
   c) One from: Elle aime jouer au football. / Elle joue au football tous les samedis.
2) a) Naima   b) Lena   c) Faiz

Page 28: Writing Questions

2) J'ai rencontré mes deux meilleures amies au club des jeunes. Edith est très amusante / drôle et bavarde, comme moi. Delphine est timide mais gentille et généreuse. Elles sont très différentes mais elles sont très sympathiques et nous passons beaucoup de temps ensemble. Nous nous entendons bien. Quelquefois il est difficile de se faire des amis.

Section Three — Daily Life

Page 30: Everyday Life

I get ten euros of pocket money per / a week. But I have to work to earn this money. I do household chores every day to help my parents. In addition, last Saturday I babysat. I buy lots of music online, but I'm going to try to save up because I would like to go on holiday with my friends.

Page 31 — Food

1) a) B   b) A   c) A   d) B

Page 33 — Shopping

1) a) You can't ask an assistant for advice.
   b) You don't have to queue. **or** You save time.
      or The supermarkets deliver your shopping.
   c) if the clothes will be the right size

Page 35: Technology

J'ai reçu / eu un nouveau portable pour mon anniversaire. Ma mère me l'a acheté. C'est très utile parce que je peux contacter mes parents et mes amis quand je veux. Je peux aussi télécharger de la musique et des jeux d'Internet. Demain, je l'utiliserai pour acheter un livre en ligne.

Page 36: Social Media

1) Elle tchatte avec ses amis.   3)   Elle regarde ses photos.
2) Ils sont indispensables.

Page 38: Listening Questions

1) (i) a strawberry cake / a bottle of red wine
   (ii) She had forgotten her purse.
2) (i) B and D   (ii) B and C

Page 40: Reading Questions

1) a) B   b) C
2) I have to use social networks for my work. I find them practical / convenient for organising my life. However, I believe that it is important to be responsible because others can see what you upload. I write a fashion blog but I would never share personal details / information.

Page 41: Writing Questions

2) Marie doit acheter un cadeau pour sa petite amie / sa copine parce que c'est son anniversaire cette semaine. Hier elle est allée au grand magasin. Elle a trouvé une jolie robe mais ce n'était pas la bonne taille. Elle a vu un chapeau aussi, mais c'était trop cher. Marie n'aime pas faire les magasins / faire du shopping / faire des courses.

Section Four — Free-Time Activities

Page 45: Celebrations and Festivals

1) a) A   b) B   c) B

Page 46: Music

1) (i) a) le violon   b) son professeur
   (ii) a) en groupe   b) répéter

Page 47: Film and TV

Mon ami(e) et moi sommes allé(e)s au cinéma le week-end dernier. Nous avons regardé un film d'horreur. Je n'avais pas peur, mais mon ami(e) a crié pendant le film. J'aime aller au cinéma. C'est toujours divertissant. Le mois prochain, j'irai voir le nouveau film d'action.

Page 48: Sport

B, E, F

Page 49: Listening Questions

1) B, D and F

2) a) It allows people to watch films.

   b) 38 seconds

   c) Two from: It took place on 28th December 1895. / It took place in the basement of the Grand Café in Paris. / It lasted around 20 minutes. / Ten films were shown.

Page 51: Reading Questions

1) B, E, F

2) a) Annabelle   b) Annabelle   c) Bastien

Page 52: Writing Questions

2) Le 14 juillet est la Fête nationale en France. Beaucoup de touristes vont à Paris pour voir les défilés. Cette année, je suis allé(e) à un parc près de la tour Eiffel pour regarder les feux d'artifice. C'était une expérience formidable / chouette / géniale. Mes ami(e)s aimeraient visiter Paris l'année prochaine, donc nous célébrerons ensemble.

Section Five — Where You Live

Page 54: Talking About Where You Live

1) by the second year
2) one for men and one for women
3) He gave them a job and bread.
4) unemployment and poverty

Page 56: Weather

1) true   2) true   3) false

Page 57: Listening Questions

1) a) A   b) A   c) B

2) a) C   b) D

Page 59: Reading Questions

1) a) C'est la capitale de la Belgique. [1 mark] La plupart des institutions de l'Union européenne y sont situées. [1 mark]

   b) un grand nombre de bâtiments anciens et intéressants

   c) quelquefois ils l'énervent

2) B, D, A

Page 60: Writing Questions

2) Aujourd'hui il y a du soleil et il fait très chaud dans le sud de la France. Dans le nord de la France, c'est nuageux. Demain il y aura du vent dans le sud mais le temps sera beau / il fera beau. Cependant, dans le nord, il pleuvra et il fera assez froid, mais il y aura des éclaircies (dans) l'après-midi.

Section Six — Travel and Tourism

Page 62: Where to Go

1) Elle veut aller en Angleterre. Elle veut voir un match de football.
2) Elle veut passer les vacances au bord de la mer. Elle veut aller chaque jour à la plage.
3) Il veut rester en France. Il veut faire du camping.

Page 63: Accommodation

1) It seemed as though he hadn't left England.
2) on the ground floor
3) Two from: dried meat / oyster soup / biscuits / cheese
4) Two from: They didn't have to pay for the food. / The restaurant was comfortable. / They were served a lot of food.

Page 65: How to Get There

Next week, I'm going to go on holiday to the United States. In particular, I would like to see New York. I've reserved / booked a luxury hotel there with a big swimming pool. However, the journey worries me a lot. I'm scared of flying, and I will be on the plane for seven hours.

Page 69: Giving and Asking for Directions

1) a) C   b) A   c) A   d) B

Page 70: Listening Questions

1) a) 1

   b) more information about the different types of room (available)

   c) your name; your telephone number; the dates of your stay

2) (i) a) meat / burgers
   (ii) a) beef
      b) She is allergic to egg. [1 mark]
         She has to wash her hair. [1 mark]

Page 72: Reading Questions

1) a) You turn right and cross the street.

   b) You take the street next to it and go straight ahead.

   c) at the end of the street (opposite the Hôtel Magnifique)

2) a) drôles   c) l'hospitalité
   b) l'histoire du pays   d) partir

Page 73: Writing Questions

2) L'année dernière, ma famille a logé / est restée dans un petit hôtel en Angleterre. Quel désastre ! Notre chambre était très petite. La salle de bains était vraiment sale, c'était dégoûtant. La nourriture au restaurant était affreuse et le serveur était impoli. L'année prochaine, nous irons en Chine et visiterons un parc d'attractions.

Section Seven — Current and Future Study and Employment

Page 76: School Routine

1) a) son frère   b) le mardi   c) libres

Page 77: School Life

1) Vusi   2) Karine   3) Alain

Page 79: School Events

1) (i) D   (ii) A

Page 80: Education Post-16

Pour célébrer la fin des examens, j'ai regardé des films avec mes amis. Nous sommes très heureux / heureuses parce que c'est les vacances. En septembre prochain, j'irai au lycée pour faire le bac(calauréat) et j'aimerais / je voudrais obtenir de bons résultats. Cependant, mon / ma meilleur(e) ami(e) veut / a envie de faire un apprentissage.

Page 81: Career Choices and Ambitions

When I was younger, I wanted to be a baker because I loved to make cakes. Today, I'm still interested in cooking, and I would like to be a chef when I leave school. I have a part-time job in a restaurant kitchen. I don't earn a lot of money, but I hope that the experience will be useful in the future.

Page 82: Languages for the Future

1) Because she would travel the world.
2) Because if she marries someone from abroad, she will be able to speak to them in their native language.
3) the culture of a country

Page 84: Listening Questions

1 (i) a) A
   (ii)a) C   b) A
2 a) Two from: practical / hard-working / honest
   b) a driving licence / being able to drive
   c) send a copy of her CV [1 mark] send a copy of her passport
     [1 mark] (before the 30th November)

Page 86: Reading Questions

1 a) On a trouvé son journal intime après la guerre.
   b) One from: mettre des affiches / fabriquer des costumes / vendre des
     billets / jouer un rôle
   c) Elle a dû / C'était difficile de faire ses devoirs et apprendre son texte
     en même temps.
2 a) Marc   b) Lucie   c) Ankit

Page 87: Writing Questions

2) J'apprends le français et l'italien depuis cinq ans. J'irai au lycée
parce que j'espère étudier les langues étrangères à l'université / la
faculté. J'aimerais / Je voudrais être / devenir interprète parce que je
pourrais parcourir le monde / voyager autour du monde. Cet été, je
vais aller en Italie pour pratiquer mon italien.

Section Eight — Global Issues

Page 89: Problems in Society

There are lots of social problems in my area / region, such as
unemployment. Also, there are people who live on the street. Yesterday I
saw some homeless people and they were malnourished. In my opinion,
we must do something to help these people. We must combat inequality.

Page 91: Environmental Problems

Samit pense que nous devons / qu'il faut protéger la planète. Il croit
que le réchauffement de la Terre a causé des problèmes graves, comme
des sécheresses et des ouragans. À son avis, les gens gaspillent trop de
ressources naturelles. Il pense que, dans le futur / à l'avenir, nous devrons
utiliser l'énergie renouvelable au lieu du charbon et du pétrole.

Page 93: Global Events

Pour son anniversaire, j'ai donné à mon père deux billets pour un match
de la coupe du monde de rugby. Nous allons aller au match ensemble.
Nous aimons regarder la sport. En 2012, nous sommes allés aux Jeux
olympiques et c'était incroyable. Il y avait une ambiance agréable avec
des gens de beaucoup de pays différents.

Page 94: Listening Questions

1) a) sa peau   b) agace   c) le racisme
2) a) B   b) A   c) A

Page 96: Reading Questions

1) a) Blaise   b) Amir   c) Blaise
2) The football world cup will take place in June. It's a sports event
that I love because there are famous players who come from all over
the world / all corners of the world. Unfortunately, I was not able
to / I couldn't buy tickets because they were too expensive. I hope
that the French team will score lots of goals.

Page 97: Writing Questions

2) Je pense qu'il est très important de protéger l'environnement. Il y a
beaucoup qu'on pourrait faire à la maison. Par exemple, en hiver
j'éteins toujours le chauffage central pendant la journée. Hier, j'ai
pris une douche au lieu d'un bain parce que ça utilise moins d'eau.

Section Nine — Grammar

Page 99: Words for People and Objects

1) le cadeau — les cadeaux   4) le cheval — les chevaux
2) la piscine — les piscines   5) la voiture — les voitures
3) le citron — les citrons   6) la pâtisserie — les pâtisseries

Page 100: 'The', 'A' and 'Some'

1) L'homme a un peu **de** pain.   4) Nous avons **des** bananes.
2) Les étudiants viennent **du** Maroc.   5) Ils n'ont pas **de** raisins.
3) Je vais **au** pays de Galles.   6) Il va **à la** bibliothèque.

Page 101: Words to Describe Things

1) La mère fière.   5) Les chiens vifs.
2) Une fille triste.   6) Les voitures blanches.
3) Le chat lent.   7) Une femme gentille.
4) Une maison bleue.   8) Une veste chère.

Page 102: Words to Describe Things

3 and 6 are correct. The others should be:
1) C'est un jeune chien.   4) Tu as lu un livre ennuyeux.
2) Le train long est bleu.   5) J'ai une nouvelle voiture rouge.

Page 103: Words to Describe Things

1) **Mon** père n'aime pas **sa** nouvelle voiture.
2) **Tes** amis ne vont pas à **notre** lycée.
3) **Cet** hôtel est grand.
4) **Cette** cuisinière a **quelques** légumes.

Page 104: Words to Compare Things

1) Navid et Pauline sont les plus forts.
2) Ta / Votre grand-mère est plus vieille que mon grand-père.
3) Ce magasin est le moins cher.
4) Julie est aussi active que Thérèse.
5) Ses idées sont les pires.
6) Le français est le meilleur.

Pages 105-106: Quick Questions

1 a) m   c) f   e) f   g) m   i) f   k) f   m) f   o) f
   b) m   d) f   f) m   h) m   j) m   l) f   n) m
2 a) f   c) m   e) f   g) m   i) m   k) m   m) f   o) m
   b) m   d) f   f) f   h) f   j) f   l) f   n) f
3 a) la maison   c) le professeur   e) la robe   g) l'abricot
   b) le jardin   d) l'orange   f) l'hôpital   h) l'hiver
4 a) des   c) de l'   e) de   g) du
   b) de   d) de la   f) de   h) des
5 a) facile   c) vieux   e) triste   g) bonne
   b) amusants, gentils   d) belle   f) grande   h) long, ennuyeux
6 a) Alexandre a les yeux **bleus**.
   b) J'habite dans une maison **moderne**.
   c) La **première** question est très **difficile**.
   d) Susanna porte un chapeau **rouge** et des chaussures **orange**.
   e) Mes frères sont assez **sportifs**.
   f) Le cochon d'Inde est **heureux** et **mignon**.
7 a) longues   b) nouvelle   c) toute   d) rigolo
8 a) blanche   b) étrangers   c) dernières   d) chère   e) sèches
9 a) J'ai une chemise **bleue**.
   b) Nous sommes au **premier** étage.
   c) Loïc habite dans un **petit** appartement.
   d) Il chante des chansons **étrangères**.
   e) C'est une **bonne** peinture.
10 a) mon chien   e) ses chaussures
   b) leur voiture   f) son frère
   c) ta / votre maison   g) nos parents
   d) mon copain / ma copine   h) ton / votre cheval
11 a) Mon vélo est rouge.
   b) Est-ce que ton manteau est bleu ?
   c) Sa mère habite en Irlande.
   d) Avez-vous parlé à votre grand-mère ?
   e) Ils n'ont pas fait leurs devoirs.
   f) Est-ce que tu as vu son argent ?
12 a) Je joue au rugby **chaque** week-end.
   b) Eric a acheté **quelques** légumes.
   c) **Chaque** élève doit faire des devoirs.
   d) Il a trouvé **quelques** livres intéressants.
13 a) ce   b) Cet   c) ce   d) Ces   e) cette
14 a) Cette fête est la plus passionnante.
   b) Je suis étrange / bizarre, mais il est le plus étrange / bizarre.
   c) Ces arbres sont les plus verts.

Page 107: Words to Describe Actions

1) tristement   4) fièrement   7) mauvais
2) négativement   5) absolument   8) constamment
3) sérieusement   6) lentement

Page 108: Words to Describe Actions

1) Je joue au tennis là-bas.
2) Tu chantes tous les jours.
3) Normalement, je vais en ville en bus.
4) Elles vont là-bas.
5) Par conséquent, j'aime mes matières.
6) J'aime ce nouveau professeur maintenant.

Page 109: Words to Compare Actions

1) Thomas joue du piano **le mieux**.
2) François va à l'étranger **le plus fréquemment**.
3) Lucie court **plus que** Emmanuel.
4) Je regarde la télévision **le moins souvent**.
5) Tu ris **autant que** moi.
6) Je chante **pire que** toi.

Page 110: Words to Say How Much

1) Elle est **très** vive.
2) Ils ont **un** peu d'eau.
3) Le musicien est **vraiment** doué.
4) C'est **assez** intéressant.
   'Assez' (quite) isn't followed by 'de' here because it's an intensifier.
5) Tu as beaucoup **de** chaussettes.
6) L'homme a trop **de** chocolat.

Page 111: Quick Questions

1 a) facilement b) précisément c) heureusement
  d) évidemment g) clairement j) calmement
  e) gentiment h) stupidement k) incroyablement
  f) complètement i) deuxièmement l) honnêtement

2 a) Zanna écrit autant qu'Étienne.
  b) Le chien noir est le plus âgé / vieux.
  c) Les gâteaux au chocolat sont les meilleurs.
  d) Je joue au tennis mieux que ma sœur.

3 a) Julian joue du banjo **mieux** que Claude.
  b) Ayesha nage **le pire** dans la mer.
  c) Lucie écrit **le moins** au collège.
  d) Mathieu cuisine **plus** à la maison que Charles.

4 a) Hier b) souvent c) Normalement d) demain e) déjà

5 a) Je l'ai vu **là-bas**.
  b) Elle a perdu son portable **quelque part**.
  c) Mon père a ses papiers **partout**.
  d) L'aéroport est assez **loin** de la ville.
  e) Venez **ici**, s'il vous plaît.

6 a) in general / generally d) next year g) last week
  b) absolutely e) late h) at the same time
  c) from time to time f) in any case

7 a) a little bit / a little bit of / a little
  b) enough d) little / not much / not many
  c) too much / too many e) lots of / many / a lot of

8 a) Elles ont **assez de** poissons. c) Mon ami a **beaucoup de** serpents.
  b) Elle a **trop d'**argent. d) Le magicien a eu **peu de** succès.

Page 112: I, Me, You, We, Them

1) Hélène **lui** donne le livre. 4) Avez-vous le livre? Non, elle **l'**a.
2) **Elle** aime les chiens. 5) **Nous** allons au cinéma.
3) Tu peux **les** voir? 6) Non, **elles** ne sont pas ici.

Page 113: Something, There, Any

1, 4 and 6 are correct. The others should be:
2) **Tout** le monde sait que c'est vrai.
3) A-t-elle des livres? Oui, elle **en** a.
5) Tu connais le château? J'**y** suis allé(e).

Page 114: Position and Order of Object Pronouns

1) Il le lui donne. *He gives it to him / her.*
2) C'est moi qui l'ai écouté. *It's me who listened to him.*
3) Tu l'as écrit toi-même. *You wrote it yourself.*
4) Vous y êtes allés avec nous. *You went there with us.*
5) Elle t'a dit. *She told you.*
6) Je vais lui en parler. *I'm going to talk to him / her about it.*

Page 115: Relative and Interrogative Pronouns

1) L'homme qui est sportif.
2) La pizza que j'aime manger.
3) J'ai cinq crayons qui sont rouges.
4) Tu cours avec qui? / Avec qui cours-tu?
5) La voiture qu'elle conduit est lente.
6) À quoi penses-tu?

Page 116: Possessive and Demonstrative Pronouns

1) Le stylo là est **le tien**. 4) Ces chiens sont **les nôtres**.
2) Celle-là est **la sienne**. 5) Où as-tu vu **ça / cela**?
3) **Cela** n'est pas drôle! 6) C'est **le / la vôtre**.

Page 117: Quick Questions

1 a) **Elle** aime le chocolat. d) **Il** joue au football.
  b) **Il** a mangé mes chaussures. e) **Elle** est sous la table.
  c) **Ils** détestent les filles. f) **Elles** sont allées au cinéma.

2 a) Je **la** regarde. b) Paul **le** lit. c) Je **les** déteste.

3 a) quelque chose c) tout le monde e) plusieurs
  b) quelqu'un d) chacun(e)

4 a) On **y** va s'il fait beau.
  b) Est-ce que tu peux m'**en** acheter ?
  c) Je n'**y** vais pas à cause des monstres.
  d) Les vacances, parlons-**en**.
  e) Tu **y** es déjà allée ?
  f) On ne s'**en** sortira jamais !

5 a) Nous pouvons le leur donner. d) Elle les y rencontre.
  b) Mon père t'y attend. e) Je la lui avais offerte.
  c) Vous lui en achetez. f) Il leur a téléphoné hier.

6 a) Le lapin **que** tu as tué était délicieux.
  b) C'est un homme **qui** aime le poulet.
  c) Les sandales **qu'**il porte avec des chaussettes sont laides.
  d) Le gendarme **qui** a volé ma voiture était vieux.

7 a) The farmer has a hen whose eggs are perfect.
  b) He had three cakes, two of which were filled with fruit.
  c) The illness from which she suffers gives her a blue nose.

8 a) le nôtre b) la sienne c) les miennes d) la sienne

9 a) I don't like this dress. I prefer that one.
  b) Have you read these books? This one is very good, but that one is boring.
  c) I like dogs, but those ones are really nasty.

Page 118: Joining Words

1) d 2) b 3) e 4) a 5) c 6) f

Page 119: Prepositions

1) Je joue au foot. 5) Je joue de la clarinette.
2) Elle rend visite à Manu. 6) Ils / Elles habitent en France.
3) Il s'agit d'un jeune garçon. 7) Il va à la banque.
4) un pull en laine 8) Tu viens du pays de Galles.

Page 120: Prepositions

1) Je suis **chez** Paul avec Dima.
2) Le magasin est **sous** le pont.
3) Je vais aller en vacances **pour** deux semaines.
4) Je travaille à la pharmacie **depuis** six mois.

Page 121: Quick Questions

1 a) but d) like, as g) since j) or else
  b) neither...nor e) or h) while k) after
  c) when / as soon as f) when i) because l) then

2 a) Je voudrais une pomme **et** une poire.
  b) C'est mon anniversaire **mais** je ne sors pas.
  c) **Si** tu manges le champignon, je te tuerai.
  d) Je me douche, **puis** je m'habille.
  e) **Comme** j'étais en retard, j'ai manqué le bus.

3 a) à c) dans e) en g) dans
  b) aux d) à f) en h) aux

4 a) sous c) sans e) chez g) avec
  b) sur d) après f) vers h) avant

Answers

5 a) My father is very tired because he works all the time.
b) Take a chocolate if you want.
c) I'm tired so I'm going to go to bed.
d) What are you going to do during the holidays?
e) I play football with my brother.

6 a) de la c) à la e) du g) à la i) du
b) aux d) au f) de h) de la j) à

7 a) L'école est en face de la piscine.
b) Je suis resté(e) à la maison / chez moi à cause de la pluie.
c) Il y a un supermarché à côté du parc.
d) Aix-en-Provence est / se trouve près de Marseille.

Page 122: Verbs in the Present Tense
1) je parle
2) il établit
3) nous remplissons
4) tu réponds
5) elles entendent
6) vous commencez
7) vous perdez
8) ils grossissent
9) j'allume
10) on vend

Page 123: Irregular Verbs in the Present Tense
1) nous **devons**
2) je **veux**
3) vous **êtes**
4) tu **dois**
5) elle **va**
6) ils **font**
7) elles **peuvent**
8) on **sait**
9) ils **ont**
10) nous **faisons**

Page 124: More About the Present Tense
1) Je commence à comprendre.
2) Je veux manger de la pizza.
3) J'étudie le français depuis deux ans.
4) Aimes-tu / Aimez-vous les prunes?
5) Joues-tu / Jouez-vous du piano?

Page 125: Quick Questions
1 a) je parle
b) tu écoutes / vous écoutez
c) nous jouons
d) ils / elles détestent
e) il écoute
2 a) agis d) choisissent g) bat j) vends
b) achetez e) partagez h) attendez
c) finis f) punissent i) mord
3 a) e, e b) ons, es c) e, ent d) ez, e
4 a) boit c) lis e) ferme
b) disent d) ouvrez f) pouvons
5 a) fais c) veut e) faites g) allons i) doivent
b) vas d) devons f) fait h) voulez j) vais
6 a) Nous sommes heureux.
b) Mon père est ingénieur.
c) Les devoirs sont ennuyeux.
d) Vous êtes anglais.
e) Je suis fatigué.
f) Elle est belle.
7 a) J'apprends à jouer de la guitare.
b) Je n'arrive jamais à manger mon petit-déjeuner.
c) Il commence à pleuvoir.
d) J'arrive toujours à faire mes devoirs.
8 a) (j') ai c) a e) avez
b) as d) avons f) ont
9 a) Mange-t-elle de la viande ?
b) Vas-tu en ville ce matin ?
c) Aime-t-il le chocolat ?
d) A-t-elle un petit ami ?
e) Savez-vous parler chinois ?
f) Devons-nous partir bientôt ?

Page 126: Talking About the Future
1) il va aller / il ira
2) je vais avoir / j'aurai
3) nous allons finir / nous finirons
4) tu vas regarder / tu regarderas
5) elles vont dire / elles diront
6) vous allez faire / vous ferez
7) tu vas pouvoir / tu pourras
8) elle va venir / elle viendra
9) ils vont être / ils seront
10) on va vendre / on vendra

Page 127: Talking About the Past
1) j'ai parlé
2) il a élargi
3) nous avons fini
4) tu as vendu
5) on a grandi
6) elles ont mangé
7) j'ai répondu
8) vous avez cherché

Page 128: Talking About the Past
1) elles ont mis
2) nous avons lu
3) tu as dit
4) je suis allé(e)
5) elle est arrivée
6) nous avons dû
7) ils sont retournés
8) je me suis lavé(e)

Page 129: Talking About the Past
The imperfect verb phrases are:
1) nous venions
3) elle faisait
4) vous veniez
8) tu étais

Page 130: Talking About the Past
1) J'ai couru. (perfect)
2) Ils / elles ont mangé. (perfect)
3) Tu riais. (imperfect)
4) Il était pénible / embêtant. (imperfect)
5) C'était terrifiant. (imperfect)
6) Elle a pleuré. (perfect)
7) Je jouais au basket. (imperfect)
8) Je rangeais (imperfect) quand elle est arrivée. (perfect)

Pages 131-132: Quick Questions
1 a) je vais choisir c) ils vont finir
b) tu vas manger d) vous allez prendre
2 a) elles arriveront c) il jouera
b) on dansera d) nous vendrons
3 a) demanderez c) écriront e) entendra
b) donnerai d) finirai
4 a) I will go d) they will say g) you will have
b) we will be e) he will have to h) I will do
c) you will be able to f) she will want
5 a) j'ai joué d) elles ont dormi g) nous avons fini
b) tu as vendu e) il a écouté h) on a choisi
c) vous avez regardé f) j'ai mangé
6 a) lu d) mort g) conduit j) voulu
b) eu e) craint h) mis k) su
c) été f) dû i) pris l) né
7 a) Hier soir mon frère **est sorti** avec ses amis et il **est rentré** très tard.
b) J'**ai voulu** te téléphoner mais j'**ai dû** faire mes devoirs.
c) Le film **a fini** à huit heures, donc nous **avons pu** en voir un autre.
d) Quand vous **êtes allée** à la discothèque, est-ce que vous **avez mis** votre robe rouge ?
8 a) s b) e c) es d) —
9 a) a lu b) as mis c) ont écrit d) avez vécu
10 a) je suis allé(e) e) nous sommes monté(e)s
b) vous êtes devenu(s) f) ils sont partis
c) elle est sortie g) tu es tombé(e)
d) il est arrivé h) elle est entrée
11 a) Il y avait un concert au théâtre.
b) C'était trop facile.
c) Dans ma chambre, il y avait un lit et une armoire.
12 a) Les moutons faisaient du bruit au centre-ville.
b) Nous étions bronzées après nos vacances.
c) Tu avais la grippe.
d) Tu étais très content de recevoir le paquet.
e) Je faisais la vaisselle avec mes doigts de pied.
f) J'avais un melon et une courgette.
13 a) je dormais d) tu devais
b) ils finissaient e) vous écoutiez
c) il semblait f) nous restions
14 a) Susie **a téléphoné** pendant que tu **faisais** tes devoirs.
b) J'**ai mangé** tout le gâteau pendant que ma mère **regardait** la télévision.
c) Il **s'est cassé** la jambe pendant que nous **jouions** au rugby.
d) Pendant que vous **rangiez** votre chambre, j'**ai pris** une douche.
15 a) I was watching television.
b) She was dancing in the dining room.
c) We were waiting for the postman.
d) They were making a lot of noise.

Answers

16 a) I used to play the piano.

b) We used to go to the park every day.

c) We used to watch the news.

d) You used to believe in Father Christmas.

e) You used to buy the newspaper.

f) He used to eat green beans.

Page 133: Reflexive Verbs and Pronouns

1) nous nous couchons
2) vous vous disputez
3) elles se lèvent
4) il s'intéresse à
5) tu t'es amusé(e)
6) je vais me détendre
7) elle s'est sentie
8) nous allons nous plaindre

Page 134: Negative Forms

1) Je ne mange jamais de viande.
2) Il n'a pas de chien.
3) Tu ne bois que de l'eau.
4) Ils n'aiment personne.
5) Nous ne vivons / habitons plus ensemble.
6) Vous n'y allez jamais.

Page 135: Would, Could and Should

1) tu améliorerais
2) il élargirait
3) nous rendrions
4) je ferais
5) elles iraient
6) vous viendriez
7) on serait
8) elle aurait
9) ils se laveraient
10) vous chercheriez

Page 136: Giving Orders

1) Finissez vos devoirs!
2) Organisons une fête!
3) Écoute!
4) Mangeons!
5) Ne va pas!
6) Ne courez pas!
7) Couche-toi!
8) Ne vous disputez pas!

Page 137: Quick Questions

1 a) m'excuse b) nous lavons c) vous amusez d) se trouvent e) se sent / se sentait f) se couchent

2 a) e b) s c) — d) es

3 a) Je ne mange pas de viande.

b) Elle n'aime pas faire les courses.

c) Tu n'as pas beaucoup d'argent.

d) Nous n'allons pas au cinéma ce soir.

4 a) Je ne mange ni petit pois ni carottes.

b) Elle ne porte que des chaussettes bleues.

c) Nous ne sommes jamais allé(e)s en Russie.

d) Elles ne parlent à personne.

5 a) préférerais b) détesterions c) jouerais d) prendraient

6 a) J'irais au cinéma, mais je n'ai pas assez d'argent.

b) Nous aimerions aider.

c) Tu devrais arriver à onze heures.

7 a) Mange b) Soyez c) Allons d) Finis

8 a) Prête-moi ton stylo ! b) Couche-toi ! c) Taisez-vous ! d) Assieds-toi ! e) Asseyez-vous ! f) Levons-nous !

9 a) Ne sors pas ! b) N'allons pas à la piscine ! c) Ne te couche pas ! d) Ne te lève pas !

Page 138: 'Had done' and '-ing'

1) j'avais joué
2) nous nous étions disputé(e)s
3) vous étiez arrivé(e)s
4) elles avaient été
5) en aidant
6) en restant
7) après être parti(e)(s)
8) après avoir détruit

Page 139: The Passive

The passive sentences are:

1) L'homme est heurté par la voiture.
4) La pomme sera mangée par mon oncle.
6) La tasse a été cassée.

Page 140: Impersonal Verbs and the Subjunctive

The phrases containing a verb in the subjunctive are:

3) avant que vous alliez
4) bien qu'elles soient
6) pour que nous puissions
8) bien qu'il puisse

Page 141: Quick Questions

1 a) il avait décrit b) vous aviez fait c) elles étaient parties d) il avait vécu e) ils avaient dit f) tu avais manqué g) nous étions allé(e)s h) j'avais mangé

2 a) I had finished.

b) Mark had forgotten to close the window.

c) Michelle and Sharon had arrived.

d) She had got up at three o'clock.

e) We had lost the cow.

f) I had left by car.

3 a) voulant b) donnant c) achetant d) finissant e) rendant f) choisissant g) perdant h) faisant i) disant j) allant k) sachant l) buvant

4 a) We entertain ourselves by reading comics.

b) He stays fit by playing tennis.

c) I do my homework while watching the TV.

5 a) Après avoir fait le gâteau, je l'ai mangé.

b) Après être parti, il est revenu.

6 a) She is knocked over by the snail.

b) I am watched by everyone at the theatre.

c) Louis and Carlo were punished by their teacher.

d) You have been found by the fire-fighters.

7 a) you / one must b) it is necessary to c) it seems d) it's about e) it's snowing f) it's hot

8 a) iv b) i c) ii d) iii

9 a) Il faut que tu viennes — tout le monde sera là !
You must come — everyone will be there!

b) Il semble qu'ils aient une maladie grave.
It seems that they have a serious illness.

c) Je veux qu'il me dise toute l'histoire.
I want him to tell me the whole story.

d) Il est possible que nous y allions ce soir.
It is possible that we will go there this evening.

Practice Exam — Listening Paper

Question Number	Answer	Marks
1 a	A	[1 mark]
b	B	[1 mark]
c	C	[1 mark]
d	A	[1 mark]
e	B	[1 mark]
2 a	ennuyeuse	[1 mark]
b	histoire	[1 mark]
c	chimie	[1 mark]
d	EPS	[1 mark]
e	informatique	[1 mark]
3 a	D	[1 mark]
b	C	[1 mark]
c	B	[1 mark]
d	A	[1 mark]
4	A	[1 mark]
	C	[1 mark]
	G	[1 mark]
5 a	the experience outside lessons / provision of non-sports clubs	[1 mark]
b	students who aren't sporty / have other interests	[1 mark]
c	one from: music / drama / theatre	[1 mark]
6 a	B	[1 mark]
	C	[1 mark]
b	A	[1 mark]
	D	[1 mark]
7 a	They post photos.	[1 mark]
	They organise parties.	[1 mark]
b	It's practical.	[1 mark]
	It lets him keep his conversations private.	[1 mark]
c	She can keep in touch with family who live abroad.	[1 mark]
d	It is not necessary.	[1 mark]
8(i) a	Two from: It's in the USA. / It organises summer camps. / It helps disadvantaged children.	[2 marks]
b	It's a unique experience.	[1 mark]
c	protecting endangered species / helping an environmental organisation in Madagascar	[1 mark]
(ii) a	to help poor villages (in the mountains)	[1 mark]
b	His grandfather lives there.	[1 mark]
c	Two from: He cooked. / He cleaned. / He spent time with the residents.	[2 marks]
9(i) a	B	[1 mark]
	C	[1 mark]
(ii) a	A	[1 mark]
	C	[1 mark]
b	B	[1 mark]
	D	[1 mark]
10(i) a	people who like to discover new things	[1 mark]
b	watch the birds	[1 mark]
(ii) a	medieval castles	[1 mark]
	fortified cities / towns	[1 mark]
b	fish soup / lobster bisque / lobster soup	[1 mark]
c	a (kind of) cake	[1 mark]

Total marks for Listening Paper: 50

Answers

Practice Exam — Speaking Paper

Role play sample answer

1) Ma maison est assez grande et elle a une porte rouge.
2) J'aime ma ville parce qu'il y a beaucoup de magasins.
3) Quand j'étais plus jeune, j'habitais dans une vieille maison à la campagne.
4) Est-ce qu'il y a des activités pour les jeunes dans ta ville ?
5) Est-ce qu'il y a quelque chose dans ta ville que tu veux changer ?

Picture-based task sample answer

1) Sur la photo, il y a un groupe de gens qui font de la natation. C'est probablement une compétition où ils veulent tous gagner.
2) Oui, j'aime le sport parce que c'est bon pour la santé. Je joue au tennis deux fois par semaine. Mon sport préféré est le hockey car c'est très compétitif.
3) Mon week-end de rêve serait plein d'activités. J'aimerais lire et écouter de la musique. S'il faisait beau, j'aimerais faire de la randonnée avec ma famille.
4) À mon avis, je n'ai pas assez de temps libre pour me détendre car on nous donne trop de devoirs.
5) Je suis allé(e) au cinéma avec mon ami. Nous avons vu un film d'action, c'était passionnant mais un peu trop violent. Normalement, je préfère les films policiers.

Conversation sample answers

International and global dimension

1) Je voudrais faire du travail bénévole dans une école primaire pour aider les enfants à lire et à écrire. Je pense que c'est important d'encourager les élèves qui n'ont pas confiance en eux en classe.
2) Selon moi, le travail des associations charitables est extrêmement important parce qu'il aide les gens défavorisés qui n'ont pas les moyens d'améliorer leurs situations. Quand on vit dans une situation difficile, c'est souvent impossible de s'en échapper sans l'aide des autres.
3) J'ai participé à une vente de charité qui avait lieu à l'hôtel de ville. Nous avons vendu des gâteaux et des tasses de thé. Le but était de collecter des fonds pour une organisation charitable qui trouve des logements pour les sans-abri.
4) On pourrait construire des centres de refuge pour donner un lieu sûr aux sans-abri où ils pourraient manger et dormir. On pourrait aussi donner de la nourriture aux banques alimentaires.
5) Les conséquences du réchauffement de la Terre sont nombreuses. Les animaux qui habitent dans les zones froides doivent s'adapter à des températures plus chaudes. Quelques zones chaudes deviennent de plus en plus sèches.
6) Moi, j'essaie d'être vert(e) dans ma vie quotidienne car je pense que les petites actions peuvent avoir un grand effet. Je trie mes déchets et j'évite d'acheter des choses qui ont beaucoup d'emballage. En plus, je me douche au lieu de prendre un bain.

School

1) Je crois qu'il y a trop de devoirs au collège. Quand j'étais plus jeune, on avait beaucoup moins à faire en dehors de la classe. Quelquefois, je m'inquiète de mes notes parce que je voudrais être médecin et j'ai besoin de très bonnes notes.
2) Mon collège est assez petit. Il y a environ cinq cents élèves, donc on connaît presque tout le monde. Nous avons deux terrains de foot et une piscine à côté de la cour. L'année prochaine, il y aura un nouveau proviseur du collège.
3) Une journée typique au collège est assez longue. On commence à neuf heures, et la journée scolaire termine à quinze heures trente. Normalement, on a cinq cours chaque jour — deux avant la récréation, un entre la récré et le déjeuner, puis deux leçons avant la fin de la journée.
4) La matière que j'aime le plus, c'est l'histoire car je suis fasciné(e) par le passé. Je m'intéresse surtout à l'époque victorienne. En étudiant le passé, nous pouvons mieux comprendre notre société actuelle.
5) À mon avis, les échanges scolaires sont une bonne idée en théorie, mais ils ne marchent pas toujours. Moi, j'ai participé à un échange scolaire en France l'année dernière mais mon partenaire ne voulait pas me parler. Je me sentais vraiment seul(e).
6) J'aimerais aller dans les Alpes pour faire du ski car je préfère les excursions actives. Toutefois, j'avoue que cela coûterait très cher ! Je voudrais aussi visiter Londres parce que je n'y suis jamais allé(e).

Practice Exam — Writing Paper

1 a) — Sample answer

Il y a deux ans, j'ai fait un stage dans une clinique vétérinaire pendant trois mois. J'ai fait beaucoup de tâches pour lesquelles j'avais besoin d'une bonne connaissance de la biologie. Je pense que les stages sont très utiles, parce qu'il faut avoir de l'expérience professionnelle pour trouver un vrai travail. Mon travail idéal serait d'être vétérinaire parce que j'adore les animaux. Je pense que ce serait un métier très intéressant car je pourrais travailler avec beaucoup d'animaux différents. Pourtant, c'est une carrière difficile parce que les animaux sont plus difficiles à traiter que les humains.

1 b) — Sample answer

À mon avis, les voitures sont la cause principale du réchauffement de la Terre. Il y en a trop sur les routes et cela a augmenté les émissions de gaz d'échappement. Une stratégie pour réduire les émissions est d'utiliser plus les transports en commun. Un autobus peut transporter soixante personnes au lieu d'une voiture qui peut en transporter seulement cinq. Si tout le monde prenait l'autobus, on pourrait réduire la pollution. Le week-end dernier, je suis allé(e) au cinéma à vélo. À l'avenir, j'achèterai une voiture électrique parce qu'elles sont plus propres que les voitures normales.

2 a) — Sample answer

Personnellement, je pense que les campagnes charitables sont une bonne idée parce qu'elles rappellent aux gens qu'il y a des problèmes dans la société. Sinon, tout le monde mène sa propre vie sans penser aux autres. J'avoue que les campagnes ne sont pas une solution à long-terme, mais elles peuvent quand même avoir des effets bénéfiques. Par exemple, l'été dernier les habitants de ma ville ont organisé un festival pour collecter des fonds pour les réfugiés. Il y avait de la musique dans la rue, des jeux pour les enfants et des compétitions. À mon avis, ça a été un grand succès car nous avons collecté beaucoup d'argent pour les gens qui en ont vraiment besoin. C'est mon rêve d'assister à un grand concert de charité un jour, car je pense que l'ambiance serait chouette. Les événements mondiaux réunissent les gens et cela est très important de nos jours.

2 b) — Sample answer

Moi, j'utilise les réseaux sociaux pour faire de la recherche. Par exemple, la semaine dernière j'ai voulu aller au cinéma mais je n'avais aucune idée quel film aller voir. J'ai posé la question sur les réseaux sociaux et mes amis ont décrit les films qu'ils ont vus et m'ont donné leur avis. C'était très pratique et je pense que les réseaux sociaux nous offrent beaucoup de possibilités. Les familles et les amis qui vivent à l'étranger peuvent utiliser les réseaux sociaux pour rester en contact et pour partager des photos. Pourtant, un des risques des réseaux sociaux est qu'on pourrait les utiliser pour harceler les gens. Récemment j'ai été victime du cyber-harcèlement. Quelqu'un a laissé des commentaires négatifs sous des photos que j'avais postées, ce qui m'a vraiment choqué(e). Il faut toujours faire attention à ce qu'on met en ligne parce que les gens qu'on ne connait pas peuvent y accéder.

3 — Sample answer

Quelquefois, Damien aime faire des achats / des courses sur Internet / en ligne parce que c'est plus rapide. Cependant, la semaine dernière il est allé au supermarché pour faire les courses. Il a acheté des fruits, des légumes et du pain. Maintenant, il veut de nouvelles chaussures et il devra aller aux magasins pour les acheter parce qu'il aura besoin de / il devra les essayer.

Practice Exam — Reading Paper

Question Number	Answer	Marks
1 a	Susi	[1 mark]
b	Susi	[1 mark]
c	Étienne	[1 mark]
d	Susi	[1 mark]
2 a	It has increased dramatically.	[1 mark]
b	They are male.	[1 mark]
c	20 refuge centres are being opened in the city.	[1 mark]
d	find a long-term solution	[1 mark]
3 a	B	[1 mark]
b	D	[1 mark]
c	A	[1 mark]
d	C	[1 mark]
4 a	C	[1 mark]
b	A	[1 mark]
5 a	the boss / head of a large (industrial) business / industry	[1 mark]
b	six	[1 mark]
c	either side of the street	[1 mark]
6 a	C	[1 mark]
	E	[1 mark]
	F	[1 mark]
b	He found it difficult to follow the plot.	[1 mark]
c	It was spectacular. / There were lots of special effects.	[1 mark]
d	find her first love	[1 mark]
7 a	Two from: accessing the Internet / listening to music / watching films / taking photos / finding your way	[2 marks]
b	They send messages during meals.	[1 mark]
	They post every detail of their life on social media.	[1 mark]
c	The light can disturb sleep (patterns).	[1 mark]
8 a	une robe	[1 mark]
	une paire de chaussures	[1 mark]
b	La montre ne marche / ne marchait pas.	[1 mark]
c	Elle avait perdu le reçu / le ticket de caisse.	[1 mark]
9 a	B	[1 mark]
b	D	[1 mark]
c	B	[1 mark]
10 a	Il aime travailler avec les animaux.	[1 mark]
b	Il a travaillé dans un refuge pour animaux.	[1 mark]
c	Elle s'intéresse à la mode.	[1 mark]
d	Elle est travailleuse.	[1 mark]
11 a	C	[1 mark]
b	B	[1 mark]
c	A	[1 mark]
d	D	[1 mark]
12	What a terrible holiday! I have just returned from my trip to Germany and it was truly / really awful. I went to Berlin with my cousins. The city was incredible, but the hotel where we stayed was unpleasant. There wasn't any / There was no hot water! If I were to return / go back to Berlin one day, I would find different accommodation / somewhere else to stay.	[7 marks]

Total marks for Reading Paper: 50

For the translation question, you get 7 marks if you fully communicate the meaning of the passage. You get 4-6 marks if you mostly communicate the meaning of the passage, and you get 1-3 marks if you only partially communicate the meaning of the passage.

Speaking Exam Mark Scheme

It's difficult to mark the practice Speaking Exam yourself because there isn't one 'right' answer for most questions. To make it easier to mark, record the exam and use a dictionary, or get someone who's really good at French to mark how well you did. Use the mark schemes below to help you, but bear in mind that they're only a rough guide. Ideally, you need a French teacher who knows the Edexcel mark schemes well to mark it properly.

Role play (10 marks)

In the Role play, you're marked separately for your response to each of the five bullet points (tasks). There are two marks available for each task.

Marks	Quality of Response (per task)
2	You produce a clear, appropriate response with accurate pronunciation.
1	Your response is partially clear or partially appropriate. Your pronunciation may make your response hard to understand.
0	Your response isn't clear or accurate.

Picture-based task (24 marks)

You are scored out of 24 for the Picture-based task and there are two separate sets of criteria.

Marks	Communication and Content
13-16	Your responses are appropriate and developed. You give and justify opinions and consistently use accurate pronunciation.
9-12	Your responses are mostly appropriate and developed. You give and justify opinions and mostly use accurate pronunciation.
5-8	You give reasonable responses and develop several of your answers. You give an opinion and can be understood.
1-4	Your responses are generally short and require prompting. You give an opinion, but sometimes can't be understood.
0	You don't say anything that's relevant.

Marks	Linguistic Knowledge and Accuracy
7-8	You use grammatical structures correctly, including speaking in past, present and future tenses. Mistakes are very minor.
5-6	You use grammatical structures and refer to past, present and future events mostly accurately. Mistakes are minor.
3-4	Generally, you use grammatical structures and refer to past, present and future events successfully. However, mistakes sometimes affect your communication.
1-2	You use some grammatical structures and different tenses correctly, but your responses sometimes don't make sense.
0	You don't say anything that's correct.

Conversation (36 marks)

The Conversation should last between five and six minutes, and you are marked on three separate sets of criteria.

Marks	Communication and Content
10-12	You give well-developed answers, use language creatively and justify your opinions, all using accurate pronunciation.
7-9	You give detailed answers, use a variety of vocabulary and justify some opinions, using mostly accurate pronunciation.
4-6	Your answers are relevant and use some varied vocabulary. You give opinions and your pronunciation is mostly clear.
1-3	You give mostly short answers, using basic vocabulary. You give some opinions and can mostly be understood.
0	You don't say anything that's relevant.

Marks	Interaction and Spontaneity
10-12	You respond spontaneously to questions and are able to hold and develop a natural conversation.
7-9	You respond to most questions spontaneously, and are able to hold and develop a mostly natural conversation.
4-6	You respond to some questions spontaneously. You can sometimes develop the conversation, with some prompting.
1-3	You occasionally respond to questions spontaneously. The conversation is quite stilted, and regular prompting is needed.
0	You don't respond to any questions correctly.

Marks	Linguistic Knowledge and Accuracy
10-12	You use grammatical structures correctly, including complex grammatical structures. Mistakes are very minor.
7-9	Your use of grammatical structures and past, present and future tenses is mostly accurate. Mistakes are minor.
4-6	Generally, you use grammatical structures and relevant tenses successfully. Mistakes sometimes affect your communication.
1-3	You use some grammatical structures and different tenses correctly, but your responses sometimes don't make sense.
0	You don't say anything that's correct.

Answers

Writing Exam Mark Scheme

Like the Speaking Exam, it's difficult to mark the Writing Exam yourself because there are no 'right' answers. Again, you ideally need a French teacher who knows the Edexcel mark schemes to mark your answers properly. Each of the writing tasks has a different mark scheme.

Question 1 (20 marks)

Marks	Communication and Content
10-12	Your answer is relevant, with convincing opinions, a range of vocabulary and expressions, and an appropriate register.
7-9	Your answer is relevant, with creative language, a variety of common vocabulary and some use of an appropriate register.
4-6	Your answer has some relevant points, with simple opinions, mostly familiar language and an appropriate register at times.
1-3	Your answer has few relevant points, with very basic opinions, simple language and some appropriate use of register.
0	Your answer doesn't have any relevant points.

Marks	Linguistic Knowledge and Accuracy
7-8	You use a variety of grammatical structures (some complex) and frequently produce extended sentences that are linked together. You also successfully refer to past, present and future events, and there are few errors that affect meaning.
5-6	You use different grammatical structures and produce extended sentences that are linked with some simple conjunctions. Your references to past, present and future events are mostly correct, but there are some larger communication errors.
3-4	You mostly use simple grammatical structures and short sentences, with some use of longer sentences. You make some successful references to past, present and future events, but frequent errors often make your meaning unclear.
1-2	You use simple grammatical structures and sentences, with some repetition. You make some successful references to past, present and future events, but sentences are often ambiguous and errors mean that your meaning is often unclear.
0	You haven't written anything that's suitable for the task.

Question 2 (28 marks)

Marks	Communication and Content
13-16	Your answer is detailed, relevant and develops the key ideas. You express and fully justify a wide range of thoughts and opinions, using a wide variety of vocabulary and expressions, and an appropriate register and style throughout.
9-12	Your answer is detailed, mostly relevant and develops many of the key ideas. You justify most of your thoughts and opinions, and use a variety of vocabulary and expressions. Your use of register and style is mainly appropriate.
5-8	Your answer contains some relevant information and it develops some of the key ideas. You express some opinions and justify some of them. You use a variety of vocabulary and expressions and mostly use an appropriate style and register.
1-4	Your answer contains some relevant information, but rarely develops any of the ideas. You occasionally justify your opinions. The majority of the language used is simple. The register and style is generally appropriate with some mistakes.
0	Your answer doesn't have any relevant points.

Marks	Linguistic Knowledge and Accuracy
10-12	You use a variety of grammatical structures and complex language, and your answer is fluent, with frequent extended sentences linked together. You successfully refer to past, present and future events, and errors don't obstruct meaning.
7-9	You use a variety of grammatical structures, some complex language and your answer is mostly fluent, with some linked extended sentences. Your references to past, present and future events are mostly correct, with some errors.
4-6	You use some grammatical structures and complex language. There are some longer sentences that are linked together. You make successful references to past, present and future events, but errors sometimes make your meaning unclear.
1-3	You use a variety of simple grammatical structures and occasional complex language. There are occasional extended sentences linked together. You make some correct references to past, present and future events, but errors affect meaning.
0	You haven't written anything that's suitable for the task.

Question 3 (12 marks)

Marks	Quality of Response
9-12	You've fully communicated the meaning of the passage. Your language and structures are accurate, with no major errors.
7-8	You've mostly communicated the meaning of the passage. Your language and structures are mostly accurate, and there are only rare errors that may affect the meaning.
4-6	You've partially communicated the meaning of the passage. Some of your language and structures are accurate, but there are some errors that prevent meaning being communicated.
1-3	You've communicated the meaning of some words or phrases. Some simple structures are accurate, but frequent errors mean that the meaning of phrases and sentences is not communicated correctly.
0	You haven't written anything that's suitable for the task.

Transcripts

Section One — General Stuff

Track 01 — p.3

E.g. **F1**: Et maintenant, écoutez le proviseur pendant cinq minutes, lorsqu'il fait des annonces.

1) **M1**: D'abord, nous avons les résultats de notre sondage sur les habitudes de nos élèves. Le sondage nous a montré que la plupart des élèves se lèvent à sept heures moins le quart. Les cours commencent à huit heures et demie. La plupart des élèves pensent qu'ils commencent trop tôt.

Deuxièmement, il y a maintenant des cours de danse le mardi et le jeudi dans le gymnase — inscrivez-vous !

Et pour finir, ce collège a été établi en mille neuf cent quatre-vingt-seize, donc cette année il y aura une fête pour célébrer son vingtième anniversaire.

Track 02 — p.10

1 (i) **F1**: Quelquefois j'aime faire du sport. J'adore jouer au foot car c'est bon pour la forme. Je m'amuse bien avec mon équipe. Mais je n'aime pas faire du sport quand je suis fatiguée. Je n'aime pas lire. Moi, j'adore les films. J'en regarde beaucoup — les films d'action, les films d'horreur... même les films romantiques.

(ii) **M1**: Je ne m'intéresse pas trop au sport, mais la natation me plaît car c'est relaxant. Personnellement, je préfère les livres. En ce moment, je lis un roman formidable. L'histoire est vraiment intéressante. Les comédies m'énervent. Mais regarder un film me plaît si les acteurs sont bons. La semaine dernière, j'ai vu un film d'action. C'était formidable.

Track 03 — p.11

E.g. **M1**: Mon week-end était génial ! Tout d'abord, j'ai fait du shopping et j'ai acheté deux T-shirts et un jean.

1) **M1**: J'adore regarder les films et heureusement j'ai trouvé beaucoup de DVD dans un magasin de disques — j'en ai acheté une dizaine.

Finalement, j'ai choisi trois nouvelles casquettes de base-ball. Elles sont chouettes. Tout ça m'a coûté deux cent cinquante-six euros.

J'ai passé le samedi soir avec cinq de mes copains. Nous avons regardé un film ensemble. C'était le seizième anniversaire de mon meilleur ami, donc il a reçu beaucoup de cadeaux.

Track 04 — p.11

2 (i) **M1**: Salut Claire ! Comment ça va ?

F1: Salut Georges ! Ça va très bien, merci. Je viens d'assister à un concert chouette de ma chanteuse préférée, Lilette Laurent. C'est une chanteuse vraiment douée. À mon avis, elle a beaucoup de talent et en plus elle est très sympathique.

Elle travaille avec les enfants défavorisés. J'ai regardé une émission à son sujet et ça m'a vraiment impressionnée. À mon avis, sa nouvelle chanson est géniale. Sa musique rend les gens heureux et moi, je crois que ça, c'est la chose la plus importante.

(ii) **M1**: Personnellement, je trouve qu'elle n'a pas de talent. Elle est riche et stupide. J'avoue qu'elle est assez belle, mais c'est tout. En plus elle n'écrit pas ses propres chansons. Toutes les vedettes sont ainsi : leur seul objectif, c'est de gagner de l'argent.

Elle veut simplement attirer l'attention du public. Elle en a besoin, car sa musique est affreuse ! Moi, j'aime le rock. La musique pop m'énerve, surtout les chanteurs gâtés comme Lilette Laurent.

Section Two — About Me

Track 05 — p.18

E.g. **F1**: Alors, Fabien, tu habites toujours à la maison. Parle-moi un peu de ta famille.

1 (i) **M1**: Chez moi, il y a toujours du bruit — ma famille est très vive. J'ai deux sœurs et un frère qui sont tous plus jeunes que moi. Mes sœurs sont jumelles. Elles ont toutes les deux les cheveux roux et les yeux verts. J'ai aussi un demi-frère aîné qui n'habite plus à la maison.

(ii) **M1**: Ma mère est toujours calme et souriante. Elle a les yeux bleus et les cheveux blonds, courts et raides. Mon père est sympa. Il est grand et il a une barbe. Physiquement, je ressemble plus à ma mère qu'à mon père.

Track 06 — p.20

1) **M1**: Chaque semaine, je promène le chien de mon voisin. Duc est un très beau chien, avec des poils tout noirs et de grands yeux adorables. Pourtant il est très jeune, donc il n'aime pas rentrer à la maison quand je l'appelle.

J'adore les cochons d'Inde car ils sont mignons et affectueux. Pourtant, j'aime surtout les chats — je les trouve très élégants. J'aimerais avoir des chats, et aussi des chiens, quand je serai adulte.

À l'avenir, je voudrais habiter à la campagne où je pourrais avoir beaucoup d'animaux autour de moi. J'en ai marre d'habiter en ville.

Track 07 — p.25

E.g. **M1**: Je m'appelle Samir. Pour moi, être à la mode c'est très important.

1) **M1**: J'essaie de mettre toujours des vêtements à la mode, et je lis des magazines pour me donner des idées. Les vêtements des années soixante-dix sont à la mode cette saison et je veux acheter un blouson à pois.

F1: Moi, je suis Maya. Je ne mettrais pas un gilet moche simplement parce que c'est à la mode — je trouve ça nul. Par contre, j'ai un style personnel, et j'aime me faire coiffer au salon tous les quinze jours.

Track 08 — p.25

2) **F2**: Les grands événements familiaux, comme les mariages et les fêtes d'anniversaire, sont super car on voit toute la famille en même temps. Mes grands-parents habitent très loin de chez nous, donc nous ne nous voyons que quelques fois par an. En mai, ma tante s'est mariée et tout le monde était là.

Mes amies sont très importantes pour moi aussi. Ma meilleure amie s'appelle Kelise et nous nous amusons bien ensemble. Je peux lui parler de tout et nous avons les mêmes intérêts, surtout la musique classique. Elle joue de la flûte et moi, je joue du piano.

Section Three — Daily Life

Track 09 — p.31

E.g. **F1**: Comme je suis musulmane, je ne peux pas manger de porc parce que ma religion me l'interdit.

1) **M1**: J'adore les légumes, en particulier les petits pois et les champignons. Je mange aussi du chou-fleur de temps en temps. Qu'est-ce que tu aimes, Élodie ?

F2: J'aime beaucoup la nourriture épicée, mais ma petite sœur déteste ça ! Elle mange beaucoup de nourriture sucrée. Ce n'est pas bon pour la santé !

M1: Moi, je suis végétarien. Je ne mange jamais de viande. Ma mère me cuisine des plats avec des légumes. J'aime manger des pommes de terre avec des tomates et des petits pois.

F1: Je préfère les fraises aux framboises, et je déteste l'ananas : c'est trop acide. Je ne peux pas manger les noix car je suis allergique.

Track 10 — p.33

E.g. **F1**: À mon avis, faire des courses en ligne est plus facile que de les faire en magasin.

1) **F1**: Cependant, on ne peut pas demander conseil au vendeur — je n'aime pas ça, parce que parfois c'est utile de demander l'avis d'une autre personne.

M1: J'aime le fait qu'on ne fait pas la queue à la caisse, alors on gagne du temps. J'ai toujours beaucoup de choses à faire donc c'est un avantage important pour moi. Aussi, les supermarchés vous livrent vos courses quand vous le désirez. Par contre, c'est difficile d'acheter des vêtements en ligne parce qu'on ne peut pas les essayer et qu'on n'est pas certain si la taille sera bonne.

Track 11 — p.38

E.g. **M1**: Je suis Abdoul. Moi, je préfère faire du lèche-vitrine et je n'ai pas acheté grand-chose.

1 (i) **M1**: Je suis Frédéric et je suis allé au supermarché. J'avais l'intention d'acheter seulement du pain et du fromage, mais en fait je viens d'acheter pas seulement le pain et le fromage, mais aussi un gâteau aux fraises et une bouteille de vin rouge.

(ii) **F1**: Je m'appelle Manon et je suis allée à la parfumerie. Ma mère adore le parfum et j'avais envie d'acheter un flacon de parfum spécial à lui donner. J'ai choisi un parfum chouette, mais quand j'ai voulu payer, j'ai découvert que j'avais oublié mon porte-monnaie. Quelle idiote !

Track 12 — p.38

E.g. **M1**: Tu utilises les réseaux sociaux, Cho ?

F1: Oui, j'aime utiliser les réseaux sociaux. Cependant, je sais que cela peut être dangereux et il faut faire attention à ce qu'on partage.

2 (i) **F1**: Et toi, Jules ?

M1: Moi, j'utilise les médias sociaux pour partager des photos et des vidéos. Je pense que c'est génial de pouvoir montrer aux autres ce qu'on fait. Par exemple, si on sort le soir, on peut mettre des images en ligne, pour que tout le monde sache que tu t'amuses. En outre, on peut voir les photos que les autres ont mises en ligne, ce qui est toujours intéressant parce qu'on sait ce qu'ils font.

(ii) **M1**: Et toi, Clara : est-ce que tu aimes les réseaux sociaux ?

F2: J'aime partager mes photos, mais je demande toujours la permission de mes amis avant de les mettre en ligne. S'ils ne sont pas d'accord, je ne les mets pas. Il faut accepter que les photos soient visibles à tous. En plus, on ne peut jamais vraiment effacer les choses qu'on a mises en ligne. Il me semble qu'elles restent sur Internet pour toujours.

Section Four — Free-Time Activities

Track 13 — p.45

E.g. **M1**: Je m'appelle Youssou. La semaine dernière, j'ai célébré mon seizième anniversaire.

1) **M1**: Mon anniversaire était jeudi. J'ai dû aller au lycée, donc j'ai décidé d'ouvrir mes cadeaux le soir. Je n'ai pas voulu me lever tôt pour le faire le matin ! On m'a offert des baskets, un jeu vidéo et un livre d'histoires mythologiques. J'ai fêté le jour de mon anniversaire avec ma famille. Mon père m'a cuisiné mon plat préféré et ma sœur m'a préparé un gâteau.

Le week-end après mon anniversaire, j'ai retrouvé mes amis pour le célébrer encore. C'était la fête du travail donc il y avait des feux d'artifice. C'était bien de fêter ça avec ma famille et mes amis.

Track 14 — p.46

1 (i) **F1**: Bonjour Joël. Merci d'avoir accepté de répondre à nos questions. Depuis quel âge joues-tu d'un instrument de musique ?

M1: J'ai appris à jouer de la guitare quand j'avais 12 ans, mais mon premier amour, c'est le violon. J'ai commencé à en jouer à cinq ans, et à l'âge de sept ans, je jouais déjà dans un orchestre.

F2: C'était difficile d'apprendre à jouer d'un instrument ?

M1: Oui, au début ce n'était pas facile car je ne m'entendais pas avec mon professeur. Il était trop strict. Heureusement, ma mère m'a trouvé un nouveau professeur.

(ii) **F1**: Et pourquoi l'envie de faire partie d'un groupe plutôt que de faire une carrière solo ?

M1: À l'âge de 15 ans, j'ai assisté à mon premier concert. J'ai trouvé l'ambiance géniale et j'adorais la musique du groupe. Au concert j'ai compris que faire partie d'un groupe était plus amusant que jouer tout seul.

F1: Et qu'est-ce qu'il faut faire pour réussir à devenir un musicien célèbre ?

M1: Naturellement il faut aimer la musique. Mais le plus important, c'est de répéter régulièrement et de toujours essayer de faire de son mieux.

F1: Merci Joël, et bonne continuation.

Track 15 — p.49

1) **M1**: L'Aïd est la fête qui marque la fin du ramadan. Pour le célébrer, les musulmans vont prier à la mosquée ensemble au petit matin. Tout le monde met ses plus beaux vêtements.

Vers midi, on partage un repas festif avec la famille, les voisins et les amis. Ce qu'on mange dépend de la tradition du pays. Les invités font une grande fête — ils écoutent de la musique et dansent. Les gens offrent de petits cadeaux aux enfants. Selon la tradition, les enfants doivent porter de nouveaux vêtements.

Track 16 — p.49

2) **F1**: En 1895 les frères Lumière ont inventé le cinématographe, et grâce à cet appareil, l'art du cinéma est né. Le cinématographe était une caméra qui permettait aux gens de regarder des films.

Leur premier film s'appelait 'La Sortie de l'usine Lumière' et ça durait seulement 38 secondes.

Ils ont organisé la première représentation publique payante des films le 28 décembre 1895 au sous-sol du Grand Café à Paris. La séance a duré environ 20 minutes et on y a projeté dix films.

Section Five — Where You Live

Track 17 — p.57

1) **F1**: J'habite dans un joli appartement au premier étage, qui se trouve près des magasins. C'est très pratique pour faire les courses.

Mon appartement n'est pas très grand : il y a seulement trois pièces. J'habite seule, donc c'est parfait pour moi. Je ne voudrais pas avoir un colocataire car j'ai besoin d'espace personnel.

La cuisine est ma pièce préférée parce qu'il y a un petit balcon où je prends mon café le matin.

Track 18 — p.57

2) **F1**: J'habite à Nice. Nice est une grande ville qui se trouve dans le sud de la France, sur la côte méditerranéenne. Il y a de belles promenades à faire le long de la côte.

M1: J'habite à Lille, une grande ville dans le nord de la France, près de la frontière entre la France et la Belgique. J'aime habiter à Lille mais ce n'est pas une ville qui est jolie ou touristique. Lille est un centre industriel très important, et la ville se développe de façon dynamique.

Section Six — Travel and Toursim

Track 19 — p.69

1) **M1**: Après l'école, nous nous retrouverons au café de la Belle Époque. Pour y aller, prends l'autobus numéro 15. Descends à la gare routière et change d'autobus. Prends le numéro 23 vers le centre-ville. Descends à la Grand-Place, à côté du marché.

J'espère que tu vas te rappeler de tout ! Attends, malheureusement je n'ai pas fini les instructions, bon alors, puis tourne tout de suite à gauche et continue jusqu'à la bibliothèque.

Traverse la rue aux feux et continue dans le même sens. Après environ cent mètres, tu trouveras la Belle Époque à gauche.

Track 20 — p.70

E.g. **F1**: Bonjour. Bienvenue à l'Hôtel de la Paix, Cannes.

1) **F1**: Pour faire une réservation pour les mois de mai, juin, juillet ou août, tapez un. Pour une réservation pour les mois de septembre jusqu'à avril, tapez deux.

Si vous désirez plus de renseignements sur les différents types de chambre qui sont disponibles, regardez notre site internet.

Pour parler avec un membre de notre équipe, laissez votre nom ainsi que votre numéro de téléphone et les dates du séjour prévu. Merci de votre appel.

Track 21 — p.70

2 (i) **F1**: Allô ?

M1: Salut Juliette, c'est Leo à l'appareil.

F1: Leo ! Quelle surprise… Ça va ?

M1: Ça va bien merci. Je t'appelle car je voulais te demander si tu avais envie de dîner avec moi ce soir. Il y a un nouveau restaurant en ville où on prépare des plats délicieux. La viande là-bas est superbe, surtout les steaks hachés.

(ii) **F1**: Ben… en fait, je suis végétarienne. Quel dommage !

M1: Tu es devenue végétarienne ?

F1: Oui, c'est vrai. Avant, j'aimais bien manger du bœuf mais je trouve que la viande est très mauvaise pour la planète.

M1: Pas de problème, je suis sûr que nous pouvons trouver un restaurant qui te plaira. Est-ce que tu aimes le fromage ?

F1: Ben… malheureusement je ne mange pas de fromage.

M1: Ben… et si nous allions manger des crêpes ?

F1: Je suis allergique aux œufs. Je l'ai découvert hier. Et en plus, il faut que je me lave les cheveux ce soir. Au revoir !

Section Seven — Current and Future Study and Employment

Track 22 — p.76

E.g. **M1**: Je m'appelle Nicolas. Ma matière préférée c'est la chimie parce que c'est vraiment intéressant, et je crois que cette matière me sera utile dans l'avenir.

1) **M1**: Je pense que l'école commence trop tôt — mon premier cours est à huit heures et demie ! En plus, je suis souvent en retard parce que j'y vais avec mon petit frère, et il marche trop lentement. J'étudie neuf matières à l'école. Je n'aime pas le mardi parce que j'ai deux heures de chimie et deux heures de physique et, en tout, ça fait quatre heures de science. Je trouve ça fatigant. Mais heureusement, nous n'avons pas d'école le mercredi.

Track 23 — p.79

E.g. **F1**: L'année dernière, j'ai fait un échange scolaire en France.

1 (i) **F1**: Je suis allée chez mon correspondant, Marc, pendant deux semaines. Avant d'aller en France, j'écrivais à Marc régulièrement. En France, je suis allée à l'école. C'était différent car les cours étaient plus longs que mes cours ici en Angleterre.

(ii) **F1**: Aussi, je ne déjeunais pas à la cantine comme je fais ici : Marc habite près du collège et sa mère nous préparait à manger tous les jours. Après avoir mangé à la maison, nous retournions aux cours. Le soir, après avoir fini nos devoirs, Marc et moi bavardions ou regardions la télé. J'ai adoré mon échange car la famille de Marc m'a très bien accueillie et j'ai pu améliorer mon français.

Track 24 — p.84

1 (i) **M1**: Salut Karine ! Est-ce que tu aimes les langues ?

F1: Pour moi les langues ne sont pas aussi utiles que les sciences. Je préfère la chimie mais je trouve que de nos jours, toutes les sciences sont indispensables. En plus, les langues sont plus difficiles pour moi.

(ii) **F1**: Qu'en penses-tu, Nadia ?

F2: Je ne suis pas d'accord avec toi. Moi, j'adore communiquer avec les autres, donc savoir parler une autre langue, c'est important. Pourtant, pour moi, la matière la plus importante c'est l'informatique, car il faut comprendre la technologie pour survivre dans le monde. Heureusement, j'adore passer mon temps sur l'ordinateur parce que je pense que c'est l'avenir.

Tu n'es pas d'accord, Salim ?

M1: Si, mais je crois que les jeunes comptent trop sur les ordinateurs et passent trop de temps devant l'écran. Je trouve aussi qu'il est nécessaire d'être fort en maths, en sciences, en français et en anglais. Il ne faut pas toujours utiliser un ordinateur.

Track 25 — p.84

2) **M1**: Allô ! C'est Gino Ponroy à l'appareil.

F2: Allô, ici Annette Calvel. Je viens de voir le poste de facteur / factrice sur Internet et j'aimerais avoir plus d'informations.

M1: D'accord. C'est un emploi à mi-temps — c'est 25 heures par semaine. On cherche quelqu'un de pratique, travailleur et honnête.

Ce serait utile d'avoir votre propre voiture, mais pour faire cet emploi il faut absolument savoir conduire. Avez-vous le permis de conduire ?

F2: Oui, j'ai mon permis depuis deux ans.

M1: Bien. Si vous voulez poser votre candidature, vous devez nous envoyer une copie de votre CV et une copie de votre passeport avant le 30 novembre. On va organiser les entretiens pour la semaine du 14 décembre.

F2: Très bien, merci beaucoup. Au revoir monsieur.

M1: Au revoir madame.

Section Eight — Global Issues

Track 26 — p.94

1) **F1**: Henri, est-ce que tu penses que notre société est égalitaire ?

M1: Malheureusement, non, elle n'est pas égalitaire. Par exemple, je suis né et j'ai grandi en France, mais certains me traitent différemment parce que je suis noir. C'est raciste et ça me gêne beaucoup.

F1: Mischa, qu'est-ce que tu en penses ?

F2: Je pense qu'il faut lutter contre le racisme, c'est affreux, mais on ne devrait pas oublier qu'il faut aussi mettre fin aux autres genres de discrimination. Par exemple, la discrimination religieuse reste un problème. Je suis musulmane et certains me regardent bizarrement quand je porte des vêtements traditionnels, comme mon foulard.

Track 27 — p.94

2) **M1**: La semaine dernière, les habitants de notre ville ont organisé une journée d'événements sportifs. Le but était de collecter des fonds pour les personnes atteintes du cancer du sein.

C'était l'idée de la mairesse de la ville. Sa mère est morte du cancer et elle voulait faire quelque chose pour collecter de l'argent pour la recherche sur le cancer.

Il y avait beaucoup d'événements différents, y compris un tournoi de foot et une course autour de la ville. Beaucoup de participants se sont habillés en vêtements bizarres pour amuser les spectateurs.

Practice Exam — Listening Paper

Track 28 — p.148-157

E.g. **F1**: Aujourd'hui, de plus en plus de gens ne font pas d'exercice.

1) **F1**: Tout le monde sait qu'il faut faire de l'exercice pour rester en bonne santé, mais beaucoup de gens disent qu'ils n'ont pas le temps. Si vous pensez que vous ne pouvez pas prendre le temps de faire de l'exercice, je vous conseille de réfléchir à votre routine quotidienne et d'envisager comment vous pourriez l'adapter.

Par exemple, vous pourriez aller au travail à pied ou à vélo, au lieu de conduire. Si vous prenez l'autobus pour aller au travail, vous pourriez descendre un arrêt plus tôt pour marcher.

E.g. **M1**: L'allemand ne me plaît pas parce que c'est trop compliqué.

2) **M1**: Il y a beaucoup de matières que je trouve ennuyeuses — la géographie est la pire. Je préfère l'histoire parce que c'est vraiment intéressant, mais on doit trop lire. La matière qui me pose le plus de problèmes est la chimie parce que je n'arrive pas à faire les calculs. Je fais de l'EPS — cela me permet de rester en bonne forme, mais ce n'est pas une matière très utile pour l'avenir. Je voudrais être informaticien donc l'informatique est la matière la plus pratique.

E.g. **F1**: Toutes mes fêtes favorites se célèbrent à la fin de l'année.

3) **F1**: J'adore Noël. Ma tradition de Noël préférée, c'est le sapin de Noël — mon frère et moi le décorerons la semaine prochaine après avoir rendu visite à notre tante. Cette année je vais passer Noël avec ma famille dans le sud de la France. Normalement, c'est difficile d'organiser une réunion familiale parce que nous sommes très nombreux. Je dois acheter beaucoup de cadeaux. Je vais offrir un collier à ma belle-mère et j'ai une figurine d'un cheval pour ma cousine. Il me reste un cadeau de Noël à acheter — un train électrique pour mon petit frère.

E.g. **M1**: À Liège, on prévoit des nuages pendant toute la journée.

4) **M1**: Dans le nord du pays, surtout à Bruges, on prévoit des averses continues jusqu'à minuit. Après 2h, on s'attend à de la grêle dans les zones élevées et il y a un risque de neige.

Alerte pour les citoyens de Bruxelles : des vents très forts en provenance du sud-est souffleront pendant toute la journée. On prévoit des temperatures plus basses et on conseille aux Bruxellois d'éviter les voyages superflus.

Il fera froid dans le sud, surtout à Charleroi, où la température tombera en dessous de zéro. On avertit tous les citoyens du temps brumeux qui réduira la visibilité dans un rayon de 50 mètres ou moins.

E.g. **F1**: L'expérience en classe est bonne, mais il y a quelques élèves qui aiment déranger les leçons.

5) **F1**: J'aime mon collège mais je pense que le collège pourrait faire plus d'effort pour améliorer l'expérience des étudiants en dehors des heures de classe. Il y a beaucoup d'équipes sportives mais ce serait mieux si on pouvait aussi organiser des clubs pour les étudiants qui ne sont pas sportifs mais qui ont d'autres intérêts, comme la musique ou le théâtre.

6) **F2:** Les services de diffusion musicale en ligne sont accessibles en quelques clics et la popularité des services de musique en continu a augmenté. J'accueille le groupe musical suisse Les Moutardiers qui va nous donner leur opinion. Alors, qu'en pensez-vous Alain ?

M1: Il est facile de trouver la musique qu'on veut sur les services de diffusion musicale en ligne. Par contre, la qualité de son est inférieure aux CDs.

F2: Et vous, Michelle, qu'est-ce que vous en pensez ?

F1: Il est possible d'écouter les chansons tout de suite et cela me convient parfaitement. Malgré tous les avantages, je crois que cette nouvelle manière d'écouter de la musique n'est pas très utile pour les nouveaux groupes parce qu'ils ont besoin de vendre leurs albums afin de gagner de l'argent.

E.g. **F2:** Alors, Paul, comment expliques-tu la popularité des réseaux sociaux ?

M1: De nos jours, c'est la façon la plus facile de contacter les gens — et ça ne coûte rien.

7) **F2:** Et tes amis ? Comment s'en servent-ils ?

M1: Normalement, mes amis postent des photos car on aime se tenir au courant de tout ce qui se passe dans nos vies. Quelquefois, ils organisent des fêtes sur les réseaux sociaux parce qu'il est possible de communiquer en groupe sans être ensemble.

F2: Quel moyen préfères-tu pour y accéder ?

M1: Si j'ai l'intention de lire les postes et regarder des vidéos, je préfère utiliser mon ordinateur. Cependant, j'utilise toujours mon portable pour envoyer des messages parce que c'est plus pratique et ça me permet de garder mes conversations privées.

F2: Est-ce que ta famille y accède ?

M1: Pour ma mère, les réseaux sociaux représentent la façon la plus facile de parler aux membres de sa famille qui habitent à l'étranger. Cependant, mon frère pense que les réseaux sociaux ne sont pas nécessaires.

8) (i) **F2:** Florian, mon amie m'a dit que tu avais choisi de travailler aux États-Unis avec une association caritative qui organise des colonies de vacances pour les enfants défavorisés. C'est vrai ?

M1: Oui, c'est vrai, j'y suis allé. Si on cherche une expérience unique, je recommande ces colonies de vacances. J'ai passé deux mois là-bas et j'ai l'intention d'y retourner l'année prochaine.

Et toi, Sandrine, est-il vrai que tu as passé une année à Madagascar ?

F2: Oui, j'ai aidé une organisation environnementale et c'était incroyable. J'ai participé à beaucoup de projets — j'ai même passé neuf mois dans les forêts pour protéger les espèces en danger.

(ii) **F2:** Zayna, comment décrirais-tu ton expérience au cœur des Andes ?

F1: Quelle expérience ! C'était une expédition au Pérou qui avait pour but d'aider les villages pauvres dans les montagnes. Nous avons passé deux mois dans un petit village presque inaccessible. La communauté avait grand besoin d'un hôpital. Le travail m'a énormément plu mais c'était très fatigant !

Et toi, Kassim, qu'est-ce que tu as fait ?

M1: Mon grand-père habite dans une maison de retraite dans ma ville, donc j'ai choisi d'y passer cinq semaines. J'ai aidé à cuisiner et à nettoyer, mais j'ai passé la plupart du temps avec les résidents parce que beaucoup d'entre eux se sentaient seuls.

9 (i) **F2:** Jamil, as-tu des projets pour l'avenir ?

M1: Mon rêve, c'est d'être journaliste. Écrire est ma passion et je regarde les informations à la télévision tous les jours. Pour acquérir de l'expérience j'écris des articles pour le journal scolaire et en été j'ai l'intention de passer quelques mois dans le bureau de mon cousin parce qu'il travaille comme secrétaire pour un journal régional.

(ii) **M1:** Et toi Marie, quels sont tes projets pour l'avenir ?

F1: Moi, vraiment je ne sais pas. Quand j'étais plus jeune, je voulais être artiste parce que j'aimais peindre. Pourtant, mes parents pensaient que ce n'était pas un métier important comme avocat ou médecin. Alors, j'ai changé d'avis et maintenant je pense que je voudrais être agent de voyage car je suis forte en langues.

10 (i) **F1:** La Bretagne est la destination idéale pour ceux qui aiment découvrir de nouvelles choses. Explorez les 2700 km de côtes et de nombreuses îles qui montrent la beauté de la région. Visitez l'île d'Ouessant, le lieu le plus à l'ouest de toute la France, ou voyagez aux Sept-Îles pour observer les oiseaux.

(ii) **F1:** Découvrez la grande richesse historique de la Bretagne en visitant les châteaux médiévaux et les cités fortifiées. Plongez-vous dans la culture bretonne et assistez aux festivals tels que la 'Fête des Remparts' ou le 'Festival du Chant de Marin.'

N'oubliez pas — aucun voyage en Bretagne n'est complet sans goûter ses fameuses soupes de poisson et sa bisque de homard. Si vous préférez quelque chose de sucré, essayez les kouign-amanns. Ces gâteaux datent du 19e siècle et ils se font avec de la pâte à pain, du beurre salé et du sucre.

Index

Index